BOOKS BY *James Trager*

WEST OF FIFTH: *The Rise and Fall and Rise of Manhattan's West Side*   1987
LETTERS FROM SACHIKO: *A Japanese Woman's View of Life in the Land of the Economic Miracle*   1982
THE PEOPLE'S CHRONOLOGY: *A Year-by-Year Record of Human Events from Prehistory to the Present*   1979
AMBER WAVES OF GRAIN   1973
THE BELLYBOOK   1972
THE FOODBOOK   1970

West of Fifth

JAMES TRAGER

West of Fifth

The Rise and Fall and Rise
of Manhattan's West Side

NEW YORK   ATHENEUM   1987

Library of Congress Cataloging-in-Publication Data
Trager, James.
  West of Fifth.

  Bibliography: p.
  Includes index.
  1. Manhattan (New York, N.Y.)—History. 2. New York
(N.Y.)—History—1898–1951. 3. New York (N.Y.)—History—
1951–   . 4. Historic buildings—New York (N.Y.)
5. Manhattan (New York, N.Y.)—Buildings, structures, etc.
6. New York (N.Y.)—Buildings, structures, etc. I. Title.
F128.5.T78   1986   974.7'104   86-47665
ISBN 0-689-11775-2

FIRST EDITION

Acknowledgments

It takes many people to make a book accurate, only one to make a mistake. The views expressed herein are mine; any errors are my fault alone. I wish to express my thanks to the following people who gave of their time and knowledge in the interest of accuracy: Janice Aubrey of Carnegie Hall; Paul Beresford-Hill and Gina Shapira of the Anglo-American School; Abraham B. Beller of the Fiorello H. La Guardia High School; Selma Berrol of Baruch College; Chaim Botwinick of the Board of Jewish Education; Bruce Breimer of Collegiate School; Clarence Bruner-Smith and George Herland of Trinity School; Robert Carswell; Lawrence and Nancy Creshkoff of West 78th Street; Leonard X. Farbman of the Lincoln Square Community Council; Jere Farrah of the Mannes College of Music; Simon Felder, former manager of the Benjamin Franklin; Joan Franklin of West 75th Street; Lewis Freedman; William Lee Frost of the Lucius N. Littauer Foundation; Mrs. Leopold Godowsky (Frances "Frankie" Gershwin); Ruth Granet of West 72nd Street; David Greer of the Bloomingdale House of Music; Tessa Harvey of the New York City Department of Education, District 3; Elissa Keiser of the St. Michael's Montessori School; Jacqueline Lebenthal of the Evanston; Gerald E. Maslon of the City University of New York; David Ment of Teachers College; Elizabeth Murphy of the Red House; Nora S. Murphy of the New York Archdiocese; Alfred Palca of 175 Riverside Drive; Mrs. William Prager of the San Remo; Joseph M. Puggelli and Lawrence N. Tallamy of the McBurney School; Joan Rudd and Richard J. Soghoian of Columbia Grammar and Preparatory School; Ruth Shapiro of the Bank Street School; Caroline Shookhoff; Monroe S. Singer of Lincoln Towers; George Soter of the Strathmore; Philip Tama of the Board of Education; Roseanna Watson of the Phipps Houses; and librarians at the New-York Historical Society. Chie Nishio's contribution went far beyond her photography. Thomas A. Stewart of Atheneum proposed the project and supported it; Atheneum's Ann Rittenberg did what all too few editors still do, going over the manuscript word for word and making brilliantly sensible suggestions.

Contents

Illustrations

West of Fifth

Introduction

Its buildings run the gamut from crumbling to brand-new, from well preserved elegance to already deteriorating "project" housing, from subsidized to extravagantly priced. On any given day, at least half a dozen of these buildings are coming down or going up; and just as many or more are being renovated to produce additional income for their owners.

New York, like any city, is buildings. Its West Side alone has more than twenty-five hundred, some more than a century old. Much of this book will be about buildings—big ones, small ones, old ones (all but a few of them still with us), new ones, Italian palazzos, Second Empire French extravaganzas, utilitarian structures of no distinction, mosques, edifices that would feel more at home on Queens Boulevard standing cheek by jowl with some of the grandes dames of early twentieth-century architecture. New York has lovely old buildings near Union and Washington squares, in downtown commercial districts, even on Fifth Avenue; only on the West Side can they be found in such profuse variety. Smile and surprise wait round every corner for the pedestrian (or bus rider) who will but lift his or her eyes above the storefronts and see the richness of architectural detail that remains from decades past. While the Museum of Natural History has yet to complete its collection of dinosaurs, the ones outside are disappearing. And as the mellow old buildings give way to mammoth structures that yield more income (and more tax revenue), the city grows poorer even while profiting monetarily.

Low-and middle-income housing does not make good copy. Of the scores of buildings discussed (and in some cases illustrated) in the pages that follow, most were built as luxury housing for people who could afford the best, West Side or East. No reader should be misled into thinking that such people ever represented a large percentage of the population; if they seem to be conspicuous on the upper West Side in the closing years of the twentieth century it is partly because the poor of the city remain, as always, largely invisible. The poor, nevertheless, probably represent 15 percent of the city's population. Despite recent emphasis on the tax base rather than on human need, many of the poor still live on the upper West Side, some of them in housing projects, some in pitifully substandard dwellings, virtually none in the elegant Central Park West, West End Avenue, or Riverside Drive buildings that in a superficial way have come to symbolize the West Side.

Beyond bricks and mortar, the story of the West Side is one of diversity, heterogeneity, snobbery, prejudice (racial and religious), ani-

mosity (between landlord and tenant, between rich and poor), speculation, greed, growth, apathy, community involvement, and—above all—
continual change. A bronze plaque in the vestibule of the Holy Name of
Jesus Church on the northwest corner of Amsterdam Avenue and 96th
Street memorializes the "Boy Heroes of Holy Name Parish" who gave
their lives in World War I. Most of the names are Irish, yet services at the
church have been in Spanish for some years. One block to the west, on
the northwest corner of Broadway and 96th, is the glitzy Columbia apartment house of the mid-1980s. Eight blocks down Broadway from the Columbia is the handsomely appointed Central condominium, until the early
1980s the Central Hotel, an open market for drugs and prostitutes. Such
changes continue.

Perhaps more than any other city in the world, New York has
always been home to people struggling for success, and success has always
been measured in terms of address. For over half a century, New Yorkers
tended to relate the East Side with genteel safety and prestige while view-
ing the West Side as bohemian, seedy, down-at-the-heel, sometimes posi-
tively dangerous. Earlier generations took a different view. As the nineteenth century wore on, Fifth Avenue came to be lined on both sides with
fine residences, some of which spilled over to Madison Avenue. Gramercy
Park and Murray Hill on the East Side were New York's fashionable residential areas in the 1870s, but thereafter many people of money and taste
built houses and purchased, or rented, apartments not on the mostly
shabby East Side but on the vibrant West Side. To the east, the smells of
Turtle Bay abattoirs sometimes pervaded the air, and steam trains ran
down a Fourth Avenue ditch into large, noisy yards north of Grand Central. The life of the city was to the south—at Union Square, on Newspaper
Row, on Ladies' Mile—and to the west. On the West Side were to be
found the city's piers, exchanges, commercial houses, department stores,
private schools, libraries, museums (even the Metropolitan Museum of
Art is, technically, west of Fifth), theaters, opera houses, concert halls,
sports arenas, private clubs, and restaurants.

Developers of upper Eleventh Avenue, north of 72nd Street, succeeded in having its name changed in 1880 to West End Avenue, hoping
to make the West Side an echo of London's posh West End. What originally had been intended as a commercial thoroughfare was later closed to
trolley cars and, later still, to trucks and buses. Town houses at first, then
prestigious apartment houses, sprang up along West End Avenue and on
neighboring streets.

Yet somewhere along the way the West Side lost its image of elegance. While the West Sider regarded the East Side as a smug matron
whose silk bonnet matched her silk shoes with excruciating exactness,
whose bookcases were empty of any volume save the Social Register, and
who retired at ten ("I went to the East Side but it was closed"), the East
Sider began to see the West Side as an overaged hippie in running shoes,
topped by a muskrat coat, wearing too much makeup, with the ashes of

her cigarette falling on her sleeve as she waited in line at the health food store. The East Side was cold, stuffy, overpriced. The West Side was déclassé.

The West Side was where Norman Mailer stabbed his wife in a West End Avenue apartment, where gangsters were gunned down in hotel barbershop chairs or Central Park West apartment house lobbies, where Herman Wouk's Marjorie Morningstar dreamed her dreams and Philip Roth's Portnoy did those things in the bathroom, where residents shrugged off Needle Park and muggers ruled the streets. The East Side was where parents balked at letting their children marry people who spoke with accents of other boroughs (and were even a tad uneasy about prospective in-laws who lived on the West Side), where apartment co-op boards found ways to keep out Jewish applicants.

Both views were obviously exaggerated; neither was without some truth. Although the East Side probably had just as many Jewish residents as the West Side, East Side co-ops did close ranks against prospective tenants who were black or had Jewish names. The West Side was a polyglot haven for European refugees, arty types, former East Siders who had sold their old co-ops for what seemed at the time enormous prices, Hispanics and blacks living either on welfare or on the fringe of middle-class respectability, young people newly arrived in New York who could not afford the prices of East Side apartments.

Jewish tenants had begun moving into the West Side even before the turn of the century. E. Idell Zeisloft, in his book *The New Metropolis*, wrote in 1899 about the upper West Side, "The dwellers here are not as a rule of the old and historic New York families, or very wealthy as a class, but all are people exceedingly well to do. A fair proportion of them are Hebrews and many are former residents of other cities who have found here the best value for their money." More and more Jewish families moved into West Side apartments after World War I. Many came from the lower East Side. That section below 14th Street and east of Broadway had the highest population density in the world as late as 1910; some 542,000 people were crowded into one and a half square miles of space. More than 90 percent were Jewish immigrants, refugees from czarist pogroms who, like their predecessors from so many other countries, came looking for work in the booming economy of America. In the 1920s most of them moved to Brooklyn or the Bronx; the more successful moved to the upper West Side. By 1934 Jews constituted more than half the population of the area from 72nd Street to 96th between Central Park West and Riverside Drive. More than a third of the Jewish families in this section were headed by a parent born in Europe, most likely Russia or Poland.

Said *Fortune* magazine in 1939, "The West Side is inhabited chiefly, though by no means exclusively, by New York's foreign Jews, who have standards of their own, but whose interest in social prestige is practically nil. These people have behind them generations of city life, often originating in poverty; they are not only wedded to the city but know how to get the most out of it for their money. They take more pleasure than the Ivy Leaguers in cultural activities; their theater is a necessity; and they habitually cultivate a wide variety of tastes from food to music."

And specifically because it was so heavily Jewish, the West Side tended to be shunned by certain East Side White Anglo-Saxon Protestants, even though it was possible to have more space for less money on the West Side.

Then, beginning in the late 1960s and early 1970s, more people began to realize that the West Side *is* New York, that no other part of the city reflects so truly the mix of people who make New York what it is, and that the tensions and ferment of this mix produce an excitement not to be found on the East Side—or anywhere else. The West Side began to attract the now ubiquitous young upwardly mobile professionals, gentile as well as Jewish, who disdained suburban life, who could often afford the East Side but found it sterile, who discovered that in what some people called Fun City the West Side was more fun, and who had the wherewithal to bid up prices of apartments in buildings on Riverside Drive, on West End Avenue, on Central Park West, and on the avenues and streets in between—buildings like the Beresford, where Mike Nichols had a triplex; the Dakota, where Lauren Bacall had her apartment and where John Lennon lived with his wife, Yoko Ono; the Apthorp, where Sidney Poitier had an apartment; the Belnord, where Isaac Bashevis Singer and Zero Mostel were longtime tenants. Some of the buildings were older than the century, others had been up for only a few years. The West Side has been a long time a-building.

I. Wild and Woolly

The West* Side of Manhattan, from Central Park West to the Hudson River and from 59th Street north to 110th—roughly two hundred blocks, nearly half of which are virtually double the size of corresponding East Side blocks. Excursions into peripheral areas aside, this is our focus.

No other large city in America is so easy to navigate as New York. The configuration of Manhattan's avenues and streets is based on a grid pattern laid out in 1811 after a four-year survey undertaken when the city's population had grown to 83,503 and the city fathers discerned a need to give direction to such undisciplined growth. North of City Hall, then being completed, Manhattan consisted almost entirely of farmland. (City Hall, completed in 1811 at a cost of $500,000, was left with its north side unadorned to save $15,000; it faced a rural landscape that was not expected to change for many years.) Spanish colonists had pioneered grid plans in the Caribbean islands. That New York adopted such a foreign plan for the area north to 110th Street rather than permit a continuation of the haphazard cowpath style of development, still evident in the area south of 14th Street, which preexisted the 1811 plan, suggests remarkable foresight on the part of the early city fathers. Later generations would leave city planning and development largely to market forces, and there would be departures from the original grid plan.

Even ignoring the odd-shaped blocks created by the diagonal slash of Broadway, Manhattan blocks are not uniform in size. West Side blocks are longer east-west than East Side blocks which, between Fifth and Third, are in fact half-blocks: the grid plan was modified by law in 1832 and 1833 to introduce Lexington and Madison Avenues. Lexington, opened north from Gramercy Park to 42nd Street in 1836 and to the Harlem river in 1873, cuts in between Fourth (formerly the Boston Post Road, later Park Avenue) and Third. Madison, opened north from 26th Street at Madison Square to 42nd Street in 1836, reached 124th Street by 1869, dividing the space between Fifth and Fourth. On the upper West Side between 100th and 124th Streets, Manhattan Avenue divides the blocks between Central Park West and Columbus Avenue, but that is a relatively recent development. Upper West Side blocks measure 204.4 feet from north to south below 86th Street but only 201.5 feet above 86th Street—a

*The *North*west Side, sticklers cavil. Early colonists called the Hudson the North River, the Delaware being the South River. The George Washington Bridge is considerably to the east of the Queens Midtown Tunnel. Westbound Manhattan streets actually run northwest.

petty difference but one that observant city walkers have noticed in their perambulations.

The upper West Side extends no more than 3,200 feet from Central Park to the Hudson River as compared with as much as 5,000 feet between the Park and the East River on the East Side. The area encompasses about two square miles—a small fraction of Manhattan's 22.2 square miles, a tinier fraction of the city's more than three hundred square miles. (Manhattan is the city's smallest borough; Queens has nearly one hundred and ten square miles, Brooklyn more than seventy-four, Staten Island about sixty, the Bronx nearly forty-three.) Both sides of Manhattan today are well served by bus routes, but only the West Side has two subway lines. No place on the West Side is more than a few blocks from a subway station; no destination in the city's financial area, garment district, entertainment centers, or midtown office area is more than about twenty minutes away. Few East Siders live so convenient to rapid transit facilities.

Yet the West Side was slow to develop as a prime residential area. Through the East Side ran the well-traveled Boston Post Road (later Fourth and Park avenues); the Albany Post Road, or Bloomingdale Road, laid out in 1816 on the West Side, carried far less traffic. Parts of the West Side were swampy, and the rocky Manhattan schist discouraged construction. The upper West Side was left ungraded for years, without sewers or paved streets. When it finally was built up, the building material was mostly brownstone. Before 1846, when architect Richard Upjohn completed Trinity Church on the west side of Broadway at Wall Street, brownstone had been used chiefly for window sills and other special purposes. Trinity Church was built primarily of brownstone and marked the start of a revolution in New York construction, which for many decades would make heavy use of brownstone even though it is a sandstone composed of sheets that, in time, separate. (The church, dark with a century and a half of soot, cannot be cleaned for fear its facade will disintegrate.)

A builder completed a row of modest frame houses in 1847 on West 40th Street between Sixth Avenue and Broadway (and rented them for less than $11 per month), and a similar row of two-story houses (each with four bedrooms, two parlors, kitchen, piazza, and front veranda) went up in 1850 on West 52nd Street between Tenth and Eleventh avenues. Chelsea in 1850 was not even half built up. Then, just to the north, William Backhouse Astor began in 1851 to build two hundred brownstones, each three to five stories high, in the blocks between Broadway and Ninth Avenue from 44th to 47th Streets.

The land on which Astor built had been part of the seventy-acre Medcef Eden Farm, which extended from 42nd Street up Broadway to 46th and across to the Hudson River. It had been purchased in 1803. John Jacob Astor, father of William B., and William Cutting bought the farm for $25,000, Astor's half of the property being on high ground nearest Broadway; Cutting took the the western half. Astor had sold his fur interests in 1833 and invested in New York real estate at a time when farms and gardens occupied five-sixths of the land area of Manhattan, whose numbered streets were not yet divided into east and west numbers depending on which side of Fifth Avenue they were. His five-story Astor House hotel downtown, built in 1836 of Quincy granite with a central courtyard, was on Broadway between Vesey and Barclay Streets; its vast rotunda would remain a popular luncheon spot for merchants to the end of the century.

Coinciding with William Astor's development was the inauguration in 1849 of the Hudson River Railroad's line to East Albany; the railroad had several stops along the upper West Side. In order to open the area north of 44th Street, Astor's contractors cleared away rocky outcroppings along Sixth Avenue. And as each block was graded, builders put up tenements and row houses along the avenue and in the side streets. By the mid–1850s Tenth and Eleventh Avenue addresses in the West 40s were considered perfectly respectable, albeit moderately priced.

The West Side, said James Gordon Bennett's *New York Herald* in 1860, had "a superior class of residents than those on the East Side of town." And according to *Frank Leslie's Illustrated Newspaper*, the West Side had "a good English or rather American population." Both references were primarily to Chelsea and sections to the south.

More New Yorkers began to look with favor on areas west of Fifth Avenue after the city acquired land for Central Park in 1856. The West 40s and 50s had an elevation that was regarded as healthful, and street railroad lines made the area convenient to downtown offices; by 1860, according to the *Herald*, Seventh Avenue was "very wide and well paved . . . [with] a number of fine edifices . . . in course of erection, under the pressure of the Central Park excitement."

Not until 1865, at the end of the Civil War, did the state legislature order the Central Park Commission to correct defects in the 1811 grid plan, which had been drawn without regard to topography. The grades of upper West Side streets were so steep as to make traffic practically impossible. Andrew Haswell Green, comptroller of Central Park, worked for the next decade to improve the West Side grade, a project that was delayed for three years while city planners agonized over whether to keep Riverside Drive and Morningside Heights for parkland or use it for housing.

By this time New York was already the nation's largest port, its docks crowded with sailing vessels as well as steamships. It was the center not only of American finance, insurance, and publishing but also of manufacturing, with blast furnaces, forges, workshops, breweries, distilleries, sugar refineries, and carriage factories. Its chief residential areas were still the lower East Side and—for the moneyed classes—Washington Square, lower Fifth Avenue, and Murray Hill. Most people lived in boardinghouses or tenements, relatively few of them as far north as 42nd Street, and most lived on the East Side. New Yorkers had enjoyed good Croton water since 1842, but even in the early 1880s only 2 percent of city houses had water connections. Tenement builders installed rudimentary plumbing facilities (communal toilets at the ends of floors) in order to save space; private houses and boarding houses had backyards, some of them with privies, which were otherwise in basements.

Some real estate investors had formed the West Side Association in 1866 to promote rapid development of the area north of 59th Street, where the Jacob Harsen Farm was subdivided into five hundred lots that were sold strictly for residential use, but few people even thought of putting up houses on the upper West Side, which remained a remote bucolic region.

Green's Central Park Commission, working to improve the upper West Side between 59th and 155th Streets, redefined the area's main artery, the Boulevard, formerly called the Bloomingdale Road. Originally thirty-three feet wide, this thoroughfare had been widened by 1849 to seventy-five feet and was for a while called Broadway, like its continuation to the south. The commissioners renamed it the Boulevard and made it one hundred and sixty feet wide with a thirty-foot planted median separating two carriageways, each fifty feet wide with broad sidewalks. Between 78th and 105th Streets, the old Bloomingdale Road ran so close to Tenth Avenue that it cut off the depth of many avenue lots; the Commissioners made it nearly equidistant between Tenth and Eleventh Avenues for those twenty-seven blocks and then merged it into Eleventh, thus saving the cost of opening a new thoroughfare to the north. The Boulevard would remain unpaved north of 92nd Street until after 1891.

New York had tenements as early as 1833; where a private house on a standard twenty-five-by-one-hundred-foot lot could accommodate only one family, a five-or six-story tenement occupying the same property could house four families per floor. In 1869 and 1870, Richard Morris Hunt, the architect, put up the five-story Stuyvesant apartments, or French Flats, in East 18th Street for the developer Rutherford Stuyvesant, who hoped to attract the kind of tenants that heretofore had lived only in private houses. This is generally considered the first American apartment house, although buildings containing apartments with private toilets and hallways may have been put up at least fifteen years earlier in Wooster Street and Hudson Street. Hunt modeled the structure on Parisian apartment buildings, and he provided quarters for a concierge. The apartment layouts were not well planned: two of the bedrooms were at the opposite end of the apartment from its one bathroom, closet space was inadequate, the long and narrow inner hall had numerous right-angle turns, and considerable distances separated kitchen from dining room from service entrance from dumbwaiter. Six rooms and a bath rented for $83.50 to $125 per month, rates that few New Yorkers could afford. Besides, as one observer put it, "Gentlemen will never consent to live on mere shelves under a common roof." But whether or not it was the first multiple dwelling designed for the gentry, the Stuyvesant apartments did begin the era of the apartment house, although that term would not come into use until about 1880.

Even in 1880 New Yorkers of means would scarcely consider living in an apartment, and many considered apartment houses immoral. It was then that the idea of co-operative apartment houses, or home clubs, was introduced to make apartment residences appear socially acceptable.

The co-operative concept dates to the Rochdale Society of Equitable Pioneers, founded by poor English weavers in Lancashire in 1844. In 1868, the *New York Evening Post* reported that families of limited means in a midwestern city had pooled their resources to build or purchase a building that they could own jointly, share the cost of taxes and maintenance, and thereby enjoy appreciable savings. The architect who promoted the co-op idea in New York was Philip Gengembre Hubert, who had adopted his English grandmother's name, Hubert, because Americans could not pronounce Gengembre. Born in 1830 at Paris, Hubert was the son of an architect and civil engineer who was wounded in the revolution of 1830 and financially ruined. The family moved to America and eventually settled in Cincinnati, where Philip studied under his father. Architects were not much in demand, and the young man turned to writing in English and teaching French. At twenty-three, he was professor of French, Spanish, and history at Girard College, Philadelphia. While still in his twenties, he received a patent for a self-fastening button, which he sold for $120,000, a great fortune in the 1850s. He moved to Boston in 1860 and did so well teaching French that he refused an assistant professorship at Harvard. At the end of the Civil War, Hubert went abroad to study architecture. He was back in New York in 1870, starting a firm in partnership with James L. Pirsson. Initially the two built churches and other public buildings, along with some private houses.

Philip Hubert grew increasingly convinced that the residential future of New York lay in apartment buildings. London, Tokyo, and some other cities might continue to expand horizontally via sprawling single-family houses, but the population of New York, which did not yet include Brooklyn or much else besides Manhattan, had grown to 1,164,673 by 1880, up from 942,292 in 1870. Manhattan would have to build upward to accommodate a growing population.

Hubert's first co-op, built for a club of artists, was the Rembrandt Studios in West 57th Street. Erected in 1880 on a site slightly to the left of what would later be Carnegie Hall, it was a great success, even though one bath served as many as four bedrooms.

Sarah Gilman Young, writing in 1881, observed that Americans were always trying to appear better than they were. "Especially do we seek an exterior air of respectability and wealth in our homes. The desire to live in a fine house is peculiarly American. There are no objections to apartment houses in American cities except prejudice, and this is stronger in the United States than elsewhere. To Americans it is a matter of rank. Anything which resembles what we term a tenement is tabooed. There being no fixed caste in America, as in the foreign states, we have established a certain style of living and expenditure, as a distinctive mark of social position."

The vast majority of New Yorkers did live in tenements or boarding houses, and it seemed to Mrs. Young that Americans knew little about how to build apartment houses. "To pack people at night like herrings in casks, in dark, unventilated sleeping rooms, may suit the idea of a soulless New York landlord," she said, but it would not be tolerated in Europe. American landlords acted as if tenants were made for houses rather than houses for tenants. Apartment houses, she insisted, should be constructed around gardens or courts to provide for proper lighting and fresh air.

Philip Hubert may have read Mrs. Young's book. His Central Park Apartments, the largest in the world when they were built, were bright and airy residences for the well-to-do. Built by José de Navarro and commonly known as the Navarro apartments or Spanish Flats, although "Iberian Flats" would have been more appropriate*, these eight-story buildings went up beginning in 1883. They were built of granite, stone, brownstone, and brick to look as if they comprised one large block and occupied a plot of land two hundred feet wide by four hundred and twenty-five feet long. Only the most westerly four of the eight were finished by 1885. They were among the first apartment houses to have passenger elevators.

Elisha Graves Otis, a Yonkers mechanic, had invented his "safety hoister" in 1852; visitors to the New York industrial fair of 1854 had seen Otis hoisted aloft, screamed when he plunged earthward after ordering the ropes to be cut, and gasped in relief and amazement when safety ratchets engaged to halt his descent. Five years later, the world's first commercial passenger elevator was installed in a five-story store at the corner of Broadway and Broome Street. The six-story Fifth Avenue Hotel, built at about the same time at 23rd Street, had an Otis elevator, but until the late 1870s no apartment building had one, and few New Yorkers who could afford better lived above the second or third floor.

Each of the Spanish Flats buildings contained twelve eight-to sixteen-room apartments, three of them duplexes, with drawing rooms sixteen feet by thirty, libraries seventeen by twenty-two, dining rooms eighteen by twenty, chambers (bedrooms) eleven by fifteen, and kitchens fifteen by sixteen. Maid's rooms and storage space were in the basement, reached by a vehicular tunnel in which delivery wagons could be unloaded under cover and off the street. Rooms facing the rear enjoyed the fresh air, sunshine, and quiet of a long common courtyard containing flower beds and fountains. Half the apartments were sold as co-operatives. The buildings were completed as rental structures but had trouble finding tenants. Put up at a time when the surrounding blocks were filled almost entirely by private houses and stables, the Spanish Flats would stand until 1927.

In 1884, Hubert built the eleven-story Chelsea apartment hotel in 23rd Street between Seventh and Eighth avenues. Sixty of its ninety original three- to nine-room suites were in effect co-op apartments, owned by shareholders in the Chelsea Home Club. The other thirty were for rent at $50 to $100 per month and the projected $10,000 in annual rental income was expected to ensure the financial stability of the club, easing the burden of the shareholders. Most flats lacked full kitchen facilities, so the ground

*The first of the Spanish Flats, at the northeast corner of 58th Street and Seventh Avenue, was the Lisbon, built in 1883. It was joined in 58th Street by the Barcelona, Salamanca, and Tolosa and, in 59th Street, by the Madrid, Cordova, Grenada, and Valencia.

floor contained a restaurant along with several private dining rooms.

More talked about than the Chelsea in 1884 was the Dakota at 1 West 72nd Street (corner of Central Park West, as Eighth Avenue above 59th Street was called beginning in 1882). Edward Severin Clark, the Singer Sewing Machine Company magnate who had financed the $2 million building, envisioned the West End as a magnificent new enclave of the city. In 1877 he paid August Belmont $280,000 for the blockfront from 72nd Street to 73rd together with land extending several hundred feet down the side streets. The *Real Estate Record and Builders' Guide* for October 13, 1877, carried a piece entitled "East Side and West Side," which observed that the West Side, isolated from the main line of city development and cut off from the East Side by Central Park, seemed destined to become "the cheap side of the city." Clark was not impressed. On December 20, 1879, he read a paper at a meeting of the West Side Association.

The New York Central & Hudson River grain elevator began operations on the Hudson River at 61st Street in 1879

Clark appreciated the desirability of diversity. The new section of the city, he said, would combine apartment buildings with single-family dwellings to house rich and poor, "Some splendidly, many elegantly, and all comfortably . . . the architecture should be ornate, solid and permanent, and . . . the principle of economic combination should be employed to the greatest possible extent."

Clark's enthusiasm for the upper West Side may have been inspired by Egbert L. Viele, a Civil War general and civil engineer who wrote in 1879 that Murray Hill, for so long "regarded as a synonym of fashion," would in time "be more strictly synonymous with shabby gentility." The upper West Side, said Viele, was "the section of the city that has been held in reserve until the time when the progress of wealth and refinement shall have attained that period of development when our citizens can appreciate and are ready to take advantage of the situation . . . Moreover, this entire region combines in its general aspect all that is magnificent in the leading capitals of Europe. In our Central Park, we have the fine Prater of Vienna, in our grand Boulevard (Broadway) the rival of the finest avenues of the gay capital of France, in our Riverside Avenue the equivalent of the Chiara of Naples and the Corso of Rome, while the beautiful 'Unter den Linden' of Berlin and the finest portions of the West End of London are reproduced again and again."

It was Viele who suggested to the West Side Association in 1880 that Eleventh Avenue north of 63rd Street, where it was clear of railroad tracks, be called West End Avenue. But to share his vision, one had to look beyond the fact that his "West End" was still a wasteland of asylums, athletic fields, breweries, grain elevators, rocky promontories, swamps, and slaughterhouses. The Home for Respectable Aged Females (later the Association Residence for Women), designed by Richard Morris Hunt at a time when he was devising a pedestal for the Statue of Liberty and completed in 1883 at the southeast corner of 104th Street and Amsterdam Avenue, lay surrounded by vacant lots and open fields (the Home accepted only Protestant women who had not been servants). Riverside Drive had opened in 1880 but still lacked the finishing touches that would make it handsome. Sewer mains were still lacking in much of the area, and thirty-four streets between West 59th and 125th Streets were not yet fully opened; there were dirt roads everywhere; even the avenues remained partially unpaved.

Critics pointed to the tenements, cheap houses, and empty lots that dominated this "West End." One could not expect many elegant neighbors if one moved there, they said. Besides, it was simply too far from the "Ladies Mile," on Broadway in the 20s, where fashionable women of the carriage trade saw each other on their daily shopping rounds. The dearth of public transportation was also a factor in real estate speculators' uncertainty about the future of the upper West Side. A horsecar line running up the Boulevard to 125th Street provided desultory service. In 1876 a single horsecar began running at hourly intervals on Eighth Avenue between 59th and 84th streets.

Signaling a change in the area's prospects was the opening of the El. On May 1, 1878, the first train of the Gilbert Elevated Railway Company steamed from Trinity Church up Sixth Avenue to 58th Street in sixteen minutes, and on June 6 the El opened to the public. It was named for Rufus H. Gilbert, whose original patent was for trains on an elevated structure to be operated by atmospheric pressure through steel enclosures. As finally completed in 1879, with a double track road extending 6.12 miles from Morris Street to 53rd Street and Sixth Avenue, this first New York El employed the more conventional means of steam locomotion, and the name was soon changed to Metropolitan Elevated Railway Company. Pertinent to the development of the upper West Side, the Sixth Avenue El swung west at 53rd Street, used tracks paralleling those of the Ninth Avenue El, and rattled up Ninth to 106th Street. After veering east to Eighth Avenue at 110th Street, the Sixth and Ninth Avenue Els reached 155th Street in 1880 with stops at 66th, 72nd, 81st, 93rd, and 104th Streets.

Lots just to the north of the Dakota were still mostly vacant in the late 1880s because owners demanded such high prices. Most building was farther north.
(Photo courtesy Brown Brothers)

When the El opened in 1878 there were no apartment houses between 59th Street and 110th and relatively few private dwellings. Thanks in part to the new El, Sixth Avenue was becoming fashion row. Arnold Constable and Lord & Taylor were still on Broadway between 19th and 20th Streets, true, but newer stores were coming to Sixth Avenue. Hugh O'Neill's Dry Goods Store had opened in 1875 on Sixth between 20th and 21st Streets; B. Altman's on Sixth between 18th and 19th in 1876; Stern's on 23rd Street between Fifth and Sixth in 1878. The Sixth Avenue El helped these and other establishments grow.

When he decided to build the Dakota, Edward Clark was clearly banking on the El. There was a station one block to the west on Ninth Avenue, and a good many houses were going up close to the stations. In fact, a building boom had already begun in the area. Still, the Dakota was a speculative proposition in the early 1880s. There was considerable risk that well-heeled New Yorkers might refuse to live in anything but town houses—*East Side* town houses—and that the upper West Side might not have any great future as a fashionable residential section.

The Dakota, built in 1884, was in the middle of nowhere (photo, c. 1890, courtesy Museum of the City of New York)

Not until the Ninth Avenue El, and the subsequent replacement of horsecars by cable-cars on Tenth Avenue and trolleys on Eighth, did developers begin to take a real interest in the upper West Side, or West End, and even then they had their doubts. Would this become a neighborhood of tenements, of row houses for working- and middle-class families, or of town houses for the prosperous?

* * *

Henry Janeway Hardenbergh was the Dakota's architect. He had attracted Clark's attention in 1879 with his Vancorlear Hotel at Seventh Avenue and 55th Street, and Clark, seeing possibilities in the upper West Side, had commissioned him to build a row of twenty-seven town houses on the north side of 73rd Street running west from Eighth Avenue. The houses were completed early in 1880, a full year before construction of the Dakota began.

Hardenbergh was given carte blanche in designing the Dakota, which was to go up across the street from his row houses. He used a design that has been called (for lack of anything more accurate) German Renaissance, giving the new structure a copper-trimmed slate roof with chimneys, flagpoles, finials, gables, peaks, pyramids, towers, turrets, and wrought-iron fences. Its sixty-five marble-floored mahogany-paneled apartments ranged in size from four to twenty rooms and had fifteen-foot ceilings (actually fifteen and a half feet on the ground floor and slightly less on each ascending floor until the eighth, where the ceilings of the servants' quarters were a mere twelve feet high). Rent-paying tenants occupied the first seven floors, the eighth and ninth were for laundry rooms, the help, and storage, the tenth was a playroom for children. Bathroom fixtures were entirely of porcelain, with seven-foot bathtubs mounted on ball-and-claw feet.

Clark did not live to see the building completed. He died in 1882 at age seventy-two. His Dakota, which opened on October 27, 1884, was left to his twelve-year-old grandson and namesake, who also inherited the owner's apartment—a sixth-floor flat of eighteen rooms, including a drawing room forty-nine feet long and twenty-four feet wide.

Until the Dakota, few residential buildings anywhere in the world rose more than six stories, although seven-story walk-ups did exist in areas where land costs were especially high. Clark had the idea that by living on the sixth floor he could help to popularize the idea of upper-story residence at a time when New Yorkers of means were accustomed only to the first and second floors of town houses. The Dakota's nine hydraulic Otis elevators were operated for years by Irish women dressed in black bombazine. Each passenger elevator served just two apartments per floor, thus giving tenants a feeling of privacy.

The Dakota was New York's first true luxury apartment hotel. It had an inner-courtyard entrance, a large wine cellar, a dining room overlooking Central Park, drawing rooms that in many cases measured forty-eight by twenty feet, and bedrooms measuring a generous twenty by twenty. It was fully rented even before it opened. Tenants soon included the pianomaker Theodor Steinway, two bank presidents, several substantial business owners, a member of the board of governors of the New York Stock Exchange, two spinster sisters named Adams (of the chewing gum family), the sugar refiner Wiliam Arbuckle Jamison, the educator John A. Browning (who would found the Browning School in 1888), and Gustav Schirmer, the music publisher.

Schirmer and his wife entertained Herman Melville (who retired in 1885 after nineteen years as a New York customs inspector but whose work had fallen into obscurity until he was "re-discovered" by the Schirmers), William Dean Howells, Mark Twain, Senator Carl Schurz, and the Russian composer Petr Ilyich Tchaikovsky, who was passing through New York on a concert tour. Taken up to the roof after dinner to see the view, Tchaikovsky came away with the impression that Schirmer owned the entire Dakota and had his own private park across the way.

Until the Dakota went up, visitors deep inside Central Park could lift their eyes and see nothing to disturb the illusion that they were in the midst of meadows and woods with no buildings for miles around. Only church steeples rose above five stories.

While New Yorkers in the early 1880s scoffed at putting up a tall building so remote that it might as well be in the Dakota Territory (North and South Dakota were not admitted to the Union until 1889), it was Clark, not the scoffers, who named his structure. When construction began in 1881, the Dakotas were the focus of gold-mining and building ventures. General Custer's 1876 massacre at the Battle of the Little Bighorn was still fresh in the public mind, as were the exploits of Calamity Jane (Martha Jane Canary) in the 1878 smallpox epidemic at Deadwood; but names like Colorado, Dakota, Montana, Nevada, and Wyoming nevertheless symbolized wealth gained through the hazard of fortunes. Besides, given the advent of the new Ninth Avenue El, 72nd Street and Central Park West was not such a remote location in 1884.

A thirty-nine-year-old merchant named Isidor Straus moved his large and growing family in 1884 from the East 50s to a frame house at the northeast corner of 105th Street and West End Avenue, close to the new Riverside Park. The German-born Straus appreciated the value of the park. In 1866 Isidor had gone into the crockery business with his father Lazarus under the name L. Straus and Son, which in 1874 took over the pottery and glassware department of R.H. Macy's department store. (Isidor and his brother Nathan would own Macy's by 1896.) Not overly concerned that upper West End Avenue was a semirural area populated largely by squatters, Straus moved into a large house, complete with apple orchard. Other rich families were inspired to follow his example. Yet the upper West Side was still so undeveloped in 1884 that someone living in a 73rd Street house between Ninth and Tenth Avenues could look out of an upstairs window and see the elevated trains on the 110th Street curve.

Two years later, in 1886, the *New York Times* wrote, "The West side of the city presents just now a scene of building activity such as was never before witnessed in that section, and which gives promise of the speedy disappearance of all the shanties in the neighborhood and the rapid population of this long neglected part of New York. The huge masses of rock which formerly met the eye, usually crowned by a rickety shanty and a browsing goat, are being blasted out of existence. Streets are being graded, and thousands of carpenters and masons are engaged in rearing substantial buildings where a year ago nothing was to be seen but market gardens or barren rocky fields."

The mid–1880s did see a rush to grade streets and erect row houses and tenements in the West 60s, 70s, and 80s. Lending institutions looked with favor on this area and granted liberal loans. General William Tecumseh Sherman, the Civil War hero, moved into a house at 75 West 71st Street in 1886. (Sherman Square, where Broadway slashes across Amsterdam Avenue at 72nd Street, commemorates his name, as does the William T. Sherman elementary school, P.S. 87, at 160 West 78th Street, although many pupils today may not know their school is named for the man who cut a path of destruction through Georgia and South Carolina.) While parts of the area still appeared raw, real-estate values were climbing so fast that only people of some means could think of buying houses there.

Most West Side real estate activity, however, took place farther south. In 1885, one year after the Dakota opened, the red-stone Osborne Apartments, a rusticated eleven-story Renaissance palazzo designed by James E. Ware and, briefly, the tallest building in New York, accepted its first tenants at the northwest corner of Seventh Avenue and 57th Street. Apartment dwellers were coming to prefer the higher floors, as Clark had hoped they would do. Even the Osborne was considered far uptown when work on it began. Thomas Osborne, a stone contractor who started the structure, went bankrupt, and the building was completed by John Taylor, a hotel man, who did not stint on luxury. The Osborne had an elaborate front porch, a billiard room, and, on the roof, a croquet ground and garden. There were forty suites, some of them duplexes, and major rooms had fifteen-foot ceilings; sleeping rooms, in the rear, had eight-foot ceilings. Mahogany woodwork was used extensively, and there were bronze mantels, crystal chandeliers, and elaborate parquet flooring. The lobby, designed by Tiffany Studios, was of marble and stone, with mosaic-encrusted walls, bronze bas-relief panels, and two sweeping staircases.

Like the Dakota, the Osborne was in a sparsely populated part of town which, in the Blizzard of '88, must truly have seemed like the plains of North Dakota. Drifts covered some brownstones to the second story. One Osborne tenant, a rich malt-and-hops merchant named George D. Baremore, awoke on Monday morning, March 12, 1888, and trudged off into the snow en route to his office downtown. Finding the Sixth Avenue El station at 59th Street closed, he tried to reach the Ninth Avenue El. Police later found his body buried in a snowdrift.

The American Museum of Natural History had been housed until 1876 in the Arsenal, built in 1848 inside Central Park near Fifth Avenue and 64th Street. When the initial wing of the Museum (designed by Calvert Vaux and Jacob Wrey Mould) went up in the mid–1870s between Eighth and Ninth Avenues at 78th Street, it was on the outskirts of what most people thought of as New York City, facing a park that was by no means central. Squatters still occupied small farms within the park. Adjacent to the museum property in three directions were other small farms and vacant lots. Said the curator, "We can only wait and hope that the Elevated Railway Company will soon extend its lines north to 77th Street." The El arrived, but the area remained little changed in 1886. West Side building sites could be had at bargain prices as compared with sites on the East Side, where a vacant lot might easily cost $50,000 (plus a like amount for the house). For less than $25,000 one could obtain both a lot and house on the upper West Side. Developers showed increasing interest in West Side property; the problem was how to persuade affluent East Siders to relocate on the West Side.

Many row houses of this period survive, including 254 West 75th Street, built about 1885. Lamb and Rich in 1886 built row houses between

Handsome town houses sprang up in the 1890s in 81st Street between Columbus Avenue and Amsterdam (1986 photo)

161 and 169 West 74th Street and from 301 to 309 Tenth Avenue. James Brown Lord in 1887 built houses at 153, 155, 157, and 159 West 74th Street, between Ninth and Tenth avenues (called Columbus and Amsterdam beginning in 1890). A Philadelphia architect, Frank Furness, designed houses at 274 and 276 West 71st Street between the Boulevard and West End Avenue. A Spanish architect, Rafael Guastavino*, was engaged by the developer Bernard S. Levy to design houses for West 78th Street between Ninth and Tenth avenues; they went up from 1885 to 1890, and Levy himself occupied 121 from 1886 to 1904. West 81st Street between Ninth and Tenth avenues was built up with row houses between 1888 and 1892.

A building for Engine Company 74 of the New York City Fire Department, designed by Napoleon LeBrun and Sons, went up in 1888 at 120 West 83rd Street, in a day of horse-drawn red-enamel and polished brass LaFrance fire engines. Even with the rush of the El overhead, the city remained in the gaslight era; it was still the Little Old New York that later generations would sentimentalize. Only in the next two decades would a true transformation occur on Gotham's upper West Side.

---

*The Guastavino method of construction, a combination of concrete and masonry, came into use for public buildings such as Carnegie Hall.

II. The Light Fantastic

New York City's first skyscraper (thirteen stories) went up at 50 Broadway in 1889; it was a masonry building (the steel-skeleton skyscraper pioneered in Chicago would not reach New York for another eight years). Four years earlier, in 1885, a new building law had banned residential structures taller than seventy feet (eighty if they faced on avenues). Owners of

The American Museum of Natural History sprouted a new south facade between 1889 and 1900 (1909 Byron photo courtesy Museum of the City of New York)

three- and four-story town houses on the East Side had complained that nine- and ten-story apartment houses would block light and air, reducing their property values. Except for some hotels, no high-rise residential buildings would be put up until the law was repealed in 1901. In the meantime, even hotels would often be no taller than five or six floors.

Architect Edward L. Angell's six-story red-brick and terra cotta Endicott Hotel, with its central skylit palm court, opened in 1889 at Columbus Avenue and 81st Street, just north of the Museum of Natural History, bringing new prestige to an area of mostly single-family houses.

Two years later, as the museum sprouted its first 77th Street wing (designed by J. C. Cady and Company), the Colorado, Lyndhurst, and Nebraska apartment houses, each five stories tall, each with a mottled brick and stone front, all closely resembling the Endicott, went up across the avenue from the Endicott Hotel. Nearby, at 101, 103, and 105 West 77th Street, the five-story Kenmar, Renfrew, and Juanita also date to 1891. The seven-story Greylock at 61 West 74th Street (northeast corner of Columbus Avenue) is a year older.

Vacant lots accounted for more than half the total on the upper West Side in 1892. Between 59th and 96th Streets, where all but a few streets and thoroughfares remained unpaved, only a small majority of the lots were occupied, although 72nd, 86th, and other streets were heavily built up; between 96th and 110th nearly two out of three lots were vacant, but eight lots on the south side of 95th Street between Central Park West and Columbus Avenue were sold in 1892 for upward of $12,000 each—four times what they had cost in 1883.

At 72nd Street, tenants of the Dakota facing Central Park looked out on the shacks, chicken coops, and pigsties of squatters, who were periodically handed eviction notices that they fed to their goats. But if the neighborhood was still largely a shantytown area of open cesspools, blacksmith shops, and saloons it was because the high price of lots discouraged developers.

To the west of its gardens and generating plant, the Dakota did receive a next-door neighbor, the Olcott (it would be replaced in 1925 by a larger building of the same name). But some of the squatters in the lots across 72nd Street were not finally displaced until Jacob Rothschild, a German-born milliner-turned-developer, erected the six-hundred-room Hotel Majestic on the site in 1894. People that year sang "The Sidewalks of New York," a new song with lyrics about East Side and West Side. The Hotel Majestic soon became a rendezvous for more serious musicians, the opera world. Designed by Alfred Zucker, it was the largest of the hotels built opposite the west side of the park.

Carnegie Hall had opened at Seventh Avenue and 57th Street in 1891. Intellectuals of the Century Association that year moved into their new clubhouse, designed by Stanford White with a delicate Palladian facade, at 7 West 43rd Street. Henry J. Hardenbergh's American Fine Arts Society Building (later the Art Students League) came a year later at 215 West 57th Street.

Philip Hubert and his colleagues (the firm was now Hubert, Pirsson and Hoddick) complained in 1892 that, quite aside from the limitation on building heights, it was impossible to build houses with adequate light in all rooms given the limitations of Manhattan's long, narrow blocks. In their article "New York Flats and French Flats," which appeared in the *Architectural Record*, they asked, "Are we wasting millions in the building up of a city so radically defective in plan and construction, that a few decades will find it honeycombed with squalid tenement districts, ever spreading and ever tending to lower depths in fetid degradation?" A "radical change in our division of our land, our mode of building, and a study of yet unsolved and most intricate social questions" was needed, the architects insisted. The long communal inner courtyard shared by Hubert's eight-story Spanish Flats was designed to provide one solution to the problem of inadequate light and air.

Skating in Central Park late in 1894 after completion of the Hotel Majestic just south of the Dakota (photo courtesy Museum of the City of New York)

Hubert and his associates maintained that fireproof brick-and-iron buildings were no more expensive to build in the long run, considering the number of years they would last, and in 1893, New York's first stone-floored hotel, a twelve-story brownstone structure built by Hubert at a time when most hotels were still firetraps, opened at 117 West 58th Street under the name Sevillia.

Hubert retired from architecture in 1895 as economic depression deepened. More than 15,000 business firms failed in the next few years. Also in 1895 Herald Square received its name from the new building put up by McKim, Mead and White for James Gordon Bennett's *New York Herald*.

Far to the north, amid the country lanes of the upper West Side, the nation's first cancer hospital, financed by twenty-year-old John Jacob Astor IV, had opened in 1885 at Central Park West and 106th Street in a neo-French Renaissance château designed by Charles Coolidge Haight. The five towers of the New York Cancer Hospital (which in 1899 became General Memorial Hospital for the Treatment of Cancer and Allied Diseases) housed circular wards, believed to be more hygienic than rooms with corners that might collect germs. The hospital's 130 beds were used by more than 600 patients per year, two-thirds of them supported by the city, the others being charged $7 to $30 per week. The focus was on those with any chance of being cured.

New medical facilities were opening near Columbus Circle. Roosevelt Hospital, which had begun in 1871 at 70th Street and Madison Avenue (with private rooms at $3 to $4 per day at a time when other hospitals, including Bellevue, had only crowded wards, many of them crawling with rats), began a move west in 1892; its William J. Syms Operating Theater, built that year at the southwest corner of 59th Street and Ninth Avenue, would be followed within a few years by a complex of other buildings. (The philanthropist James Henry Roosevelt had died in 1863, leaving a large fortune, amassed through real estate investments, to found the hospital.)

Broadway, still called the Boulevard north of 59th Street, was becoming more attractive in the early 1890s, with hotels going up in the West 60s. The *New-York Daily Tribune* had written of the "Charms of the Boulevard" in its May 6, 1884, issue: The "driveway [is] divided for its full length by a strip of green flanked on each side by trees; [it is] the only street that does not depend upon the buildings for its beauty . . . But the development of the Boulevard is only in its incipiency." That development leaned increasingly toward multiple-dwelling residential construction. The *Tribune* quoted a resident to the effect that this was "the ideal large apartment-house street . . . its pavement of the noiseless kind."

The Sherman Square Hotel, built in 1891 at the southwest corner of 71st Streeet and Amsterdam Avenue (a twelve-story addition would extend the four-hundred-room hotel south to 70th Street in 1901), rose seven stories and was the tallest West Side building north of 59th Street except for the Dakota. The six-story Park and Tilford Building, designed by McKim, Mead and White as the uptown headquarters of a liquor company, went up in 1893 at 100 West 72nd Street, on the southwest corner of Columbus Avenue. North of 72nd Street, said the *Tribune* on June 9, 1895, there were "no less than eighty excavations for buildings" (chiefly private houses but some apartment houses, too) west of Central Park. Electric conduits, developed in the mid–1890s, were beginning to come into the area, making it possible to install the new electric elevators. Electric trolley lines would soon replace cable-cars on the Boulevard and Amsterdam Avenue.

"It would not be easy to find anywhere a better illustration of the powerful influence of transportation facilities upon the material evolution of a locality than has been afforded here," said the *Tribune*. "That this section is possessed of natural advantages superior to any other part of Manhattan Island is no new discovery."

Sounding very much like the puffery of a real estate promoter, the article went on to cite "the unequalled views, pure air, solid foundations and proximity to the city's pleasure grounds . . . substantial inducements for residential settlement." The *Tribune*, the *New York Herald*, and the *World* even had columns on social life in what they sometimes called the West End, but they were segregated from the social columns which related goings-on in more fashionable parts of town.

Columbus Circle got its name and its statue in 1892 (photo courtesy Museum of the City of New York)

It appeared for a time that this West End would indeed become fashionable, perhaps not so chic as the East Side neighborhoods built up with solid rows of brownstones years before but nevertheless providing a suitable enough address for any respectable member of New York society. On West End Avenue, covenants restricted construction to first-class private houses, and houses above 72nd Street were actually more gracious in style than most found on the East Side. They were built on the new American basement plan, so called because a wide, street-level reception hall replaced the traditional high stoop. From such a reception area a curving staircase led to a salon, music room, and dining room on the floor above.

It was obvious that a good many servants were required to run such an extravagant establishment; that was part of the attraction. Thorstein Veblen, the University of Chicago social scientist, was developing his theory of the leisure class at the time, and the houses of the upper West Side provided perfect illustrations of his theories of conspicuous consumption and conspicuous waste. New Yorkers were not averse to flaunting their wealth.

The gateway to this real estate developer's dream was Columbus Circle, so called beginning four centuries after the Great Navigator's discovery, when it was graced with Gaetano Russo's column. It rose seventy-seven feet above the carriage, wagon, and horsecar traffic that revolved below.

Churches had been built to serve the growing upper West Side population. Isaac Thomas Hecker, the priest who founded the Missionary Society of St. Paul the Apostle (the Paulist Fathers), had had the cornerstone laid early in 1876 for the Church of St. Paul the Apostle on Columbus Avenue at 60th Street. The church, with altars and a sanctuary lamp designed by the architect Stanford White and a baptistry and mural by John LaFarge, was dedicated early in 1885. St. Andrew's Methodist Episcopal Church (later the West Side Institutional Synagogue) went up at 120 West 76th Street between Columbus and Amsterdam avenues in 1889; Henry F. Kilburn's Romanesque revival brownstone West-Park Presbyterian Church, on the northeast corner of 86th Street and Amsterdam, in 1890; All Angels Episcopal Church on the southeast corner of West End Avenue and 81st Street in 1890; T. H. Poole's Roman Catholic Holy Name of Jesus Church at 96th Street and Amsterdam in 1891; Robert W. Gibson's Protestant Episcopal St. Michael's Church on the northwest corner of 99th Street and Amsterdam in 1891; George Keisler's First Baptist Church at the Boulevard and 79th Street in 1892. Dutch Reformed worshippers moved with their Collegiate School into Robert W. Gibson's West End Collegiate Church and schoolhouse at West End Avenue and 77th Street in 1892.

Construction began in 1892 (and continues today) on the Cathedral of St. John the Divine, on Amsterdam Avenue at 112th Street, in an area that was still largely open fields. The Methodist Episcopal Church of St. Paul was completed in 1897 on the northeast corner of West End Avenue and 86th Street. The Universalist Church was built in 1898 on Central Park West at 76th Street. The Roman Catholic Holy Trinity Church at 213 West 82nd Street (between Amsterdam and Broadway) came a year or two later. Church spires were still New York's tallest structures, visible for miles.

Naturally, parishioners lived in the private residences and multi-family dwellings that were springing up in the area; what surprised investors was *where* the buildings were springing up. Many had assumed that West End Avenue would become the chief business thoroughfare and that the best private residences would be on Central Park West and on the broad, treelined Boulevard. Yet more private houses were put up on West

The Church of St. Paul the Apostle, built in 1876 on Ninth Avenue at 60th Street, was followed in the next two decades by other upper West Side churches
(1986 photo)

End Avenue than anywhere else. The lots facing Central Park were filled not with imposing houses, as was Fifth Avenue across the park, but rather with "family hotels," apartment buildings, and institutions.

America's first indoor ice-skating rink, the St. Nicholas, was built in 1896 at 57 West 66th Street. Designed by Walter B. Chambers and the Beaux Arts architect Ernest Flagg, it later became the St. Nicholas Arena, where boxers the likes of Jack Johnson and Jess Willard fought before World War I.*

Columbia University's Low Memorial Library was built in 1897 (photo courtesy Columbiana collection)

In the 1890s a controversy arose about building a subway somewhere on the West Side, possibly under the Boulevard, as Broadway was still known, and property owners resisted selling in hopes that the subway would boost Boulevard land prices. As a result, the Boulevard, in spite of the little parks along its center island, remained largely unimproved, a shambles of rocks, shacks, and billboards, even after other avenues and sidestreets were built up with private houses.

*Although prizefighting was illegal in New York at the time, George Bellows painted his famous *Stag at Sharkey's* in 1907. Bellows was the youngest and most athletic artist of the Ashcan School. He had opened a studio nearby and frequently attended events held at 127 Columbus Avenue, where Tom Sharkey, a retired fighter, operated a famous athletic club. Patrons got round the letter of the law by joining Sharkey's "club" for the evening. Every handbill bore the words, "Both Members of This Club," referring to the contenders in a bout, and a well-known Bellows painting of 1909 is entitled *Both Members of This Club*. Floyd Patterson had his professional debut here in 1952; its final event, held in 1962, was a bout between two undefeated heavyweights, Billy Daniels and a young Olympic prize winner by the name of Cassius Clay. Clay (later Muhammed Ali) won. After 1962 the arena went on to enjoy a career in broadcasting. Stillman's Gymnasium, on the west side of Eighth Avenue between 54th and 55th, was founded in 1921 by Lou Stillman, who sold it in 1959. Used by fighters such as Jack Dempsey, and a source of material for the writer Damon Runyon, it was razed in 1961 to make way for a seventeen-story white-brick apartment house.

Work on a new campus for Columbia University, situated since 1857 in Hamilton Hall on Madison Avenue between 49th and 50th Streets and neighboring buildings, began in 1893 close to the cathedral site: from 114th to 120th Street between the Boulevard and Amsterdam Avenue. New York Hospital's Bloomingdale Insane Asylum had sold its spacious grounds to the university. Columbia's Low Memorial Library, donated by former university president (and former New York mayor) Seth Low and designed by McKim, Mead and White, dates to 1897.

La Rochelle, a new apartment house designed by Lamb and Rich with a columned facade, went up in 1896 at the northeast corner of 75th Street and Columbus Avenue. Its first two stories were occupied by a large restaurant containing a grand staircase, potted palms, and a quiet "Japanese garden." Tranquility was an elusive commodity on Columbus Avenue. Amsterdam Avenue, which had no El, was quieter. Not for another four years would excavation begin on Broadway (as the Boulevard was renamed on February 14, 1899) for the city's first subway line, which would eventually end the clatter of the El.

*   *   *

Greater New York after 1898 included Brooklyn, Queens, the East Bronx, and Staten Island as well as Manhattan and the West Bronx (Kingsbridge, Morrisania, and West Farms, which had been annexed in 1874); by the turn of the century it had nearly three and a half million people. Manhattan alone had 1,850,093—up from 1,441,716 in 1890. It would have nearly half a million more by 1910. A few Fifth Avenue mansions were still going up for the very rich, and row-houses continued to rise on East Side and West.

West Side houses were more eclectic than those on the other side of town, where a high-stooped brownstone uniformity prevailed: flat rooflines, symmetrically rectangular windows, few departures from the norm. Newer houses of the 1890s on the West Side were also in some cases brownstones, but they could as easily be faced with white marble, blue-gray sandstone, limestone, or brick ranging in color from gray to cream, from soft rose to deep red. In an age of architectural conformity, these houses were rebels. They displayed a defiant variety of roof styles—gabled, dormered, peaked, and pyramided—some of them not unlike the chalet roofs of the El stations. Many had bay windows, often of stained glass. Their architects seemed deliberately to strive for kitsch. The variety of its houses gave the upper West Side an air of frivolity that made it seem almost a different city from the rest of town.

But the price of a new row house, $15,000 on average in 1890, was climbing fast—by 1902 the average would be $64,000. Residential construction on the West Side at the turn of the century was therefore primarily apartment house construction, encouraged in part by the electric elevator invented in the late 1890s. Turn-of-the-century apartment buildings are listed in Appendix I under 1900, although that date is in many cases approximate. None is of any great importance except to the people who have lived in them; they are remarkable only in the vast profusion of their evocative names and in the fact that virtually all of them survived at least until the late 1980s. Taken together, they illustrate the furious pace of building that went on in so much of the upper West Side as developers anticipated the arrival of the subway.

The Turrets on Riverside Drive at 84th Street, designed by S. B. Ogden, was the first apartment building on Riverside Drive. (No row house on the Drive would be replaced by an apartment house until after World War I.) Apartments at the Turrets ranged in size from ten rooms with three baths to twenty rooms with six baths. The building had a white marble swimming pool, a gymnasium, a billiard room, a basketball court, bowling alleys, a banquet hall, and a large ballroom.

Apartment houses were beginning to rise on Riverside Drive at the turn of the century (1903 photograph courtesy Museum of the City of New York)

As the century turned, stately town houses off Central Park West in 85th Street received a couple of new apartment house neighbors when the five-story Clinton and Sudeley went up at the end of the block near Columbus Avenue. The Brockholst, a six-story apartment hotel across Columbus at 101 West 85th Street, had been standing since about 1890 with a lobby decorated by Tiffany Studios and an elegant restaurant (most large apartment houses at the time had their own restaurants, a holdover from the boardinghouse life-style and an amenity that would continue into the 1920s and, in some cases, even longer). An apartment with nine rooms and bath rented for $125 per month.

The classic 1895 limestone Bar Association building by Cyrus L. W. Eidlitz at 42 West 44th Street (and 37 West 43rd) was enhancing the West Side's claim to architectural prominence. So (more dramatically) was Daniel H. Burnham's towering twenty-story Fuller Building, commonly called the Flatiron Building, at 23rd Street and Madison Square (1902). The Algonquin Hotel in 44th Street between Fifth and Sixth Avenues (1902), John Jacob Astor IV's 660-room Astor Hotel on the west side of Times Square, the elaborate red-brick Knickerbocker Hotel, at the southeast corner of 42nd Street and Broadway, which Enrico Caruso and George M. Cohan would soon call home, and new hotels uptown were reasserting the West Side's claim to having prestigious accommodations. In the block with the Algonquin was the red-brick Harvard Club, built in 1894 by McKim, Mead and White; so was Warren and Wetmore's fanciful New York Yacht Club, put up five years later.

Spurring much of the construction was the so-called new law of 1901 permitting construction of buildings one and a half times as high as the width of the streets on which they faced. New York's 83,000 six-story "old law" masonry-and-wood tenement buildings still housed 70 percent of the city's population. Emma Lazarus had written her fine words about "huddled masses, yearning to breathe free" in 1883, three years before the Statue of Liberty went up in New York harbor, and those words would be inscribed on the statue's pedestal in 1903,* but the city's immigrant population, and most of its other residents, were huddled still. The tenements, each housing at least ten families, were strung end to end, like railroad cars, on lots measuring twenty-five feet by one hundred. Tenants shared generally rudimentary plumbing facilities at one end of each ninety-foot hall, while tiny air shafts at the ends of the halls permitted only minimal amounts of light and air. Any apartment building is, technically, a tenement, but because the word had such unpleasant associations it began to be applied strictly to apartment housing for the poor, even though the new law required that existing tenements be upgraded with skylights and additional water closets.

Some 4,425 Manhattan apartment houses, most of them very small, went up between 1902 and 1910; many were on the upper West Side. Compared with the old tenements and even the new ones, the new apartment houses were almost sinfully luxurious, the new hotels pure heaven.

Graham Court, built by the Astor family at the southwest corner of West 116th Street and Seventh Avenue (later called Adam Clayton Powell, Jr., Boulevard), had a handsome inner courtyard. Clinton and Russell were the architects. William Hamilton Russell had worked for his greatuncle James Renwick, designer of Grace Church and St. Patrick's Cathedral, until 1894, when he went into partnership with Charles W. Clinton, who had studied with Richard Upjohn, architect of Trinity Church. Clinton and Russell also designed the Astor Apartments, built for William Waldorf Astor.

The Criterion Arms, a six-story apartment house, went up at the turn of the century at 526 West 111th street, just down the street from the nascent Cathedral of St. John the Divine; it echoed the cathedral in having

---

*A replica of the statue, fifty-five feet high, was placed atop a storage warehouse at 43 West 64th Street in 1902. This Liberty lost her torch in a windstorm some years ago, but otherwise she stands intact.

The Dorilton, on Broadway at 71st Street, was ridiculed by critics in 1902 (1986 photo)

stained-glass windows at the back of its court and, in front, a row of medieval masons, builders, and other workmen carved in stone.

The Dorilton, designed by Janes and Leo, was called an architectural aberration when it opened in 1902 at the northeast corner of 71st Street and Broadway. Said the *Architectural Record*, "the sight of it makes strong men swear and weak women shrink affrighted." But it would look rather handsome, gingerbread and all, more than eighty years later. Henry Ward Ranger, an American painter, helped to organize the co-operative Sixty-Seventh Street Studios, a structure that would in time be covered with ivy. Its predecessor at 25 West 67th Street had a central kitchen that sent meals up to the apartments via dumbwaiter.

The gleaming white Ansonia was financed by William Earl Dodge Stokes, a rich speculator who had inherited $6 million and who, in 1886,

Ansonia, on Broadway between 73rd Street and 74th, dazzled the eye in 1901
(1986 photo)

had put up more than fifty row houses west of the Boulevard. Stokes had been divorced in 1900 after less than five years of marriage to the former Rita Hernandez de Alba Acosta, a noted beauty whose picture he had seen in a Fifth Avenue photographer's window. Their son Weddy had been born at 262 West 72nd Street, one of many Stokes-owned houses in the area. Ostensibly designed by the French architect Paul E. M. Duboy of Graves and Duboy, the sixteen-story Ansonia, on the west side of Broadway between 73rd and 74th streets, was actually Stokes's own creation. Stokes was heir to Phelps, Dodge copper and Ansonia Brass and Copper fortunes, and he named his hotel after his maternal grandfather Anson Greene Phelps, who had founded Ansonia Brass and Copper at Ansonia, Connecticut. Outside, it looked like a confectioner's spun-sugar fantasy of a nineteenth-century French resort hotel, with turrets and balconies galore. Inside, floor plans were based on models that Stokes had studied in

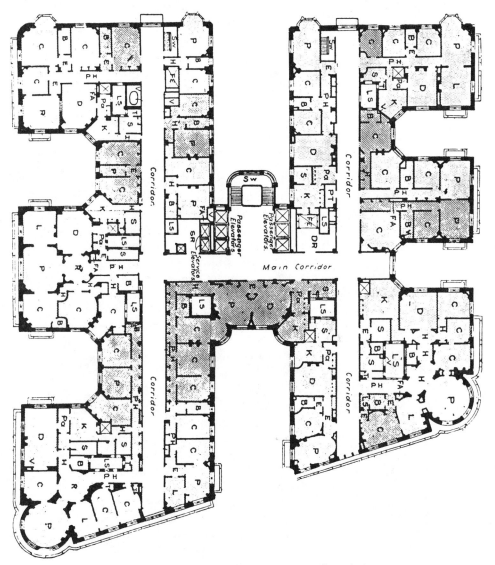

Ansonia apartments were mostly enormous (floor plan)

France, and the apartments contained some unusual rooms. One had an elliptical living room, a dining room to match, and a bedroom shaped at one end like the apse of a church. Another had an oval reception hall with a semicircular sculpture niche; it also had a circular dining room. The hotel had 400 baths plus 600 toilets and washbasins. A single room and bath rented for $50 per month, a suite of eighteen rooms with three baths and four toilets went for $625 per month. Electric blowers in the sub-basement circulated air over coils that were steam-heated in winter and cooled by freezing brine in summer to keep the Ansonia's interior at a constant 70° F. Three-foot-thick partitions of terra cotta from a Stokes plant in New Jersey separated the apartments and made the place fireproof (Stokes balked at paying high fire-insurance premiums). Elevators came from a Stokes company in Worcester, Massachusetts.

Stokes and his young son Weddy lived in a sprawling apartment on the sixteenth floor, which also housed the Ansonia's banquet hall and English Grille. The main dining room, seating 550, was on the lobby floor. Also in the lobby was a fountain containing live seals; there was a swimming pool in the basement. An orchestra played in the roof garden to entertain guests on summer evenings. Stokes used the roof garden to keep goats, a pet bear, chickens, ducks, and geese. Whatever goatsmilk he did not drink he used to make cheese, and he sold eggs to tenants at half price until stopped by a lawsuit from doing so.

The Ansonia would soon be home to Theodore Dreiser and other notables, including Florenz Ziegfeld, who in the summer of 1908, while his wife, Anna Held, was in Europe, installed his eighteen-year-old show-girl mistress Lillian Lorraine, *née* Eulallean de Jacques, in a thirteenth-floor flat just like the tenth-floor suite occupied by Ziegfeld and his wife. (Thirteen rooms and four baths at the Ansonia went for about $400 per month in those days.) Ziegfeld was a notorious lothario who had earlier in the year forced his wife to undergo an illegal abortion. Babe Ruth, the home-run king whose sexual appetites were legendary and whose amazing capacities dwarfed those of Ziegfeld, would be an Ansonia tenant in the early 1920s.

Despite all its new hotels and apartment houses, the upper West Side at the turn of the century remained an area of grassy lawns and shady trees. Broadway was for the most part neglected by developers until 1900. The social critic Lewis Mumford, born in 1895 to a serving girl who had been seduced by an East Side bachelor, spent his early years in his grand-mother's West 65th Street brownstone. He recalled the area in his memoirs, published when he was in his late eighties:

"That was before the High School of Commerce was built across the way and long before the Lincoln Arcade—which still later became a refuge for penurious artists—was razed to make way for Lincoln Center. Until the new subway tore up Boss Tweed's tree-lined Boulevard . . . , as Broadway above Fifty-ninth Street was called, this was a quite respectable street and gave no hint of becoming the sordid red-light area it later turned into . . .

"From Sixty-fifth Street up, Broadway was still full of vacant lots, with visible chickens and market gardens, genuine beer gardens like Unter den Linden, and even more rural areas. Since for the first quarter of a century of my life I lived between Central Park and Riverside Drive, wide lawns and tree-lined promenades are inseparable in my mind from the design of every great city; for what London, Paris, and Rome boasted, New York then possessed . . . "

North of 110th Street in the early part of the century, Mumford recalled, there were a few rows of houses put up by "overeager speculators or homemakers," but for the most part this was an area of vacant lots, even vacant blocks, some of them containing market gardens. Even as late as 1912 there was a market garden on the Astor estate in the lower 90s, and above 125th Street there were "many tracts that could still be called farms, interspersed as they were with roadhouses and beer gardens where the thirsty cyclists who then filled the highways on Sundays could rest in the shade and down a schooner of beer for five cents."

Elegant townhouses continued to go up in some blocks from 1902 to 1904. These, designed by Percy Griffith, are at 18–52 West 74th Street, 1902–1904 (Wurts Bros photo courtesy Museum of the City of New York)

Mumford described other West Side houses of the period: "My area of the city was relatively compact. The rows of Brownstone Fronts that had been so popular in the third quarter of the Nineteenth Century—

an ugly chocolate-colored sandstone from the quarries around Hartford had displaced the warm reddish-brown sandstone from Belleville, New Jersey, which one may still find on Brooklyn Heights—were giving way to a more variegated type of domestic architecture, first influenced by [Henry H.] Richardson, then by McKim, Mead and White, with fine ocher roman bricks and classic details; and then, on West End Avenue, this was followed by gabled houses in the Dutch style, as a new shelf of civic history books brought back into the consciousness of New Yorkers their own Dutch heritage."

Opening the upper West Side to residential living far more effectively than the El had ever done was the Interborough Rapid Transit (I.R.T.), New York's first subway system, for which Broadway was being torn up at the end of the century. Property values along Broadway soared, and many of the apartment houses listed above were built by speculators anticipating that more people would be attracted to live near the subway. It opened to the public on October 27, 1904—twenty years to the day after the Dakota had opened at 72nd Street and Central Park West—with 133 handsome kiosks, including one at Sherman Square that was later designated a city landmark.

Sherman Square (72nd Street, Broadway, and Amsterdam Avenue) after opening of first subway. Kiosk is at center, Ansonia behind it, Dorilton at right (photo courtesy Museum of the City of New York)

Private investors, led by August Belmont & Company with backing from the English Rothschilds, financed digging by the Rapid Transit Subway Construction Company of which August Belmont II was president. The work was done largely by Irish, Italian, and Polish laborers from the tenement districts. Edwin Arlington Robinson, a New Englander in his early thirties who would later be famous for his poetry, had a job checking stone weights during the removal of debris. But New York's subway, like so much of New York, was built by immigrants or their sons—twelve thousand men blasting and digging through solid rock for ten hours a day at twenty cents an hour.

In 1903, the year before the subway opened, New York's surface and elevated railroads carried more paying passengers than did all the steam railroads of North and South America combined. The subway relieved the pressure on the trolleys and El, and it also changed residential living patterns. With the subway one could live within easy reach of the city's financial, manufacturing, shopping, and entertainment districts without the noise, filth, and congestion of heavy street traffic and elevated railroads. Grand Central Railroad Station (whose great terminal still lay ten years in the future) was now only five minutes from 72nd Street, City Hall sixteen minutes. Although the subway ran only in Manhattan, and above 42nd Street only on the West Side, it covered its territory well, carrying passengers from City Hall up to 42nd Street, west to Broadway, and thence up to 145th Street.

Trolley cars were replacing horsecars except on Fifth Avenue, where horsecars continued until 1907. Proper ladies and gentlemen still went about town by private carriage or hansom cab. Stables, blacksmith shops, farriers, and the like continued to occupy an inordinate amount of real estate, sometimes in relatively high-rise structures such as the four-story Claremont Stables (circa 1889) in 89th Street between Columbus and Amsterdam, where riding horses can still be hired for a turn in the park. Dating from about the same time are stables at the northwest corner of Amsterdam and 75th Street, once the New York Cab Company, later the Berkley Garage.

Horse lovers patronized saddle and carriage shops on Broadway in the upper 40s, an area called Long Acre after a similar district in London. Longacre Square, whose north end was occupied by the Brewster Carriage Works, became Times Square on April 19, 1904, when newspaper publisher Adolph Ochs had the name changed as construction proceeded on his twenty-five-story Times Tower, built at the south end of the square on a site formerly occupied by Pabst's Hotel and Restaurant.

Times Square area hotels of the period included the nine-and-a-half-story Norfolk (later called the Remington), built at the turn of the century at 129–131 West 46th Street; the thirteen-story Patterson (later called the Wentworth), built in 1901 at 59 West 46th Street by Mrs. Frances Patterson, who had operated a large boarding house at 49–51 West 49th Street; the twelve-story Seymour at 52–54 West 45th Street; and the twelve-and-a-half-story Woodward, built in 1903 at the southeast corner of Broadway and 55th Street, which would expand to fill the blockfront between Broadway and Seventh Avenue.

Times Square was only beginning to assume its role as the world's theatrical center.

III. The New Rialto

Times Square early in the century as seen from atop the Times Tower (photo courtesy Brown Brothers)

When the subway opened in 1904, Times Square had barely embarked on its career as the city's prime source of entertainment, legitimate or otherwise. It was growing into the role as older theaters fell out of favor.

Castle Garden, at the Battery, had operated from 1824 until 1855 and could hold more than six thousand patrons; P. T. Barnum presented Jenny Lind there in the fall of 1850. But Castle Garden became New York's immigrant receiving station in May 1855 and the city's entertainment center became the Academy of Music, which had opened in 1854 in Irving Place. In 1868, Samuel N. Pike, a financier, put up a white-marble-and-iron Opera House at 23rd Street and Eighth Avenue, hoping that it would supplant the Academy of Music; but its location was not in a fashionable neighborhood, and it was sold in 1869 to the railroad speculators Jim Fisk and Jay Gould. They renamed it the Grand Opera House and used the top floors for their Erie Railroad offices. Fisk had a weakness for the French actresses who performed Offenbach at his opera house downstairs and looted the railroad's treasury to finance his private activities. When he was shot early in 1872 by a business rival (and a rival for the affections of his mistress, Josie Mansfield), he was nevertheless laid out in the railroad company offices atop the opera house.

In the 1870s Union Square was the focus of theatrical activity. Wallack's Theater was at East 13th Street, the Globe Theater (originally A.T. Stewart's Atheneum) was nearby; so were the German Theater, the Union Square Theater, and the Academy of Music.

Actor Edwin Booth had put up Booth's Theater in 1869 at 23rd Street and Sixth Avenue; although it lasted only five years it led the way to a movement north and west. A new Wallack's Theater opened in 1882 at Broadway and 30th Street, and the Casino Theater opened that same year at Broadway and 39th. The New Park Theater of 1883 at Broadway and 35th (its interior taken from Booth's Theater) later became the Herald Square Theater; it was initially leased for a few years by the vaudeville team Harrigan and Hart.

When the Metropolitan Opera House opened on October 22, 1883, on a site that occupied a full city block at Broadway and 39th Street diagonally opposite the Casino Theater, its location was considered fairly remote from the city's fashionable residential and shopping center to the south and east, but was not that far from the mansions of London Terrace, built in the 1840s for the nouveau riche of the day, who were called Shoddyites. The city's Old Guard—Astors, Bayards, Beekmans, Belmonts, Cuttings, and Schuylers—had blocked new millionaires, notably the Vanderbilts, from obtaining boxes in the relatively small Academy of Music. Within three years the Academy of Music was forced to close as the city's moneyed classes flocked to the new Met, which had 3,700 seats, including seventy boxes for such as George F. Baker, James Gordon Bennett, J. R. Drexel, Cyrus Field, Elbridge T. Gerry, Ogden Goelet, Jay Gould, James Harriman, Collis P. Huntington, Adrian Iselin, D. Ogden Mills, William Rhinelander, William Rockefeller, and William C. Whitney, as well as the Vanderbilts.

In 1884 New York's theaters—mostly vaudeville houses—had seating capacity for 41,000. The Casino Theater, on the southeast corner of Broadway and 39th Street, had opened in October 1882; in 1900 it launched the Floradora Girls, first in a long string of Broadway chorus lines. The Broadway Theater opened on March 3, 1888, on the southwest corner of Broadway and 41st Street; Edwin Booth and Sir Henry Irving would be among the many notable actors to appear there in the 1890s. Ned Harrigan built a theater for himself in 1890 on the north side of 35th Street just east of Sixth Avenue; Richard Mansfield took the house in 1895 and changed its name to the Garrick. And in 1893 the real estate magnate

The Lyceum Theater in 45th Street was the last word in elegance in 1903 (photo courtesy Theater Collection, Museum of the City of New York)

Robert Goelet helped finance the Abbey Theater, which opened on land he owned at 38th Street and Broadway; Henry Irving gave the inaugural performance. The theater reopened in 1896 as the Knickerbocker and survived until 1930.

But it was the legendary Charles Frohman who built first in Times Square. He opened the Empire Theater in 1893 at 40th Street and Broadway, opposite the ten-year-old Metropolitan Opera House. Two years later the cigarmaker and impresario Oscar Hammerstein opened the Olympia, a blocklong structure on Broadway between 44th and 45th streets, to house a concert hall, a music hall, and a theater. The Lyric Theater (later the Criterion), designed to house musicals, opened on November 25, 1895; the Music Hall, intended for spectacles, on December 17.

Playwrights of the time included Philip Hubert, who retired from architecture in 1895. On December 10, 1895, *The Witch*, a five-act drama by Philip Hubert and Marie Madison, opened at Richard Mansfield's Garrick Theater with a cast of twenty-four (including Marie Hubert as Leontine, the Witch). Set in 1692 Salem, Massachusetts, the "picturesque American play" was periodically revived.

In rapid succession from 1900 to 1912 came a series of new legitimate theaters in the Times Square area: the Lyric Theater and Klaw and Erlanger's New Amsterdam in 42nd Street; the Lyceum (replacing an earlier Lyceum on Fourth Avenue); the Hippodrome, with 5,200 seats, on Sixth Avenue; the Stuyvesant (later the Belasco); Charles Dillingham's Globe (later the Lunt-Fontanne); George M. Cohan's Theater with Cohan's comedy *Get-Rich-Quick Wallingford*, which had opened five months earlier at the year-old Gaiety; the Winter Garden; the Folies Bergere (later the Fulton, then the Helen Hayes), which opened as a theater-restaurant but became a legitimate house in October 1911); the Little Theater (later the second Helen Hayes); the Eltinge (later the Empire), named for the female impersonator Julian Eltinge; and the Cort, which opened with *Peg o' My Heart*, a new play by John Hartley Manners starring his bride, Laurette Taylor. All are listed in Appendix II; some are still in use, if only for kung fu films.

There were a few theaters outside Times Square. William Randolph Hearst and some associates had financed the Majestic Theater at 5 Columbus Circle, which opened in 1903 with the musical extravaganza *The Wizard of Oz*; and the New Theater had opened six years later in a magnificent building designed by Carrère and Hastings on Central Park West between 62nd and 63rd streets. Backed by a syndicate headed by Otto Kahn and including J. P. Morgan, John Jacob Astor III, and several Vanderbilts, the New Theater and its repertory company lost $400,000 in its first two seasons. Renamed the Century, it was used for a 1914 experiment in talking pictures, for operas performed in English, for religious spectacles, and for ballet. It was to the Century that Diaghilev brought his Ballets Russes and introduced American audiences to Stravinsky's *Firebird* and a police-censored version of Debussy's *L'après midi d'un faune*. Hazel Dawn, Elsie Janis, and Leon Errol appeared at the Century in the 1916

Irving Berlin-Victor Herbert musical *The Century Girl*, and in 1918 Berlin himself sang "Oh, How I Hate to Get Up in the Morning" when he and other soldiers from Camp Upton appeared at the Century in his musical *Yip Yip Yaphank*. But Hearst's Majestic had been turned into a motion picture house by the end of 1907, and the Century was never really successful. Times Square suffered from no real competition for the title of New York's rialto.

The New Theater, later called the Century, opened in 1909 on Central Park West between 62nd Street and 63rd but lasted less than twenty years (photo courtesy Museum of the City of New York)

Weber and Fields' Music Hall opened early in 1913 in 44th Street; it was the second theater built for the song-and-dance comedians Joe Weber and Lew Fields (Shanfield), who had begun their careers at age sixteen in 1883 at Keith and Batchelder's Dime Museum in Boston under the management of Edward F. Albee, then twenty-six. The Shuberts soon gained control of the Music Hall and changed its name to the 44th Street Theater. In the meantime, the Palace Theater opened in March 1913 at Broadway and 47th Street. B. F. (Benjamin Franklin) Keith and his partner Edward F. Albee, who owned a chain of theaters and other vaudeville houses, presented a bill that included a wire act, a Spanish violinist, a one-act play by George Ade, a condensed Viennese opera, the Eight London Palace girls, comedians McIntyre and Hardy, and comedian Ed Wynn, then twenty-six. They charged $2 admission when the top price at other vaudeville theaters was fifty cents but had little success until Sarah Bernhardt opened on May 5 and a pantomime juggler, William Claude Dukenfield (who called himself W. C. Fields), joined the act in the week of May 10.

On the heels of the Palace came other new theaters, all of them built before the end of 1918, most of them still important fixtures in the Great White Way: The Longacre, Shubert, Booth, Morosco, Bijou, and Plymouth, the Broadhurst (named for a turn-of-the-century playwright), and Henry Miller's Theater all date to this period.

Times Square theater construction increased in the 1920s as West Side speakeasies defied Prohibition and playgoers flocked to see the latest by Eugene O'Neill, Philip Barry, Elmer Rice, Noel Coward, George M. Cohan, Marc Connelly, and George S. Kaufman. At least one promoter tried to move above Times Square: the Jolson Theater (later called the Century) opened in 1921 on Seventh Avenue between 58th and 59th Streets with Jolson singing "My Mammy," "Toot, Toot, Tootsie," "April Showers," and "California, Here I Come" in the musical *Bombo*. Virtually every other theater built in the 1920s was put up close to the other Times Square houses. This was the era that saw the launching of a dozen new theaters: the Ambassador, whose hit operetta *Blossom Time*, with music from Franz Schubert, opened in late September 1922; the Klaw (later the Avon), which opened with *Nice People*, a play starring Katharine Cornell, Tallulah Bankhead, and Francine Larrimore; the National (later the Billy Rose, then the Nederlander); the Music Box, Imperial, Martin Beck, Guild (later the ANTA, then the Virginia), Mansfield (later the Brooks Atkinson, named after a *New York Times* critic), Royale, and Theatre Masque (later John Golden's Theater). The Erlanger, named for Abraham Erlanger of the powerful theatrical syndicate and later called the St. James, opened in 1927 at 246 West 44th Street (Sardi's Restaurant had been on that site and was obliged to move farther east in the block). Ed Wynn, the Marx Brothers, Fred and Adele Astaire, W. C. Fields, Fanny Brice, Al Jolson, Jeanne Eagels, Will Rogers, Beatrice Lillie, and Lou Holtz were some of the stars who performed on these new stages, often accompanied by the new music of George Gershwin, Jerome Kern, Sigmund Romberg, Eubie Blake, Irving Berlin, and Richard Rodgers.

Tex Rickard's new Madison Square Garden, which opened on November 28, 1925, on Eighth Avenue between 49th and 50th Streets, was slightly to the north and west of the theater district. It replaced Stanford White's thirty-six-year-old Garden on Madison Square. White had died in the summer of 1906, shot by the jealous husband of Evelyn Nesbit at the roof garden of the old Garden. Designed by architect Thomas W. Lamb, who specialized in theaters, the new sports arena would play host until February 1968 to Ringling Brothers and Barnum & Bailey's Circus, the National Horse Show, the annual rodeo, ice shows, hockey matches, basketball games, track meets, boxing and wrestling matches (for which it was principally designed; sightlines for other events were poor), and political rallies.

When the Ziegfeld Theater opened in early 1927 (with Ziegfeld's musical hit *Rio Rita*; *Show Boat*, with music by Jerome Kern, came in late

December), it, too, was not in the traditional Times Square theater district but rather on Sixth Avenue at 54th Street. The Alvin Theater (later the Neil Simon), opened in 1927 in West 52nd Street with Fred and Adele Astaire in the new Gershwin musical *Funny Face*. But when the Ethel Barrymore Theater was inaugurated late in 1928 in 47th Street it was back in the heart of familiar theater territory. The formally dressed opening night crowd for a now almost forgotten play at the new theater included Jules Bache, Anthony J. Drexel Biddle, Jr., Mrs. William Astor Chanler, George Gershwin, Otto Kahn, Conde Nast, the Herbert Bayard Swopes, Deems Taylor, and Walter Wanger.

Few theaters were built in the 1930s, and some existing ones were converted to movie theaters or radio studios or closed. But B. S. Moss's Colony Theater (later the Broadway), which had opened late in 1924 at 1681 Broadway (53rd Street) with a Douglas Fairbanks movie, reopened as a legitimate theater late in 1930. Jimmy Durante, Lew Clayton, Eddie Jackson, Ann Pennington, and Hope Williams starred in *The New Yorkers*, a new Cole Porter musical with songs that included "Love for Sale." The Mark Hellinger, named for a *Daily News* columnist, author, and film producer, was also a movie house when it opened in 1930 in West 51st Street; it was converted to a legitimate theater late in 1934.

Radio City Music Hall opened on Sixth Avenue between 50th and 51st streets on December 27, 1932, with a seating capacity of 6,200. Its 100-piece orchestra and mighty Wurlitzer organ accompanied vaudeville acts presented by showman Samuel ("Roxy") Rothafel, but the world's largest indoor theater failed to attract crowds until it showed motion pictures and renamed its high-kicking Roxyette chorus girls the Rockettes to reflect its Rockefeller Center location. Four years earlier, in 1928, the 2,600-seat Beacon Theater designed by Walter Ahlschlager (who also did the Roxy Theater on Broadway between 50th and 51st streets) had opened on the upper West Side at 2124 Broadway, between 74th and 75th streets. It was originally a movie theater, a replica of the Roxy at 49th Street and Seventh Avenue, and its lavish interior—the lobby had stained glass, murals, and a rotunda, the theater itself carved wood, intricate ceilings, and brass ornaments—rivaled the Music Hall's.

IV. ". . . If They Ever Get It Finished"

The West Side was growing up fast. Riverside Park and Riverside Drive were twenty-four years old when the subway opened in 1904. The park extended from 72nd Street up to 145th but still lacked the tall trees and lovely fountains that would make it a true sylvan retreat. The Drive, which had been dotted with squatters' shacks, truck gardens, and what remained of century-old country estates when it first opened, was changing rapidly. The actress Lillian Russell and others attracted by its spectacular views were living there in the 1890s, when Clarence F. True, an architect and developer, bought up all available parcels below 84th Street. True put up handsome row houses of his own design.

The Schwab mansion between 73rd Street and 74th was the jewel of Riverside Drive (photo courtesy Museum of the City of New York)

In 1904 Charles M. Schwab of Bethlehem Steel Company was preparing to move into a seventy-five-room château occupying the full block between Riverside Drive and West End Avenue from 73rd Street to 74th. He had paid an astounding $865,000 for the site of the former New York Orphan Asylum, owned by Jacob Schiff of Kuhn, Loeb, who sold it

Soldiers and Sailors Monument, Riverside Drive and 89th Street, 1902 (1986 photo)

to Schwab after his wife complained tearfully that if she moved so far west she would never see her Fifth Avenue friends again. The Schwab mansion, under construction since 1901, would be completed in 1906 with turrets one hundred and sixteen feet high, a private chapel, a state drawing room copied from the Petit Trianon, a banquet hall that seated fifteen hundred, and—wonder of wonders—air conditioning, which had been pioneered in 1902 by Willis H. Carrier in a Brooklyn printing plant.

Beaux Arts houses, Riverside Drive, 105th Street to 106th, 1899–1902 (1985 photo)

Mrs. Alfred Corning Clark's huge 1900 mansion of white marble and red brick up the Drive had its own private colonnaded bowling alley. Other free-standing mansions lined the Drive, including the Villa Julia, built by the electric storage battery pioneer Isaac L. Rice for his wife in 1901 at 89th Street, across the Drive from the Soldiers and Sailors Monument, completed in 1902 by Stoughton and Paul Duboy. Henry Beaumont Herts of Herts and Tallant, who designed Villa Julia, also designed such Broadway theaters as the New Amsterdam. Rice, who may have been the city's first automobile owner, was a railroad lawyer, promoter, and publisher. His house was acquired in 1908 by a foreign tobacco merchant and was later turned into the Yeshiva Chofetz Chaim. Also built in 1901 was the limestone Lydia S. Prentiss residence at the corner of 72nd Street, designed by C. P. H. Gilbert. Gilbert's limestone residence, next door to the Prentiss house at 311 West 72nd Street, was built in 1902.

Survivors of this period—handsome French Beaux Arts town houses by Janes and Leo, Mowbray and Uffinger, Hoppin and Koen, and

Robert D. Kohn, all built between 1899 and 1902—fill the blockfront today between 105th and 106th streets and grace the Drive in a few other spots as well. An ornate freestanding French château by Wiliam B. Tuthill, put up in 1909, is at 351, at the northeast corner of 107th Street.

Lewis Mumford wrote in his late eighties about the riverview houses, "On Riverside Drive itself the houses, often spreading mansions, were done in rustic stone and had enough shrubbery around them to give them a suburban air, though in the early part of the present century Bishop Potter's new residence, near the Soldiers' and Sailors' Monument, and a few other palatial houses introduced a more urbane Italian note. Never have rich people in New York had more garden space than they did for a decade or so at this time."

While Riverside Drive, as Mumford pointed out, also had some drawbacks, it was here that the West Side had houses to rival the palaces on and off Fifth Avenue on the the other side of the park. Since the Drive had no potential for shops or offices, speculators did not bid up lot prices as they did elsewhere. And despite any negative aspects to living near the river's edge in the first decade of the twentieth century, apartment houses were joining the single-family dwellings on Riverside Drive and were also beginning to fill the rest of the West Side. Many were quite magnificent—and some remain so.

Outstanding among them are the Apthorp, Alwyn Court, Belnord, 44 West 77th, and the St. Urban, but others deserve further mention. The Red House at 350 West 85th Street was designed by Harde and Short, who went on to design 44 West 77th Street and Alwyn Court. Architectural critic Paul Goldberger has called the Red House "an absolute gem . . . a six-story Elizabethan manor house." It rose just to the west of some English red-brick row houses that had stood since 1895. The Manhasset, on the west side of Broadway between 108th and 109th streets, was designed by Janes and Leo with salmon brick, grey brick, limestone, and a two-story mansard roof. It had two- to four-bedroom apartments complete with libraries, "lounging halls," and drawing rooms renting for between $150 and $290 per month. Servants' rooms had no bathtubs.

At George F. Pelham's Riverdale, on the southeast corner of Riverside Drive and 79th Street, each floor had two ten-room apartments with monthly rents from $160 to $290. An apartment of five bedrooms, three baths, maid's room, kitchen, pantry, entry gallery, living room with wood-burning fireplace, dining room with woodburning fireplace, and library, with a view of the Hudson, rented in 1905 for $225 per month. French windows supported by elaborate corbels looked out through wrought-iron balconies.

The Chatsworth, at 346 West 72nd Street, by John E. Schlarsmith, had upper floor apartments ranging in size from a one-bedroom flat (with maid's room, living room, dining room, and kitchen) at $83 per month to a fifteen-room suite with five large bedrooms, four and a half baths, two maid's rooms, laundry, kitchen, butler's pantry, dining room, library, and living room at $380 per month. A sun parlor ran across the entire top floor,

The Red House, at 350 West 85th Street, dates to 1904 (1986 photo)

complete with conservatory and potted plants, and the ladies of the building often gathered there of an afternoon to play whist. Tea was provided from the café in the basement, which also contained a billiard room, barbershop, hairdresser, valet, and tailor. The management maintained an electric bus service along 72nd Street to Central Park West. An annex to the Chatsworth, added in 1906 at 340 West 72nd Street, contained eight apartments, each with eleven rooms and four baths. In addition to having their own electric generator and refrigerator plant, the Chatsworth and its annex shared a common ground floor and entrance. With their splendid views of the Hudson and Riverside Park, they represented very nearly the best possible accommodations New York had to offer.

The Gotham Hotel of 1905 and Henry J. Hardenbergh's Plaza Hotel of 1907 were perhaps only slightly to the west of Fifth Avenue, but they and their sisters on the West Side marked the beginning of a new mode of life for the very rich, who had heretofore lived exclusively in private houses. Just south of the new Plaza Hotel, in fact, was a colossal château of red brick and white stone that would stand until 1927; this was the home of Cornelius Vanderbilt II and his wife, the former Alice Gwynne, together with the army of thirty servants that waited on them. The Plaza, rising fourteen stories, called itself a home hotel and had, according to the *New-York Daily Tribune*, 753 rooms for about 600 guests and the "hundreds of servants" they required. "Among the persons who have engaged suites for the year," said the *Tribune*, "are some whose names are well known in social and financial circles, many of whom have heretofore always occupied their own houses. Among these are Alfred G. Vanderbilt, George J. Gould, Mr. and Mrs. Oliver Harriman, Mrs. James Henry Smith . . . and John W. ("Bet a Million") Gates, whose apartment consists of sixteen rooms."

While its original tenants were far less illustrious, the Apthorp apartment house of 1908, with its large inner court, huge rooms, and fourteen-foot ceilings, left little room for doubt that upper West Side addresses were becoming socially desirable. The Apthorp, built on a steel frame for William Waldorf Astor and modeled on the smaller Graham Court of 1901, occupied the full block between Broadway and West End Avenue from 78th Street to 79th and was named for the Apthorp farm which had once occupied much of the surrounding area. The handsome country home of Charles Ward Apthorp (or Apthorpe) had been built in 1764 at what would later be 91st Street between Amsterdam and Columbus avenues. A stalwart supporter of George III, Apthorp was a Tory who left New York during the Revolution. Some of his property was subsequently acquired by Gerrit Stryker, namesake of what was once Stryker's Bay in the Hudson at 96th Street, and remained in the hands of Stryker's heirs until 1856. William Jauncey, a rich landowner who lived in Wall Street, bought a two-hundred-acre piece of Apthorp farmland and named it Elmwood. The southern part of the farm had been conveyed to Apthorp's daughter and her husband, John Cornelius Vandenheuvel, who put up a mansion in 1792 on the site that would later be occupied by the Apthorp apartment house. The mansion became Burnham's Hotel in 1833 and was not torn down until 1905, by which time the property had been in Astor hands for forty-five years. William B. Astor bought this part of the old Apthorp farm in 1860, when it was at the southern fringes of the village of Bloomingdale, paying $16,875 for property that was worth about $10 million in 1908.

The Apthorp, built in 1908, occupies the block bounded by Broadway, West End Avenue, 78th Street, and 79th (1986 photo)

The Apthorp has a facade of beautifully carved limestone. Its first floor originally included a bank, a pharmacy, and several doctors' offices, with five duplex apartments to provide living quarters as well as professional space for physicians. Apartments opened off four elevator halls and contained glass-paneled French doors throughout. On the third floor were twelve apartments of six rooms with bath up to nine rooms with three baths. The fourth to eleventh floors had eleven apartments each, making a total of one hundred and four. Servants' quarters and guest rooms occupied the twelfth floor as did a laundry with one hundred and forty tubs, two large drying rooms with steam dryers, and an open area for sun drying. Shaded promenades above the twelfth floor graced the 78th and 79th Street sides of the building, and the formal garden in the courtyard contained unusual plants, two fountains, benches, and lighting fixtures. The Apthorp boasted its own refrigeration system and was two-thirds rented by the time it opened in the fall of 1908. Rents initially ranged up to $460 per month.

Shearith Israel synagogue, at Central Park West and 70th Street, was built in 1897
(1986 photo)

New houses of worship had gone up on Central Park West and were still a-building. Congregation Shearith Israel, founded in Nieuw Amsterdam by Spanish and Portuguese colonists in 1655, was in a new synagogue by Brunner and Tryon on the southwest corner at 70th Street; Andrew Carnegie was attending Sunday morning services at the 1898 Fourth Universalist Church on the southwest corner of 76th Street; the Second Church of Christ, Scientist, designed by Frederick R. Comstock, was built in 1900 on the southwest corner of 68th Street; the Ethical Culture Society built an Art Nouveau building on the southwest corner of 64th Street in 1910. There was also the Progress Club (actually a German-Jewish social club, later the Walden School), built in 1904 at the northwest corner of 88th Street.

Robert L. Lyons' St. Urban apartment house, put up in 1904 at Central Park West and 89th Street, Clinton and Russell's Langham of 1905 from 73rd Street to 74th, just north of the Dakota, and the Kenilworth of 1908 a block north of the Langham (three apartments to a floor, one of nine rooms, two of ten) gave Central Park West some distinguished additions. The St. Urban, with its great porte-cochere entrance and copper roof, had forty-seven apartments, each with eleven rooms and three baths, which rented at $250 to $333 per month; the Langham, with four apartments per floor, had an ornate lobby, a central refrigeration system instead of iceboxes, a built-in vacuum-cleaning system with connections in the wall, a mail-conveyor system that carried mail directly to each apartment, and a wall-safe in each apartment. Rents began at $375 per month. The twelve-story banded limestone Prasada, designed by Townsend, Steinle, and Haskell in a version of the Second Empire style, had an interior court and three apartments per floor, each with a long interior hall.

The Bownett apartment house (later the Hayden) at 11 West 81st Street, a twelve-story 1908 Beaux Arts structure, brought new beauty to the Central Park West area north of the Museum of Natural History, whose Romanesque revival West 77th Street facade by Cady, Berg and See, completed from 1889 to 1900, added to the original structure of 1872 to 1877 (which would eventually be concealed from view by other interconnecting units). York and Sawyer's New-York Historical Society building (1908) on Central Park West between 76th and 77th Streets also contributed architectural grace to the area (north and south wings by Walker and Gillette would be added in the 1930s). Rossleigh Court had gone up in 1906 at 1 West 85th Street, the Central Park View (later Orwell House) a year earlier at 86th Street. The Brentmore, a twelve-story-and-penthouse building at 88 Central Park West (2 West 69th Street), was completed in 1910.

Private houses for Frederick Ambrose Clark of the Clark estate, designed to be leased, not sold, went up in 1906 from 18 to 52 West 74th Street, but a *New York Times* editorial two years later said, "The time is coming when there will be comparatively few private dwellings on this island, except the palaces of the rich." This, said the *Times*, was partly because land values had increased and partly because of the "universal demand of the public for more comfort, with less care and expense than entailed in private house maintenance."

An article in the *Architectural Record* in 1908 suggested a reason for the co-operative club building concept pioneered by Philip Hubert in the 1880s, a reason that had little to do with economics. Unless the "co-operators unite to constitute themselves a vigilance committee," the article said with little subtlety, "some day there will elude the vigilance of the janitor and the real estate agent a 'peroxide Juno' . . . or a hooknosed tenant, of the kind of hooknose you know and apprehend." The ignorant winks and sneers of prejudice were unabashedly blatant in 1908.

For the city home, according to the *Real Estate Record and Builders' Guide* of November 6, 1909, "apartments are coming to be preferred over the private dwelling for one reason, because a private dwelling may not be obtainable in a particular neighborhood where the family wishes to reside when in town. The really high class apartments offered to tenants of wealth and standing, the choice of the finest location in Swelldom. Emerson says that there is a price on everything—pay the price and the thing is yours. If one wishes to live in the most fashionable neighborhood in America he must pay the price fixed by the market."

Charles W. Buckham's Gainsborough Studios, built in 1908 ostensibly for painters and would-be painters, was at 222 Central Park South, between Seventh Avenue and Columbus Circle. Fourteen duplex co-op apartments faced north across the park; twenty-five simplex apartments faced south and rented for $125 per month. There was also a ladies' reception room.

Alwyn Court, designed by Harde and Short, at Seventh Avenue and 58th Street, amazed New Yorkers in 1909 with the lavish terra cotta ornamentation of its French Renaissance exterior. Rising across the street from Philip Hubert's old Lisbon, it provided accommodations for just twenty-two families in apartments that were immense—from fourteen rooms and five baths (at just over $500 per month) to thirty-four rooms with nine baths (at a bit more than $1800 per month)—with wood-paneled walls, fitted closets, marble mantelpieces, and similar luxuries.

The Belnord, which opened in the fall of 1909, was another vast apartment house in the Graham Court-Apthorp mode, occupying an entire block between Amsterdam Avenue and Broadway from 86th to 87th Street. It was much larger than the Apthorp, if less fine. E. Hobart Weekes, of Hiss & Weekes, architects, made the Belnord's inner courtyard more than two hundred and thirty-one feet long, more than ninety-four feet wide, and, where six million common bricks went into the street-side Italian Renaissance exterior, the courtyard walls were of limestone with terra cotta trim. The building's one hundred and seventy-five apartments, opening off six elevator halls, were each of seven to eleven rooms, with one to four baths and one to three servants' rooms. Most of the upper floors contained sixteen two- to four-bedroom apartments each. Four of the upper floors had apartments with double-size living and dining rooms. In some suites, doors connecting parlor to library to dining room could

Alwyn Court, Seventh Avenue at 58th Street, 1909 (1986 photo)

44 West 77th Street, 1909 (photo courtesy Museum of the City of New York)

". . . IF THEY EVER GET IT FINISHED"

be thrown open to create a space spanning the entire fifty-eight feet between inner court and avenue. Nearly every bedroom faced on the courtyard to assure peace and quiet. Each apartment had a built-in vacuum cleaning system, a wall safe, and an electric refrigerator that made ice (at a time when the iceman still came to almost every house and apartment). Beneath the courtyard, placed so as not to create disturbing vibrations, were boilers and a generating plant that made the building independent of city power sources.

Rents at the Belnord ranged between $167 and $583 per month. Tenement accommodations rented at the time for between $7 and $20 per month, apartments for as much as $2,000 per month. At the Apthorp, no apartment rented for more than $550 per month.

Farther north on Broadway, the Cornwall at 90th Street is a twelve-story red-brick apartment house. The Turin at 333 Central Park West (93rd Street) consists of four tower-like sections and originally had six apartments per floor, each of six to nine rooms with a long, narrow hall separating sleeping chambers from living room, dining room, and reception room; the latter in most cases had windows. A co-operative apartment put up in 1909 at 44 West 77th Street resembles a Gothic cathedral of fourteen floors; designed by Harde and Short with a groined, vaulted lobby and stone foyers, it originally had two apartments per floor, each with eleven or twelve rooms including an elaborately paneled dining room, and most with extra-height studios (top-floor apartments have eighteen-foot ceilings).

Gaetan Ajello, who had designed the turn-of-the-century Miramar at Riverside Drive between 117th and 118th streets, was the architect for the Lucania, a nine-story luxury apartment house built in 1910 at 235 West 71st Street with circulating hot water and filters to screen out any impurities in the city water supply. Built on an H-plan, it had four apartments per floor, two of them providing for sleep-in maids, three having formal dining rooms. These assymetrical six-room suites rented at $75 to $167 per month.

Pennsylvania Station opened on September 8, 1910, giving new importance to the West 30s, which had been the city's Tenderloin area. The first tunnel under the Hudson had opened two years earlier, but commuters from New Jersey continued to arrive mostly by ferry. Penn Station, which received trains from Chicago and points west as well as from Long Island, covered two square blocks between Seventh and Eighth avenues from 31st Street north to 33rd. McKim, Mead and White modeled the $112 million granite and travertine terminal on the warm room of the Baths of Caracalla in ancient Rome.

Penn Station was in the heart of the old Tenderloin district, home for many years to much of New York's tiny black population. So was Macy's, which had opened at Herald Square in 1901, and Gimbels, which opened a large new department store in Greeley Square in 1910. Blacks were forced to move.

A real estate boom had begun in 1901 on Lenox Avenue, in Harlem, where a black real estate operator, Philip A. Payton, was soon guaranteeing premium rates to landlords who would accept black tenants. By 1910 there were 90,000 blacks in New York—less than 2 percent of the population. By 1920 there were 150,000—about 3 percent, and at least two-thirds of New York's blacks lived in Harlem, still a model community. Harlem's Kortwright Apartments, put up in 1904 at 1990 Seventh Avenue on Sugar Hill with twenty-nine luxury units, did not accept its first blacks until 1926, but by that time few whites were left in Harlem. Most—including many of the section's Jewish communities—had moved to the upper East or West Side or to the Bronx. Before the end of the 1920s New York had 327,000 blacks. Few if any lived on the upper West Side except for a group in the low 60s, a once predominantly Irish area known as San Juan Hill.

San Juan Hill's name, by some accounts, commemorated the Spanish-American War battle of July 1–2, 1898, which saw black troops in action against the Spanish in Puerto Rico (Colonel Teddy Roosevelt gained all the headlines with the charge of his Rough Riders, but it was black troopers who took the hill). By other accounts, an on-looker saw police charge up during a racial fight and bestowed the name then and there. Henry Phipps, the steel magnate and philanthropist whose Fifth Avenue mansion stood on the northeast corner of 87th Street, built model six-story apartment houses for working-class people in West 63rd and 64th streets in 1907 and 1911 (the more famous Henry Phipps houses on the East Side were not built until the 1920s). Scores of black families still lived in the area: the men in many cases worked as stevedores on Hudson River piers or in the Horn and Hardart commissary on Eleventh Avenue, which prepared food for the many Automats found in various parts of town.

The New York Public Library which opened in May 1911 on the west side of Fifth Avenue between 40th and 42nd streets, was a white marble Beaux Arts masterpiece designed by Carrère and Hastings. It stood on a site occupied since 1842 by Croton Reservoir, a four-acre lake surrounded by fifty-foot-high Egyptian-style walls. To the west of the reservoir, in 1853, there had been a replica of the Crystal Palace, built by the royal gardener Joseph Paxton for the London Great Exhibition of 1851. Crystal Palace had burned down in 1858; the area west of the reservoir was set aside in 1884 as a park, named for the poet William Cullen Bryant; and the reservoir was torn down in 1900 to make way for the library.

East Siders still lived almost exclusively in row houses, most of them boardinghouses, and in tenements. Twin co-operative apartment houses designed by Charles Platt were built in 1906, the first at 130–134 East 66th Street (it contained mostly duplex units with double-height living rooms, one of them Platt's own town apartment), the second, soon after, at 130 East 67th. Duplex apartments designed by Charles W. Buckham were completed in 1908 at 471 Fourth Avenue (later Park Avenue South), but there were few luxury apartment houses on the East Side until 1910, when the railroad lines running into Grand Central were electrified and some progress was made toward covering over the forty acres of railroad yards and track on Fourth Avenue (soon to be renamed Park Avenue).

McKim, Mead and White's twelve-story granite Italian Renaissance 998 Fifth Avenue, put up in 1911 opposite the Metropolitan Museum of Art at the northeast corner of 81st Street, was the first luxury apartment building on Fifth. It had one apartment per floor, each with eight master bedrooms, ten baths, nine maids' rooms, an octagonal salon, large living and dining rooms, and a reception room thirty-six feet long. The building did not attract many tenants until a young real estate agent, Douglas L. Elliman, persuaded Senator Elihu Root to give up his big brick town house at 71st Street and Park and move into 998 Fifth, taking a flat that would normally rent at more than $2,000 per month for $1,250—this in the days before income taxes.

East Siders had for years looked down their noses at West Siders as people who did not own their homes but merely rented, who might have more space for less money than on the East Side but who lived where they did only because they could not afford the East Side. Now East Siders, too, were beginning to enjoy the advantages of apartment-house living. No town house could match the sunny quiet of an apartment on a high floor, and in an apartment house one could leave worries about heating and maintenance to others.

But East Side apartment houses were not of the same breed as their counterparts across the Park. Architecturally more understated, they had exteriors that fitted in more appropriately to the staid and proper brownstones that lined every side street and many of the avenues. And where West Side apartment buildings generally had names that were either exotic or English or French, few of the new East Side buildings had anything more than house numbers.

On Riverside Drive and West End Avenue, more luxury apartment buildings were replacing mansions and row houses. The H-shaped Indiana limestone Orienta at 302–304 West 79th Street (its extreme westerly location belied its name) opened in 1904 with each floor having four apartments ranging from five to seven rooms with full fireplaces and electric and gas-lighting fixtures. Rents were $55 to $77 per month. Designed by Schneider and Herter, the Orienta advertised itself with the claim that "because of its proximity to the Hudson, Riverside Drive, and Central Park [it] enjoys the purest air." From 92nd Street to 104th the Drive breaks in two, its main section flirting into Riverside Park. The St. Denis at Riverside Drive and 92nd Street, fronting like other buildings between 92nd and 104th on a strip of grass and trees that separates it from the traffic of the Drive, had apartments of nine to ten rooms. So did the L-shaped Italianate Hendrik Hudson on the Drive at 111th Street. It had seventy-two eight-room/two-bath apartments (rents were from $125 to $250 per month), a billiard room, a basement café, a barber, and a hairdresser.

William Randolph Hearst, the publisher, moved in 1907 into the new Clarendon apartment house at 137 Riverside Drive (southeast corner of 86th Street), designed by Charles E. Birge. Hearst had arrived from San

Francisco in 1895, had later bought a four-story brownstone at Lexington Avenue and 28th Street (once the home of President Chester A. Arthur), had narrowly missed being elected mayor of New York in 1905, and had run for governor in 1906. He leased the more than thirty rooms on the top three floors of the building, using the top (twelfth) floor as a gymnasium. It was the biggest apartment on the West Side—nearly three-quarters of an acre of living space, not counting the roof garden.

Victor Herbert's musical *Mlle. Modiste*, with Fritzi Scheff singing "I Want What I Want When I Want It," had recently closed at the Knickerbocker Theater. Hearst, too, wanted what he wanted when he wanted it. In 1913, when he turned fifty, he wanted more space. His paintings, statuary, and armor, acquired through the famous dealer Joseph Duveen and others, were crowding his apartment at the Clarendon. Hearst came up with the idea of evicting the building's eighth- and ninth-floor tenants and tearing out two floors to create a three-story drawing room, with a thirty-five-foot ceiling, that would look out on the Hudson. The Clarendon's owner understandably balked at so drastic a remodeling and such cavalier treatment of his other tenants, so Hearst bought the whole building for $900,000 in order to instrument his plan. If completed—and there is uncertainty as to whether it ever was—this would have been the largest apartment anywhere in the world.* Whatever its final size, its bathtubs included a gargantuan one used in the White House by the three-hundred-and-twenty-pound President Taft.

A 1910 building, the Colosseum by Schwartz and Gross, curves round the south corner of 116th Street; in 1920 it became the home of Harlan F. Stone, dean of the Columbia Law School (and later chief justice of the United States Supreme Court). Emery Roth's H-shaped Sethlow Bachelor Apartments (named for the president of Columbia University but later called the Bancroft Apartments) of 1911 at 509 West 121st Street rise eight stories with a Spanish tiled roof and a handsome entrance court.

Builders on West End Avenue claimed that it was far less damp and windy than the Drive. The prohibition against building anything other than private houses on West End had been removed about the turn of the century and the avenue was well on its way toward becoming a densely populated boulevard of twelve-story buildings. Barring buses and trucks nonetheless gave West End Avenue a degree of peace and quiet not found elsewhere on the West Side. The Evanston of 1911, at the southeast

---

*All records were broken in 1926 when a fourteen-story apartment building was completed at 1107 Fifth Avenue, southeast corner of 92nd Street, where the town house of Post cereals heiress Marjorie Merriwether Post Hutton, wife of the broker E.F. Hutton, had stood. Mrs. Hutton had sold the property on condition that her house be virtually recreated atop the new building. And so it was—a fifty-four-room triplex connected by a private elevator to a private foyer on the building's ground floor. Occupied on a fifteen-year lease at a yearly rental of $75,000, the apartment had a gown room for hanging ball gowns, a cold storage room for flowers and furs, a silver room, a wine room, a sun porch, separate men's and women's guest closets, and separate laundry rooms for household and servants.

Memorial to Isidor and Ida Straus, lost on the Titanic, *106th Street and Broadway, 1914 (1986 photo)*

corner of West End and 90th Street, was designed by George and Edward Blum to give tenants the feeling of a private house. Its twelve floors each had four apartments, two of them duplexed with sleeping rooms on the floor higher than the rooms used for entertaining but not directly above them. A music room ajoined each living room; throwing open the connecting doors created a space that was in some cases eighty feet long. The largest room in each apartment was the windowless reception room, complete with fireplace, in which guests could be entertained without disturbing the everyday living room.

At 105th Street, north of the Evanston and near the upper end of West End Avenue was the private house of Isidor Straus, a co-owner of the R. H. Macy department store, who had lived there since 1884. Straus and his wife, Ida, were among the first-class passengers who went down with R. M. S. *Titanic* when she sank in the North Atlantic on her maiden voyage on April 15, 1912. Col. John Jacob Astor IV, New York's second largest landowner (his cousin William Waldorf Astor of London was the largest) and a man responsible for many West Side buildings, was also lost. Straus Park (formerly Bloomingdale Park), at the intersection of Broadway and West End Avenue at 106th Street, commemorates the death of the couple with a biblical verse (2 Samuel 1: 23), "Lovely and pleasant were they in their lives and in their death they were not divided." There is a bronze Beaux Arts figure of a woman gazing into a fountain pool; H. Augustus Lukeman, a sculptor better known for his Stone Mountain Memorial to General Lee near Atlanta, did the work in 1914, one year after the Clebourne apartment house had replaced the Straus residence. Everybody by that time had heard the story of Straus's gallantly refusing to enter a lifeboat until all the women and children still aboard ship had been accommodated, and of Ida's refusing to leave unless accompanied by her husband.

New York's minuscule Japanese community had a Nippon Club in this Belle Epoque. In 1912 it put up a clubhouse at 161 West 93rd Street, between Columbus and Amsterdam. (The club moved to 145 West 57th Street in 1963; its original clubhouse became the church of Iglesia Adventista del Septimo Dia.)

At about the time of the *Titanic* sinking in 1912, a marble-and-brass memorial to the men who had died in the explosion of the battleship *Maine* in Havana Harbor on February 15, 1898, was being erected at the entrance to Central Park at Columbus Circle. Before the official unveiling date, a sudden gust blew off the burlap covering of Attillo Piccirilli's heroic figures. Among those who received this unauthorized preview were some infuential artists, who protested that the work was militaristic, gaudy, tasteless, and a waste of the taxpayers' money. More acceptable was the statue of Joan of Arc, created in 1915 by the American sculptor Anna Vaughn Hyatt for Joan of Arc Park, a 1.578-acre area on Riverside Drive at 93rd Street.

Only the most affluent artists could afford to move into the Hotel des Artistes when it opened in 1918 at 1 West 67th Street. Designed

Maine Memorial, Columbus Circle, 1912 (1985 photo)

by George Mort Pollard and standing just west of a town house that faced on Central Park West, it was never really a hotel but always a co-operative apartment house; it had a communal kitchen, a swimming pool, squash courts, a theater, a ballroom, and, later, a Café des Artistes with wall murals depicting frolicking nymphs painted by resident Howard Chandler Christy. Other residents would include Noel Coward, Isadora Duncan, Norman Rockwell, Rudolph Valentino, and Alexander Woollcott.

Living at Amsterdam Avenue and 75th Street in 1917 was the violinist David Mannes; his wife, Clara Damrosch Mannes (German-born daughter of the conductor Leopold Damrosch and sister of the conductor Walter Damrosch); their seventeen-year-old son Leopold; and their twelve-year-old daughter Marya. David and Clara Mannes had founded the Mannes School of Music (later the Mannes College of Music) in 1916. Young Leopold Mannes attended the Riverdale Country Day School, where his best friend, Leopold Godowsky, Jr., son of the pianist, shared his obsession with photography. Working together, the two youths developed the rudiments of what would be introduced in 1935 as Kodachrome, the first wholly successful color film.

Riverside Drive looking northwest at 76th Street, November 1917, with S.S. Washington Irving *at pier (Byron photo courtesy Museum of the City of New York)*

V. Boom Times

The end of World War I brought a Spanish influenza epidemic and economic recession. New York's cost of living, 79 percent higher in 1919 than it had been in 1914, was too much for many, and there was a movement toward the suburbs, more readily available to commuters via tunnels beneath Manhattan's rivers. The average American worker in 1919 earned only $1,144 for the year, too little in light of the higher prices. Workers, including New York dressmakers, cloak- and suitmakers, cigarmakers, printers, subway workers, longshoremen, and actors struck for higher pay. Business picked up as the '20s roared on; so did Manhattan construction, not only on the East Side, where the Lexington Avenue subway had opened in July 1918, but also on the West Side.

That construction now had to conform to zoning laws. No city in the United States had a zoning law until New York enacted one in 1916. The Equitable Building, completed a year earlier at 120 Broadway, contained thirty times more floor space (1.2 million square feet) than was contained in its site (just under one acre). Merchants gained public support when they complained that such dense construction would ruin the city. They ran full-page newspaper advertisements headed "Shall We Save New York?" The new zoning law was followed in 1923 by a setback law that further limited the height and configuration of buildings, although height restrictions on upper Fifth Avenue were eased. Other such ordinances followed, some of them applicable to specific neighborhoods.

A surplus of housing in much of Manhattan explains the low rate of construction on the West Side after 1910. But as more people crowded into the city after the war, housing shortages became so acute that the city's Board of Estimate ruled in 1921 that "all new buildings planned for dwelling purposes" and started or completed between May 1, 1920, and May 1, 1922, were to be exempt from nearly all taxes until January 1932. This tax-abatement measure had a dramatic effect throughout the 1920s, as the deadline for building starts was continually extended. The effect was most noticeable in Brooklyn, the Bronx, and Washington Heights, where land was cheaper, and on Park Avenue, where the greatest opportunities for high return seemed to exist, but the good times of the '20s saw plenty of new buildings going up on the West Side.

Tax abatement was not the only factor behind this second boom in West Side housing construction. As with the first boom, subway transportation was the key motivating force. In 1900, retailers and hotels on Broadway below 23rd Street had opposed having their thoroughfare dug up for years while underground tracks were laid: surface transportation could not operate with torn-up streets, business would be lost, blasting for subway tunnels might damage their buildings, and faster transportation might attract undesirable elements to downtown hotels. So the first subway line ran from City Hall under Lafayette Street and Fourth Avenue up the East Side to Grand Central, turning west to Times Square before proceeding north under Broadway. But when lower West Side merchants saw lofts and showrooms move closer to Fourth Avenue and the new Lexington Avenue subway, they began to demand a subway line of their own. The Broadway line was extended south in 1918 from Times Square to South Ferry, thus bringing the upper West Side to within a few minutes' ride of the garment district on Seventh Avenue. This made the upper West Side still more attractive as a residential area, and many solidly built new apartment houses and apartment hotels sprang up to meet the growing demand. They were all comfortable buildings, although none was in a class with some that had been built earlier or would be built at the end of the 1920s.

The Ormonde (later the Hotel Embassy), whose graceful tan-brick bulk had occupied Broadway's eastern blockfront between 69th and 70th Streets since 1908, was renovated in 1920 by William H. Gompert, an architect who added two stories to the original ten-story northern building (there is also a seven-story southern wing) to give it 329 rooms, 285 baths. "A building outlives its original occupancy function after fifteen or twenty years unless wise and radical alterations are made," Gompert told a reporter. "The average owner, however, being timid and reluctant to recognize this situation, endeavors to force old properties to produce proper earning capacity and invariably fails, or is compelled to accept undesirable tenants. In this instance, however, the owner [grocery-chain magnate James Butler] has set an example for many other owners of valuable real estate."

Movies were still silent when the thirty-three-story Paramount Building rose above Times Square in 1926. The Taft Hotel (called the Executive Plaza beginning in 1985) opened that year shortly before Thanksgiving on Seventh Avenue at 50th Street; guests in rooms facing Times Square had good vantage points from which to see the third annual Macy's parade, which began at the Museum of Natural History and proceeded down Central Park West and Broadway to Herald Square in a West Side event that would continue for at least sixty years.

Bucking the trend toward large apartment houses was Pomander Walk, a double row of sixteen cottages put up in 1922 between 94th and 95th streets in the block west of Broadway. Thomas Healy, a well-known restaurateur, had closed his restaurants with the onset of Prohibition and had taken a ninety-nine-year lease on a piece of property fronting on Broadway and extending nearly to West End Avenue between 94th and 95th streets. On the Broadway footage he built an indoor ice-skating rink and other establishments, which were later converted to shops and movie theaters, including the Symphony and the Thalia. Pomander Walk was the

173–175 Riverside Drive, 1925 (1986 photo)

name of a stage play, which in turn derived its name from a small street in Chiswick, part of London. The New York version by King and Campbell was modeled on the stage sets used in a Broadway production of the play. Each cottage was originally a single-family dwelling (they were later converted to two apartments each) and rented for $225 per month (they always lost money but were subsidized by the income-producing properties on Broadway). Humphrey Bogart, Rosalind Russell, and Lillian and Dorothy Gish were all residents at one time or another.

But few New Yorkers wanted town houses in the 1920s, and those few that were built were soon turned into multiple-unit dwellings. The money was to be made in apartment buildings, and there was no lack of developers to put up more of them. The West Side Tennis Club had moved in 1913 to Forest Hills, but its old courts still occupied most of the block between Broadway and Amsterdam Avenue from 92nd Street to 93rd. Nearby, on Riverside Drive between 89th and 90th Streets, where the Hamilton Institute for Girls had stood, an enormous building by J. E. R. Carpenter opened in 1925 at numbers 173 and 175, its facade curving with the Drive in a rare departure from New York's rectilinear pattern. There were duplexes and simplexes, one of which was subsequently rented to Babe Ruth. (Half a century later, Itzhak Perlman, the violinist, had an apartment that he claimed had once been the Babe's.) Grandiose new apartment houses on Riverside Drive and West End Avenue replaced older multiple-dwelling structures, many of which had been taken over for use as gambling halls and brothels, but the Claremont Inn, built as a country manor house more than a century earlier, was still on the Drive at 125th Street, where it would remain until destroyed by fire in March 1951.

The 1920s saw a boom not only in apartment buildings but also in hotel construction; and while some were residential apartment hotels, quite a few were commercial caravanseries for transient guests. The Broadway View Hotel (later the Regent) opened in 1923 on the northeast corner of Broadway and 104th Street. Designed by R. H. Shreve of Carrère and Hastings, its bottom three floors were taken up by the Metropolitan Tabernacle Church, which had occupied the property until March 1922. Cards and dancing were prohibited in the new 307-room hotel, and entertainments in the banquet hall were subject to strict censorship, as was the hotel's guest list.

The White Hall Hotel opened as the Carleton Terrace Hotel late in 1923 on the southwest corner of Broadway and 100th Street where the two-story Carleton Terrace restaurant had stood in what was becoming a new movie theater district. The Greystone Hotel at the southeast corner of Broadway and 91st Street, which also opened in the fall of 1923, occupied the last of the vacant property along Broadway belonging to the estate of the late William Waldorf Astor. The Greystone offered two-room suites and single rooms, furnished or unfurnished. Its rooftop restaurant had a ceiling that opened to the sky. The Alamac Hotel, on the southeast corner of Broadway and 71st Street, was completed on a site occupied for nearly forty years by the Church of the Blessed Sacrament. The hotel has setbacks in accordance with the zoning law of 1923.

Demolition in 1924 of the Sixth Avenue El above 53rd Street encouraged building in the area that emerged from the El's shadow. William Randolph Hearst, whose personal income was roughly $15 million per year but who still managed to spend money faster than it came in, was convinced that a bridge would be built across the Hudson at 57th Street and

Claremont Inn on Riverside Drive at 125th Street (destroyed by fire in March 1951) (photo courtesy Museum of the City of New York)

that land in the area would become immensely valuable. He and his chief editor, Arthur Brisbane, financed the Warwick Hotel, completed in 1927 at the northeast corner of Sixth Avenue and 54th Street, with a penthouse suite for Marion Davies, Hearst's mistress since 1917 (she had formerly occupied a house built in 1902 by Janes and Leo at 331 Riverside Drive*. By the late 1920s Hearst had about $50 million invested in New York real estate, including his International Magazine Building (later the Hearst Magazine Building) at 959 Eighth Avenue, between 56th and 57th streets. Designed by Joseph Urban (originally a scene designer who had been the architect for the Ziegfeld Theater in 1927), the six-story moorish structure

---

*Davies moved with Hearst to San Simeon, his California ranch, in the 1920s. Her Riverside Drive house subsequently became the Buddhist Church Jodo Shinshue and contains the American Buddhist Academy and the New York branch of Rykuoku University in Japan. A statue in front of the house memorializes Shiruran Shonin, the first Buddhist priest to take a wife.

was put up in 1928; a seven-story office tower meant to go atop the building was never built.

The Buckingham Hotel had opened in 1925 at the northwest corner of Sixth Avenue and 57th Street, the Windsor in 1926 at the southwest corner of Sixth and 58th, and the thirty-one-story Park Central (later the Omni) in 1926 from 55th Street to 56th between Seventh Avenue and Broadway. Opened in 1927 was the twenty-five-story Navarro apartment hotel (later the Ritz-Carlton Hotel) at 112 Central Park South with 275 rooms (rents for the one-, two-, and three-room suites ranged from $75 to $400 per month, including maid service). Its name kept alive that of Philip Hubert's 1880s apartment buildings, two of which (the Madrid and the Lisbon) were coming down to make way for the New York Athletic Club's new building just as the Navarro Hotel was going up.

On the south side of 75th Street between Broadway and Amsterdam Avenues, the new Beacon Hotel had recently opened off Sherman Square, replacing the city's smallest apartment house, the St. Hélène. (The St. Hélène stood for about twenty-five years and contained only two apartments, each with all the features to be found in a much larger building.) The twenty-four-story, five-hundred-room Beacon had a beacon on its roof so powerful that on a clear night it could be seen for a hundred miles—or so the promoters claimed. The hotel incorporated the four-thousand-seat Beacon Theater with an entrance on Broadway.

The Mayflower Hotel of 1925 was giving Central Park West a comfortable new hostelry north of Columbus Circle from 61st to 62nd Street. Its neighborhood was still dominated by Cadillac, Packard, Peerless, and other automobile showrooms, filling stations, and related enterprises, much as Eleventh Avenue would be sixty years later. The fifteen-story Empire Hotel of 1922, which replaced an 1894 hotel of the same name at 63rd Street between Broadway and Columbus Avenue, was a sort of informal headquarters for auto makers. Some sixty manufacturers had exhibits at the Empire when New York's annual automobile show was running, although quite a few—including Frederick Duesenberg, Eddie Rickenbacker, and racing car drivers such as Ralph De Palma—still put up at the old Woodward Hotel at 55th Street and Broadway in the heart of "automobile row." New York City had more automobiles than existed in all of Europe. Fisk Tire and United States Rubber had put up tall buildings at 57th and 58th Streets before World War I, and in 1927 a new twenty-five-story General Motors Building (called the Central Park Plaza beginning in 1985) went up on the site bounded by Broadway, Eighth Avenue, 57th Street, and 58th, where twenty-two floors were added atop an existing three-story structure.

At the end of World War I there had been only two synagogues on the upper West Side. Now there were eight. The city's oldest Ashkenazic congregation, B'nai Jeshuran, founded in 1825, was in 88th Street between Broadway and West End Avenue in a synagogue built in 1918 by Henry B. Herts and Walter Schneider. Rodeph Sholom, in West 56th Street, would move to 83rd Street off Central Park West in 1930. Most congregations had followed their members out of Harlem. The upper West Side had become what some called a gilded ghetto, with Jews comprising 50 percent of the tenants in four of the sixteen largest apartment houses and 75 percent in two others (but no more than a third in the other ten). West End Avenue's northernmost buildings and those in nearby side streets had the greatest concentration of Jewish residents, mostly of eastern European background (German Jews tended to live on Central Park West). The magnificence of the new synagogues testified to the growing affluence of the Jews who had moved into the upper West Side.

By the end of the decade, Walker and Gillette's new East River Savings Bank building of 1927 graced the northeast corner of 96th and Amsterdam (on the northwest corner was the Church of the Holy Name of Jesus, built in 1891). A new building for the Central Savings Bank (originally the German Savings Bank, later the Apple Bank for Savings), designed by York and Sawyer in a Florentine palazzo style that made it look like a miniature of their 1924 Federal Reserve Bank in Liberty Street, went up in 1928 and occupied an entire block at the north end of Sherman Square opposite the Ansonia Hotel, where a statue of Verdi had been erected in 1906 by New York Italians to create Verdi Park. The New York Athletic Club, formerly at the southeast corner of Sixth Avenue and Central Park West, had moved into a new twenty-story Renaissance palazzo a block west; as noted above, it replaced some of Philip Hubert's old Spanish Flats in West 58th and 59th streets (others were coming down to make room for hotels).

The Twelfth Regiment Armory occupied the west side of Columbus Avenue between 61st and 62nd streets in the 1920s; west of that were freight yards for the New York Central, stockyards, and, on the river at the foot of 60th Street, the Central's grain elevator, built in 1877. New York was still a major port for shipping grain, received by rail and barge from the interior, to markets up and down the coast and overseas.

New York Central trains moved down Eleventh Avenue from the yards north of 60th Street, a man on horseback preceding each train with a red flag or, at night, a lantern, as required by law since 1849, when it was the Hudson River Railroad route. Freight trains came into the large Vanderbilt terminal between 60th and 71st streets via tracks from the Central's main line, crossing the Harlem River at Spuyten Duyvil and moving down along the Hudson. Other freight arrived by barge. To facilitate berthing of barges and lighters against the current, the terminal had floating bridges plus finger piers pointing downstream, rather than at right angles to the bulkhead line. Trains on what was known as the lifeline of New York carried produce from the yards to the perishable-food yard at 33rd Street and carried cattle by elevated track from there to a stockyard at West Houston Street. The terminal north of 60th Street played a vital role in feeding the city.

The College of Physicians and Surgeons, which had taken up half the block between 59th and 60th streets from Amsterdam Avenue to Columbus, was now close to the big Columbia-Presbyterian Medical Center,

New York Athletic Club, Seventh Avenue at Central Park South, 1929 (1986 photo)

which opened in 1928 on a twenty-acre site west of Broadway at 168th Street. DeWitt Clinton High School (later Haaren High, later offices and shops), built in 1906, was on Tenth Avenue between 58th and 59th streets, just east of the I.R.T. subway powerhouse, later a Consolidated Edison Company powerhouse, built in 1904 between Eleventh and Twelfth avenues. A few blocks away, at 5 West 63rd Street, the West Side YMCA moved in March 1929 into a new building modeled on the Davanzati Palace in Florence. The Y had earlier been at 318 West 57th Street.

New York land values increased by 75 percent in the decade between 1919 and 1929. Real estate taxes provided about four-fifths of the city's revenue in 1928, and some of the most valuable real estate was on Manhattan's upper West Side. Like many other parts of the city, it was the scene in 1929 of a tremendous building boom. And like virtually all booms, this one was destined to end in a bust.

VI. Hard Times

When Wall Street crashed in October 1929, many of New York's best-known names had West Side addresses. William Guggenheim had a private house at 3 Riverside Drive, and Michel Fokine's dance studio was next door at number 4. William Randolph Hearst still had his gigantic apartment at the Clarendon, 137 Riverside Drive, which was home also to Frank G. Shattuck of the Schraaft's restaurant chain. Samuel L. ("Roxy") Rothafel, the showman, lived at 173 Riverside Drive, and Abraham Erlanger, the theater owner, at 175.

James Montgomery Flagg, the artist, was at the Harperly Hall apartments, at 1 West 64th Street off Central Park West. Samson Raphaelson, the playwright, lived with his family at the Georgean Court apartments, 58 Central Park West. A Raphaelson play was the basis for the 1927 film *The Jazz Singer* which had launched the era of sound movies. Dr. Michael I. Pupin, the Pulitzer Prize-winning inventor whose improvement to the telephone had made him a millionaire, lived at the Dakota. Edward F. Albee, the showman, lived at the Langham on Central Park West immediately to the north of the Dakota. Mrs. Horace Saks, widow of the retailer, lived at 36 West 86th Street.

Actor Clifton Webb had just moved out of the Osborne, 205 West 57th Street, which remained home to composer Dimitri Tiomkin, *New Yorker* magazine cartoonist Peter Arno (Curtis Peters), and Baroness Hilla von Rebay, a portrait painter who was encouraging the copper magnate Solomon R. Guggenheim to buy works by the Russian painter Wassily Kandinsky. Across Seventh Avenue from the Osborne, at the Alwyn Court, lived William J. Beinecke, Lewis L. Delafield, Mrs. Frederick H. Eaton, Mrs. Jacob Wertheim, and Nicholas M. Schenck, the money man behind Metro-Goldwyn-Mayer, who three years earlier had hired mourners for the elaborate lying-in-state of Rudolph Valentino at Frank E. Campbell's funeral home, then on the east side of Broadway in the 60s. George Gershwin and his brother Ira had adjoining penthouses in a new building at 33 Riverside Drive (northeast corner of 75th Street); their parents and younger sister Frankie (who would soon marry Leopold Godowsky, Jr.) lived in a private five-story house that George had bought a few years earlier off Riverside Drive at 316 West 103rd Street.

Show Girl, running at the Ziegfeld Theater, had Gershwin music played by Duke Ellington and his orchestra with a cast that included Ruby Keeler, Jimmy Durante, and dancers performing the ballet "An American in Paris."

55 Central Park West at 66th Street, 1929 (Holy Trinity Lutheran Church of 1903 at left, newer buildings in background) (1986 photo)

As the Wall Street bubble burst, skyscrapers and lavish new residential buildings were nearing completion all over New York. Others were begun in the spring of 1930, when it looked to some investors as if the economic recession would be short-lived. Many of the new hotels and apartment houses were on the upper (and not so upper) West Side. They included the St. Moritz, the Barbizon Plaza, Hampshire House, and Essex House on Central Park South; the San Remo, the Beresford, and the Eldorado on Central Park West; and London Terrace, which covered the entire block from 23rd Street to 24th between Ninth and Tenth avenues.

The American Women's Association Clubhouse, finished in 1929 at 353 West 57th Street, was a twenty-seven-story hotel with twelve hundred rooms, a sixty-foot swimming pool, a sports gymnasium, an art gallery, a sizable library, music studios, three restaurants, six lounges, two roof gardens on the fourteenth floor, and another two on the top floor. Although the hotel was open to the public, its name discouraged transients and prospective male guests; the name would be changed in January 1941 to Henry Hudson Hotel.

The Manhattan Towers Hotel, opened in April 1930, was on a site that wrapped itself round a low building on the northeast corner of Broadway and 76th Street. The architects, Tillion and Tillion, tried to preserve the Gothic architectural style of the Manhattan Congregational Church, which had formerly occupied the site and which took the first three floors of the building. There were twenty-four stories incuding the church auditorium and gymnasium, a banquet hall, two penthouses, and some 626 rooms. The hotel went into receivership in the fall of 1931, and the church congregation disbanded shortly afterward. By that time there were perhaps half a dozen church-residential buildings in the city. In the spring of 1935 a federal judge blocked a plan to open a movie theater with adjoining café on the street floor of the building. In 1936 a black evangelist conducted services in the hotel's auditorium, was dispossessed by the trustees, and explained that he was protesting against being supplanted by the Mormon church, which held its first service on March 1, 1936, and would continue to lease the auditorium (later the Promenade Theater) on a month-to-month basis until 1944.

Another hotel that included a church was the Salisbury at 123–141 West 57th Street, which housed the Calvary Baptist Church. The 121-room hotel was finished in 1930, its lease was surrendered to the church in February 1932, and the Salisbury was run thereafter by the church.

The Paris Hotel, completed in 1931 on the southeast corner of West End Avenue and 97th Street, was a twenty-four-story structure with 900 rooms, each with bath, shower, and radio speaker, with suites of up to four rooms, including many terraced apartments. Amenities included a large dining room, a grillroom, a lounge, a swimming pool and gymnasium (free to tenants every morning), a billiard room, a mezzanine with library and card rooms, and rooftop solaria (open and closed). Put up for a foreclosure auction at the end of May 1933, the Paris was struck down to the Guardian Life Insurance Company on a bid of $200,000.

The Central Park South hotels and apartment hotels—Barbizon Plaza, Essex House, St. Moritz, and Hampshire House—met with similar fates. Luxury apartment houses on Central Park West fared only slightly better.

The Barbizon Plaza, which opened in May 1930 at 101 West 58th Street (with a rear entrance at 110 Central Park South), was a forty-story hotel with fourteen hundred rooms plus two concert auditoriums, exhibition rooms, club rooms, duplex studios for artists and sculptors, and a glass-enclosed roof for indoor and outdoor exercise. The architects, Murgatroyd and Ogden, provided three separate halls for concerts, musicales, recitals, and amateur dance and dramatic offerings. There was also a fully equipped library, and an early brochure promised that saddle horses could be brought to the hotel door for ventures into Central Park. In 1933 a room and bath went for as little as $3 per night, or $17 per week, including a Continental breakfast delivered to the room; rates for a living room-bedroom-bath-serving pantry suite began at $45. The Barbizon Plaza went bankrupt in 1933 and was sold for $2,500 to a company that assumed the hotel's debts, which totaled nearly $6 million. The hotel itself was actually worth $10 million at the time. It remained a hotel until 1985.

The St. Moritz Hotel, designed by Emery Roth and built by Harris H. and Percy Uris, opened on October 16, 1930, at 50 Central Park South with nearly one thousand rooms. A thirty-six-story structure put up where the New York Athletic Club had stood before moving a block west (the property had sold in the 1890s for a mere $75,000), the St. Moritz had a restaurant on its thirty-second floor plus the street-level Café de la Paix and Rumpelmayer's. In June 1932, the St. Moritz was bought at a foreclosure auction for $3.2 million.

The Essex House, called the Seville Towers when it opened on January 29, 1931, at 160 Central Park West, was sold at auction within a few weeks and acquired by the Reconstruction Finance Corporation, which would finally sell it, in January 1946, for $6 million. Designed by the Newark architect Frank Grad and rising forty-five stories, it had 1,286 rooms, making it the largest apartment hotel in New York.

When the cornerstone of the Hampshire House, designed by Caughey and Evans, was laid on March 24, 1931, eight of the new apartment hotel's thirty-seven floors had been enclosed with brickwork. Edward L. Bernays, the public relations man, had written an inscription for the stone: "Dedicated to Yesterday's Charm and Tomorrow's Convenience." The stone contained a selection of items considered representative of the "modern spirit of America": copies of Eugene O'Neill's *Strange Interlude*, Ernest Hemingway's *A Farewell to Arms*, and Stephen Vincent Benet's *John Brown's Body*; photographs of William Zorach's marble *Mother and Child*, of Thomas Hart Benton's murals *America Today*, and of an autogiro (forerunner of today's helicopter); and the musical score of John Alden Carpenter's *Skyscrapers*. Less than three months later, when the building was nearly complete, the contractor abandoned work on it. The New York Title and Mortgage Company, which had advanced funds for

Essex House, right, and Hampshire House on Central Park South (1986 photo)

the construction, had described itself as being "sound as the bedrock of New York." Unfortunately for some 7,295 investors, the company was in fact insolvent. After President Roosevelt declared a bank moratorium in March 1933, the title company was taken over by the New York Superintendent of Insurance, but he was powerless to deal with the situation. The uncompleted Hampshire House stood for years boarded up, a No Trespassing sign over its door, as city taxes accumulated. Its financial difficulties were finally resolved, and it opened on October 1, 1937, with 510 rooms in 219 suites under its great peaked copper roof. Interior decorations were by Dorothy Draper, and many apartments were duplexes with terraces and woodburning fireplaces. But the magnificent thirteen-room suites originally planned for the upper floors had been divided into less extravagant two-, four-, and seven-room suites, which rented for between $166 and $833 per month. And Depression or no Depression, more than 75 percent were rented by opening day.

Eight new apartment buildings had by that time gone up on Central Park West, where construction of the first line of the new independent subway system had triggered a third West Side building boom in 1925. Extending the Broadway line south from Times Square in 1918 had been of far more use to people living on Broadway, West End Avenue, and Riverside Drive than to those on Central Park West. The new independent subway line, running beneath Central Park West to Columbus Circle, and then beneath Eighth Avenue past the western edge of the garment district to Chambers Street, would make Central Park West apartments far more conveniently located.

The magnificent Beresford replaced a forty-year-old building of the same name. The earlier Beresford had stood six stories high on its 81st Street side and ten stories on its 82nd Street side; the two wings combined to create one of the largest apartment hotels on the upper West Side, occupying more than twenty-two thousand square feet. A private house at 3 West 81st Street was acquired in 1925 to extend the property. What prompted the decision to raze the old hotel was, in part, the city's plan to widen Central Park West (making it one hundred feet wide, the same as Fifth and Sixth avenues), remove its streetcar tracks, and run a subway beneath it. Emery Roth's Beresford, completed in 1929, had 179 apartments ranging in size from five to fifteen rooms (for a total of thirteen hundred rooms).

The San Remo had been described in 1893 as the highest hotel on the West Side, "an immense and imposing edifice situated on the high ground of West 75th Street and facing the lawns, woods, and waters of Central Park." Emery Roth's San Remo was built on land that had also contained a private house whose owner was compensated with a ten-year lease on a fourteen-room duplex at the new Beresford, built by the same people (Ravitch Brothers) as the San Remo. The latter building, which called itself The Hotel on the Park, was "out of the hurly burly of noise yet the subway and elevated are only five minutes' walk." David Nemerov, whose Russeks stores had made him a millionaire, moved into a big

San Remo, Central Park West between 75th Street and 76th, 1930 (Kenilworth, 1908, in foreground) (1986 photo)

eleventh-floor apartment with his family, which included his son Howard, who would grow up to become a famous poet, critic, and novelist, and his daughter Diane, who would gain renown as the photographer Diane Arbus. While a teen-age Fieldston student, she stood for as long as she could on the window ledge of the apartment, looking out at the trees and skyscrapers. Eddie Cantor, the popular singer and comedian, and his wife, Ida, took the fourteen-room triplex penthouse. Nine-room apartments with two baths rented for $200 per month. Dynamos in the basement provided electricity to the building, which had, in addition to its main dining room, a smaller dining room for children and their nurses.

Irwin S. Chanin, who had acquired the bankrupt Beacon Hotel in April 1930, was building a new Hotel Majestic on Central Park West. He had originally announced that it would be a forty-five-story affair. The twenty-nine-story apartment hotel that finally opened in 1931 replaced not only the 1894 hotel of the same name but also two rows of brownstones that had extended west from the old hotel in 71st and 72nd streets. A study of New York apartment accommodations in the late 1920s had indicated a demand for apartments of eleven to twenty-four rooms, and initial plans for the Majestic called for apartments of that size. The plans were hastily reworked after the stock market crash, and when the building opened, its largest apartment was fourteen rooms. There were also some one-room flats. Cantilevered construction at the corners on its Central Park side permitted small solaria to be placed at each corner; in addition, there was a large nineteenth-floor solarium for the general use of tenants, although the sun-worshiping fad was only beginning.

London Terrace, completed in 1930 from 23rd to 24th streets west of Ninth Avenue, replaced the area's 1880 town houses with fourteen buildings whose seventeen hundred units gave Chelsea a relatively posh new way to live. The apartment complex had a swimming pool, a solarium, a private garden, and doormen dressed as London Bobbies. It was described as the greatest single residential development the world had ever seen. A three-and-a-half-room apartment rented for $100 to $110 per month, and the leases, remarkably, were staggered. Most apartment leases until then ran from May to May or from October to October; every spring and autumn saw a large-scale migration of upwardly (and downwardly) mobile New Yorkers—East Side and West Side—moving bag and baggage from one apartment to another. There was rarely any shortage of attractive alternatives, and the steady pace of new construction maintained a constant downward pressure on rental prices.

Wrote Lewis Mumford, "The shifting of residences was typical of the old city, at least among those who did not own their own houses; it was due to the fact that, far from there being a housing shortage in middle-class quarters, there was actually a constant vacancy of around 4 percent . . .

"People were tempted to move not merely for the sake of 'modern conveniences,' like electricity and 'open plumbing,' or to lower their expenses by getting the standard concession of a free month's rent; sometimes they even moved, it would seem, as the simplest way of getting through a spring cleaning. At all events, they moved; and Moving Day, the first of May or the first of October, saw vans loading and unloading on every block. This whole scheme of moving, this game of musical chairs in domestic real estate, was based on the scandalously low wages that everyone who assisted in the game received: plasterers, painters, wallpaper hangers, moving men."

Among those taking advantage of landlords' offers of free rent for signing new leases would be Margaret Phipps Moynihan, whose husband had abandoned her in the fall of 1937 and who had to find accommodations for herself and her two sons, the older of whom, Daniel Patrick, shined shoes in Times Square. He would later achieve prominence as an educator, a United States ambassador, and a United States senator from New York.

The twenty-story Parc Vendome, put up by the builder who built London Terrace, opened in 1931 on West 57th Street between Eighth and Ninth avenues across the street from the two-year-old American Women's Association Clubhouse (Henry Hudson Hotel). Otto Kahn, the financier and arts patron, had assembled the property to provide a new home for the Metropolitan Opera House and the hotel had been built with the idea that it would be opposite the Met. The Rockefellers had leased more than eleven acres west of Fifth Avenue in the 40s and 50s for the same purpose. When the Met did not accept either offer, the Rockefeller property was used to build Rockefeller Center, and the property in West 57th Street was sold to a builder, who put up an apartment building house with 570 apartments, a gymnasium, a swimming pool, a solarium, terraced gardens, and a dining hall.

In spite of some successes, the new buildings were struggling to make ends meet as the Great Depression brought hard times to New Yorkers along with everyone else.

New York taxicabs decreased in number from 28,000 in 1929 to 13,000 (the number of licensed cabs would fall to 11,787 by the late 1940s and would remain at that level for forty years). Some taxi drivers earned only $20 per week. Woolworth salesclerks made as little as $7 a week. Men who had held important jobs were reduced in the early 1930s to selling apples in the streets and waiting in breadlines. In a day when scarcely 10 percent of young Americans attended college, men with college degrees camped out in muncipal parks. (Many parks had degenerated into weed-filled dumps by the time Fiorello La Guardia came into office as mayor at the end of 1933 and named Robert Moses as park commissioner a month later. The lions' cages at the Central Park Zoo were so flimsy that keepers carried shotguns in case an animal escaped. The park teemed with rats; exterminators hired by Moses killed two hundred thousand of them in one week.) Hundreds of people died of starvation.

Families began doubling up in houses and apartments, an illegal practice that had gone on for years in Harlem and the lower East Side and was now extended to other parts of town. Private houses became small apartment houses; apartments were subdivided.

The age of grandeur in New York housing construction was over. A few future buildings might in some ways be more comfortable, but never again would the city have apartment buildings as opulent as those built earlier in the twentieth century. Later buildings would have thinner interior walls (older structures required thick walls for the heavier pipes used in their plumbing systems) of four-inch studs with plasterboard instead of blocks and would be built with union labor, far more expensive than the labor used in the 1920s. Most of the notable New York residential buildings of the 1930s were started before the 1929 Crash.

Among the last of the pre-Depression buildings was Emery Roth's Art Deco Ardsley at 320 Central Park West. Built in 1931, it replaced the ten-story Ardsley Hall Hotel, built at the turn of the century and equipped with a billiard room and "entertainment suite." The twin-towered thirty-story Art Deco Eldorado apartment house at 300 Central Park West, also finished in 1931, had duplexes of eleven rooms and five baths each on its seventeenth and eighteenth floors. Emery Roth was the architect with Margon and Holder.

Irwin S. Chanin's thirty-one-story Art Deco Century Apartments, on Central Park West from 62nd to 63rd Street, replaced the Century Theater in 1931. Designed by Chanin and Jacques Delamarre, the Century had apartments ranging in size from a one-room unit with wraparound terrace to an eleven-room maisonette with a private entrance from the street and a step-down living room. It was the first building to have penthouse and duplex apartments of as few as three rooms. A new form of concrete construction made it unnecessary for ceilings to have beam-drops, and cantilevered floor slabs enabled the builders to eliminate corner columns and make wider terraces. Special window glass on Century apartments was said to be capable of transmitting the sun's ultraviolet rays.

New Yorkers interested in the solar system and other aspects of astronomy received a boon on October 2, 1935, when the American Museum of Natural History's Hayden Planetarium opened north of the museum (and opposite the new Beresford). Investment banker Charles Hayden had contributed $150,000 for the planetarium's Zeiss projector.

Rockefeller money fueled much of the 1930s construction. Rockefeller Center buildings, built between 1931 and 1940 partly on land owned by Columbia University west of Fifth Avenue from 48th Street to 51st, have been called the greatest urban complex of the twentieth century. Much of the land once had been the site of New York City's first botanical garden, established in 1801 by Dr. David Hosack, the physician who later attended Alexander Hamilton as he lay dying after his duel with Aaron Burr at Weehawken, New Jersey, in July 1804. Taxes on the property rose steeply after 1810 and Dr. Hosack, who had bought 256 lots for $4,807.36 plus an annual rent of sixteen bushels of wheat, turned the garden over to the state in 1814. The state had held a lottery to benefit a number of colleges, and Columbia's trustees protested when other colleges received money and Columbia did not. To appease them, the state transferred ownership to Columbia of the parcel of then almost worthless 11.7 acres in midtown Manhattan.

The university collected rents from the Rockefellers for more than half a century before selling the land under much of Rockefeller Center to the Rockefeller family for $400 million early in 1985 after fifty-two years of negotiations. Columbia had been receiving $11.1 million per year in rent from the Rockefellers, giving it a yield of only 2.8 percent. By selling the property, it would increase its $863 million endowment fund over a period of years, would diversify its investment portfolio, and would gain flexibility in its financial affairs; the eight square blocks of real estate had never produced much profit for the Rockefellers, who charged low rents and provided more service than do most landlords. Fifth generation Rockefellers needed cash in 1985. Later in the year the family offered a 60 percent interest in Rockefeller Center to the public for $1.1 billion, raising fears that new owners, in order to maximize return on their investment, would build additional floorspace atop smaller structures such as the Eastern Airlines Building.

Rockefeller Center's original structures included Radio City Music Hall (1932), the seventy-story RCA Building, the sixty-five-story RCA Building West, the British Building (originally called the British Empire Building), and La Maison Francaise (all 1933), the forty-one-story International Building (1935), the thirty-six-story Time and Life Building (1937), the fifteen-story Associated Press Building, the Eastern Airlines Building, and the nineteen-story United States Rubber Company (later the Uniroyal, then the Simon and Schuster) Building.

In 1917 John D. Rockefeller, Jr., had purchased utility magnate Cornelius K. G. Billings' Fort Tryon Hall. It had burned down in 1926, and Rockefeller later gave the estate to the city, which made it part of Fort Tryon Park. The Rockefellers, who financed the construction of the Cloisters in Fort Tryon Park in 1938 as a gift to the Metropolitan Museum of Art (the medieval nunnery was filled with art treasures, including a unicorn tapestry), also had a hand in financing the 1939 Museum of Modern Art at 11 West 53rd Street; its garden backed up on 54th Street, where the so-called Rockefeller Apartments at Number 17 had stood since 1936.

The new West Side Highway, completed in 1937, now ran along the edge of the Hudson where New York Central freight cars had run. The tracks had been remodeled in 1934 between Bank Street in Greenwich Village and 34th Street to pass through the second floors of plants and thus facilitate loading and unloading of meat, eggs, dressed poultry, and the like. Men on ponies preceded each train down Eleventh Avenue south of 60th Street, as they would do until March 1941; the tracks to the north now lay beneath Riverside Park, which had been extended over the tracks on a steel framework that added thirty-two acres to its size. Relandscaped and improved, partly to create jobs during the continuing Depression, the park made Riverside Drive an altogether more attractive thoroughfare on which to live.

There was little demand for luxury housing. Alwyn Court, which had had apartments of up to thirty-four rooms when it opened in 1909, was gutted in 1938 to make way for seventy-five apartments of between three and five rooms each. People simply could not afford such large apartments any longer, not even at reduced rents.

Men on horseback continued to escort New York Central freight trains down Eleventh Avenue and then down Tenth until March 1941 (photo courtesy New York City Department of Parks)

Only a handful of the city's super-rich still lived in private houses on Fifth Avenue. *Fortune* magazine listed them in 1939: the financial wizard Bernard Baruch (who had earlier lived in West 70th Street), National City Bank president Gordon Rentschler, the oilman Joseph Feder, the Standard Oil heir Edward S. Harkness, former ambassador to Germany James W. Gerard, the sculptor and museum donor Mrs. Harry Payne Whitney, and Mrs. Cornelius Vanderbilt, whose enormous house at the corner of 51st Street was assessed at $2.45 million. Mrs. Vanderbilt, according to *Fortune*, paid $197 per night in taxes for the privilege of sleeping in that house. Even a much smaller house, one assessed at $250,000, supported a staff of ten servants—a butler, a chef, a valet, a lady's maid, a footman, a parlormaid, a chambermaid, two kitchen maids, and a laundress (who together commanded $14,000 per year in wages, to say nothing of the $4,000 it cost to feed them). Property taxes were much lower on side streets—perhaps $27 per square foot versus $42 on Fifth Avenue.

Marjorie Merriwether Post Hutton's fifteen-year lease on her fifty-

240 Central Park South at Columbus Circle, 1941 (1986 photo)

four-room triplex apartment at 1107 Fifth expired in 1941, and she gave up the place; it remained vacant for a decade before being chopped up into six apartments. Even the richest New Yorkers now lived in apartment houses, many of them on the West Side; and while average incomes were higher in sections east of Fifth Avenue, some West Siders were very nearly as rich as anyone on the East Side.

A stark white-brick apartment house by Mayer, Whittlesey and Glass at 40 Central Park South, just east of the St. Moritz Hotel, was completed in 1940 with nineteen stories plus penthouse. When a modern apartment house designed by the same firm opened at 240 Central Park South (corner of Broadway at Columbus Circle) in 1941, it was next to a site that had been occupied by Philip Hubert's old Hubert apartment house.

America was beginning to emerge from its economic slump. The country was also, not unrelatedly, about to go to war. Government rent controls, imposed as a wartime anti-inflation measure, would have profound and lasting effects on New York housing, and few parts of town would feel those effects as intensely as the West Side.

VII. "There Goes the Neighborhood," They Said

New York, and perhaps especially the West Side, went through a shattering metamorphosis immediately after World War II.

For one thing, the city's population was becoming ethnically more diverse. Puerto Rican immigration had been growing since 1938, when the Fair Labor Standards Act inadvertently wiped out the island's needle trade by setting a minimum wage scale of twenty-five cents per hour for the first year and thirty cents for the next six years. In Puerto Rico the hourly rate for even the most skilled needleworkers had been twenty-five cents. So long as economic depression continued on the mainland, there was no great impetus to move north, but when jobs opened up in New York after the war a mass migration began. Spanish was heard more and more in streets where Yiddish, German, Italian, and Russian had once predominated. Whereas the new arrivals were initially attracted to the garment center, their followers flocked to the restaurant and hotel-service industries, where their labor was needed and appreciated. Many of these newcomers found homes on the upper West Side, where rents remained low.

Just how low these rents could be is suggested by the story of a young man who arrived in town late in 1948 to begin what would be a distinguished career as a television producer. He later recalled having sublet a floor-through basement apartment in 89th Street between Columbus and Amsterdam avenues. The regular tenant was away in Europe and continued to pay half the rent, which totaled $15 per month. (A similar apartment provided the set for the 1940 play *My Sister Eileen*, basis of the 1953 Broadway musical *Wonderful Town*. Such basement apartments became illegal in 1953, under a law requiring that the mean distance between floor and ceiling be higher than the level of the sidewalk outside.)

New residential construction had slowed to a snail's pace, largely because rent controls discouraged such investment. Mandated by federal law as a war measure in November 1943, rent controls expired in most of the country in 1950. Not in New York. Here 70 percent of the people lived—and would continue to live—in rental apartments. City controls were enacted to replace the federal controls. (Rent stabilization would replace rent control in 1971; controls mandated by state legislation subsequently replaced the city controls, city controls later replaced state controls, state legislation would control rents once again beginning in 1984; under whatever aegis, rents would remain for the most part under some

Parts of the upper West Side soon constituted a Puerto Rican community (1985 photo; Hotel Bretton Hall in background)

form of control, and anyone who suggested that tenants be left to the mercies of the marketplace had a bleak political future.)

Metropolitan Life Insurance Company, which had financed the huge Parkchester housing development in the east Bronx in the late 1930s and early '40s, financed Stuyvesant Town and Peter Cooper Village on Manhattan's lower East Side after the war. The first was built under the Redevelopment Companies Law of 1943, which allowed the city to grant exemptions on the value of the project over and above the valuation of the land and buildings that were there before the project existed; Metropolitan Life did not have to pay full taxes on Stuyvesant Town for twenty-five years. The development extended from 14th Street north to 20th between First Avenue and the East River Drive; Peter Cooper Village (which had somewhat higher rents) was just to the north from 20th to 23rd Street. The two developments had a total of nine thousand units and were for whites only (discrimination was not yet illegal).

On the West Side, Hell's Kitchen continued to live up to its name. In the 1870s and '80s it had been the slum west of Seventh Avenue from the 20s through the 30s; now it was in the area of 42nd Street west of Seventh Avenue, although the entrance to the Lincoln Tunnel, built in the 1930s, had erased ninety-one of the section's tenements. More came down to make way for the Port Authority Bus Terminal, which opened in 1950 (and was subsequently enlarged). But, if anything, the area was growing even more crime-ridden: drug use was becoming more prevalent, and addicts had to steal in order to support their habits. The West 40s and 50s, despite their obvious convenience to midtown offices, shops, and theaters, would remain undeveloped long after the upper West Side had transformed itself into a series of attractive neighborhoods.

Charles Schwab's 1906 château on West End Avenue between 73rd Street and 74th came down in 1948 (proposals that it be made the mayoral residence had been rejected) to make way for Schwab House, a redbrick high rise of no great distinction but of far more use in housing a growing population. Just to the south, at 72nd Street and West End, Hudson Towers had finally been sold three years earlier to developers who completed the twenty-three-story building and rented it. Begun in 1924 as a combination hospital and hotel, left unfinished when financing ran out, the structure had been vacant for more than two decades. The city had taken it over for nonpayment of taxes in 1940 and had been unable to sell it at auction.

Except for West End Avenue, Riverside Drive, and Central Park West, however, the upper West Side remained the depressed area it had been even before the Depression, a jumble of brownstone walk-ups, many of them rooming houses, still tenanted by people of Irish and Italian descent, with a scattering of Greeks and with some blacks in the San Juan Hill area. Amsterdam Houses, which went up in 1948 on the West Side of Amsterdam Avenue between 61st and 64th streets, were just south and east of the Henry Phipps model apartments built for blacks in 1907 and 1911. They had nearly eleven hundred units, and the initial tenants were whites.

Efforts were made to integrate the project, and Hispanics and blacks soon far outnumbered whites.

Rents remained relatively low. The influx of blacks and Hispanics had not yet put much pressure on New York housing in 1949. Hispanics were an ever-growing part of the population mix, but even in 1950 Puerto Ricans represented less than 5 percent of the city's total population. Puerto Rican immigration reached its peak in 1953; by 1955 there were roughly half a million in New York City, double the number in 1950, and by 1956 they accounted for more than 9 percent of all New Yorkers, a proportion that would increase well into the 1960s.

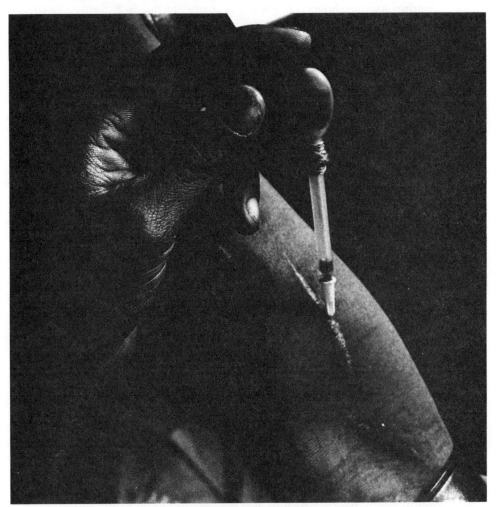

Drug addiction increased after World War II (1974 photo)

Attracted at first to east Harlem, where rents were lowest, the Hispanics soon outgrew that section. They were unable to expand to the north, where they ran into blacks who could not afford to move, or to the east, where they encountered Italians who refused to be moved. So they moved to the south Bronx and to parts of the upper West Side, notably to the San Juan Hill section, a depressed area since the late nineteenth century. By the early 1960s living standards on the home island had improved to the point where reverse immigration began; Puerto Ricans returning home outnumbered those arriving in New York, but the city's population by then included more than seven hundred thousand Puerto Ricans, and Spanish was becoming the city's unofficial second language, most noticeably in east Harlem, the south Bronx, the upper East Side above 96th Street, and the upper West Side, where in 1956 the population east of Amsterdam Avenue above 86th Street was 14 percent Puerto Rican.

The Amsterdam Houses, built in 1948 on San Juan Hill, became a black and Hispanic enclave (1986 photo)

Along with Puerto Ricans (of whom 20 to 25 percent were black) and other Hispanics, blacks from the South were flooding into New York. The Rust mechanical cotton picker, introduced commercially in 1949, picked a bale of cotton per day and cleaned it, displacing black field hands who had labored for so many generations on the plantations of the Old South. Thousands of these unskilled rural blacks moved to northern cities, including New York, where they found themselves in competition with Puerto Ricans, often in violent confrontations, for jobs and for welfare payments. The resulting fear, combined with the impact of black and Puerto Rican children on public schools, persuaded some eight hundred thousand middle-class whites to flee New York for the suburbs.

Most of the West Siders who moved to the suburbs and outlying boroughs in the 1950s and '60s were working-class people of Irish descent. They gave up tenement space that was quickly taken over by black and Hispanic newcomers to the city, many of them rural types who had never lived in a city before.

Spanish became the dominant second language on the upper West Side as in some other sections of the city (1986 photo)

Theodore H. White, in his 1978 book *In Search of History*, recalled his return to New York in October 1953 after five years in Europe. The Whites had been warned that the West Side was in a state of transition. "Obviously that meant that blacks and Puerto Ricans were moving in . . . [We] believed in integration, would have felt like traitors to join 'white flight,' if the term had been coined then, and wanted to live on the West side." So they moved into a Central Park West apartment with a view of the park at the corner of 84th Street, obtaining a foyer, living room, dining room, study, three bedrooms, two maid's rooms, and modern kitchen for $300 per month. The price was right but not much else. Writing about himself in the third person, White said, "He could not send his children to school here. . . . For the first time in all his life—in Irish Boston, in warlord China, in darkling Germany—he was afraid to walk the street outside his own house at night; . . . his children were not safe going to play in Central Park just below the window of his apartment house. . . . The problem was one of compression—two kinds of culture contesting in the pressure of closed city apartment blocks. It took White no more than six months from homecoming to pass through his particular adjustment to the confrontation. First, the blindness to the problem; then the bravado-disdain of the reality; then discomfort, and finally fear."

Half a mile to the north, birds being raised in apartment house courtyards for illegal cockfights were making their presence known each morning. The Edison Theater on Broadway near 103rd Street began showing only Spanish-language movies. The Whites left after one year for what they called the perfumed stockade of the East Side.

The Coliseum exposition hall and office building that opened in April 1956 on the west side of Columbus Circle began a revitalization of that area, but social tensions were escalating on the upper West Side. Leonard Bernstein's musical *West Side Story*, which opened at the Winter Garden Theater in September 1957, transplanted the Romeo and Juliet tragedy to New York, where black, white, and Hispanic street gangs fought as bitterly as Montagus or Capulets had ever done. Bernstein had gained fame in 1944 with his ballet *Fancy Free*, which included the 1936 Richard Rodgers number "Slaughter on Tenth Avenue." In the late 1950s there was slaughter on other West Side avenues and on side streets as well. Residents of a forty-block area on the upper West Side sealed themselves in at night out of fear. One man characterized the section as a combat zone. Citizens formed quasi-vigilante groups.

What had happened? Why had the upper West Side gone downhill while the upper East Side (with the exception of Yorkville's east 70s and 80s, where there was a good deal of racial violence) retained most of its bourgeois tranquility? According to one explanation, the difference lay in West Siders' being generally less affluent. In 1943 the manager of the Hotel Brewster at 21 West 86th Street sent a notice to his guests: "The War Labor Board . . . prevents payroll inflation; OPA rent control prohibits proper rental charges, and that prevents any move on our part to provide for an increase in wages. Therefore I appeal to you to be more liberal with your tips." The response was evidently disappointing; many of the guests did not tip at all, and it became more and more difficult for residential hotels and apartment buildings to keep their employees, many of whom left to accept higher-paying jobs in war-related industries.

Rent control permitted landlords to request voluntary rent increases of 15 percent. East Siders, who were better heeled and did not want to see their services reduced, paid the increases. West Siders, many of them European refugees struggling to survive, often could not afford the increases. So landlords of West Side apartment buildings were unable to keep up their properties and pay the taxes. Some simply walked away.

That so many poor immigrant families were living on the West Side was a major factor in its decline. When they could afford something better they moved to the suburbs, or they moved to the East Side because that had more prestige. And when they moved out, the blacks and Hispanics who moved in tended to have different cultural values.

Also contributing to the decline was the changing character of landlords. The new landlords tended not to have the same pride in their buildings that the old landlords had shown. Certainly the typical landlord profile had changed: in 1956, only 25 percent of West Side property owners lived in the buildings they rented, down from one-third in 1945. More than 20 percent of West Side rooming houses were owned by corporations in 1956, up from 9.6 percent in 1945.

Despite rent control, a couple of buildings did go up in 1957, albeit with government help: Coliseum Park at 345 West 58th Street and 30 West 60th Street are fourteen-story Columbus Avenue houses that share a common garden. The Westmore at 340 West 58th Street also dates to 1957. But middle-class New Yorkers continued to abandon the city in droves. Suburbs, especially those with good schools, attracted thousands of families. Despite an almost total lack of new building on the West Side between 1934 and 1956, the number of housing units in the area increased more than 80 percent during that period, from 7,630 to 13,928. More and more large apartments were being broken up into smaller apartments or being turned into single room occupancy (SRO) hotels, and residents of buildings in which that happened rarely needed much persuasion to move. New York City was losing its solid tax-paying bourgeoisie, some of whose places were being taken in growing proportions by unskilled and semi-skilled workers. The city's population was not increasing; on the contrary, Manhattan was losing residents: from a peak of 1,960,101 in the 1950 census, the island's population declined to 1,698,281 in 1960, mostly because of what demographers called white flight.

It was all very depressing. Marya Mannes wrote in 1961 about the thin line of Central Park West apartment houses "separating the rich from the rotting poor on the adjacent side streets" in which a few well-maintained brownstones, occupied by German-Jewish families, represented "islands of decency in a sea of squalor."

"For those fortunate enough, or determined enough, to make their own world," said Mannes, "it is possible to take the best that New York can offer by holding up a deliberate shield against its dirt, its corruption, and its indignities. It is possible, but not easy, to avert the eye from the filth on the sidewalk, the spit on the streets, when the decay blights whole areas of the city . . . It is possible, but not easy, to accept criminality and discourtesy as byproducts of a huge and affluent city. It is possible, and only too easy, to deny the open concentration camp that is Harlem.

"It is possible, too, to believe that the nadir of these various uglinesses has been reached. People in the city are rising against them, whether they are planners drafting new areas to supplant blight or citizens bent on the salvage of the young and lost, the sick and lonely, the alien and the old, or the decent many who cannot live in the city of their choice if they must choose between luxury, which they cannot afford, and squalor, which they will not afford. And all through the city, young people are now fighting for new vigor and direction, and city government, no longer able to tolerate the weakness and confusion and cowardice and

Many landlords opted to sell their buildings and values declined (1986 photo)

venality of the entrenched political machine. It is possible, but not easy, to believe that New York may have begun its arduous upward path, and that ten years may see not only a city of glass but a better way of living."

Those who believed New York was dying had only to point to the seemingly uncontrollable growth of graffiti in subways and on buildings, the increasing sale of drugs, the decline of public schools with their high dropout rates and poor scholastic levels—even the slovenly appearance of apartment house doormen who, in many cases, but especially on the West Side, no longer bothered to wear livery or even to shave regularly and often could barely speak English. Elevator operators had virtually disappeared except in a few high-priced buildings; automatic elevators, much cheaper, lacked the reassuring presence of a familiar employee and contributed to the feeling that New York was becoming a hostile environment.

For children of Puerto Rican immigrants, the upper West Side was a land of promise and opportunity (1985 photo)

The "nadir" mentioned by Mannes may have come on July 6, 1961, when a fight between a black woman and a Puerto Rican woman in West 84th Street escalated until it became a riot. One rioter was blinded when lye was thrown in his face, many others were hurt, and the episode received wide publicity. The block in which it occurred, between Columbus and Amsterdam Avenues, was labeled the worst in New York. In truth, it was little different from other blocks in which transient, unemployed blacks and Hispanics, obliged to occupy cramped and filthy quarters, made life difficult for their striving black and Hispanic neighbors.

Down the block from the scene of the riot was an Episcopalian church. Its pastor, the Reverend James Gusweller, told a *New York Times* reporter that "drunkenness, unemployment, gambling, overcrowding, prostitution, homosexuality, narcotics and despair" were at the root of the riot and of the street's other horrors. He cited the case of three starving children whose mother lay unconscious from a drug overdose. In this and other troubled streets, rooming house halls were used as toilets, robberies and car thefts were almost daily occurrences, and the noise and disorder each night so disturbed other tenement dwellers in the 1960s that more and more of them found the wherewithal to pull up stakes, even if it meant giving up rent-controlled apartments. The area's Irish Catholic population plummeted.

A violent brick- and bottle-throwing melee broke out between blacks and Puerto Ricans on August 1, 1962, in 94th Street between Central Park West and Columbus Avenue, bringing new demands for action on the part of the city. Those who saw nothing but worse times ahead seemed vindicated in 1963, when Pennsylvania Station, which had opened with such pride in 1910 and been hailed over the years for its grace and beauty, began to come down, unceremoniously demolished to make way for an undistiguished twenty-nine-story office tower, a new twenty-thousand-seat Madison Square Garden, a five hundred-seat movie theater, a forty-eight lane bowling alley, and a new rail terminal with all the aesthetic appeal of the Port Authority Bus Terminal a few blocks north. The *New York Times* editorialized on October 30, 1963, "Until the first blow fell, no one was convinced that Penn Station really would be demolished or that New York would permit this monumental act of vandalism . . . Any city gets what it admires, will pay for, and, ultimately, deserves. Even when we had Penn Station, we couldn't afford to keep it clean."

In a classic example of locking the barn door after the horse has been stolen, the Landmarks Preservation Commission was created to prevent further trashing of the city's important structures. Mayor Robert F. Wagner, Jr., defying opposition from real estate interests and developers, signed legislation on April 19, 1965, authorizing creation of the commission, whose power was consolidated by a Supreme Court decision in a case involving Grand Central Terminal. Since 1965 well-financed developers have battled in the courts against well-organized preservationists and neighborhood groups over proposed changes in the city's appearance. Lever House (on Park Avenue), the Dakota, and dozens of other buildings survive today largely because of efforts by the commission and its supporters.

Preservationism was hardly the chief motivating force in keeping the upper West Side from going down the drain in the 1950s and '60s. But, surprisingly, much of the area remained relatively untouched through the depths of that period. Even while the dominant mood appeared to be one of despair, the wheels had been set in motion for a revival that would once again make the West Side a favored place of residence for many kinds of New Yorkers.

VIII. Bouncing Back

In a *Herald-Tribune* series that began ten days before the July 6, 1961, riot in West 84th Street, Don Ross wrote that the city had plans "to halt the flight of middle-class residents from the upper West Side to outlying parts of the city and the suburbs." If the flight continued, said Ross, "it is feared the area will deteriorate into a low-income ghetto like Harlem or East Harlem."

Some 335,000 people lived in the area bounded by Central Park West, the Hudson River, 59th Street, and 125th Street. Before World War II it had been "one of the city's choicest residential sections," Ross noted. Now it was "a mixture of squalid and good living, of well-cared-for tall apartment houses next to shabby brownstones and old-law tenements that have been converted to one-room-per-family occupancy. It is a place of considerable fear, racial tension, and juvenile delinquency . . ."

That the West Side recovered as quickly as it did suggests that it never really did decline as much as Ross indicated and as was popularly believed. Its buildings were for the most part solid structures, and many West Siders stayed put, sheltered by rent control laws and by school policies that separated intellectually gifted children from those less favored.

Ironically, the seeds of the West Side's revival were being sown even as parts of it were declining. Pockets of urban decay, existing in various sections of the city and in other parts of the country, had for years been clamoring for attention, and in mid-July 1949 Congress had passed a federal Housing Act, sponsored by Senator Robert Taft of Ohio. It provided federal aid for slum clearance projects and low-rent public housing. Title I of the act encouraged municipalities to acquire substandard areas and resell them to private developers at prices below cost.

Forty thousand New Yorkers were crammed into the area between Central Park West and Amsterdam Avenue from 87th Street to 97th. More than 59 percent of apartments in the area were substandard, and serious structural defects existed in more than half the overcrowded buildings. At a seminar held in the early 1950s under the auspices of the Riverside Neighborhood Council, community leaders addressed the question of what could be done about the upper West Side. Out of that discussion emerged the West Side Urban Renewal Area.

Mayor Robert F. Wagner, Jr., after his election in 1953, had appointed a Slum Clearance Committee headed by former Parks Commissioner Robert Moses. This was the agency through which all federal monies provided under Title I of the 1949 (and 1954) Housing Acts were to be channeled. Moses wanted to clear the entire twenty-block section from 87th Street to 97th between Central Park West and Amsterdam Avenue and subsidize construction of upper-income housing—buildings that would pay full real estate taxes to the city. Samuel Ratensky had a different vision. Ratensky was associate chief of planning for the New York City Housing Authority, and in 1955 he began a process that led eventually to the large-scale urban renewal project that rebuilt the area, not as Robert Moses had intended but as a neighborhood of mixed-income housing.

Brownstones were the predominant dwellings on the upper West Side, and many were in sorry shape. Robert Moses wanted to raze them and replace them with modern high-rise buildings. With a deficit of 430,000 dwelling units, however, it was felt that the city could not afford to tear down any building in which people could live decently. In the Bloomingdale Neighborhood Conservation District between 100th and 104th streets from Riverside Drive to Amsterdam Avenue, federal government and city money helped local interests finance a program designed to spruce up buildings, reduce overoccupancy, and oblige landlords to comply with health, sanitary, and building codes. But demolition and construction was the path of least resistance. So while a good many brownstones were rehabilitated with Title I money, most such work did not begin until the late 1960s. Initially the funds went into slum clearance projects organized by the City Housing Authority to rebuild much of the densely populated upper West Side with high-rise "project" housing.

Many West Side Urban Renewal Plan buildings were built with Mitchell-Lama money. The Mitchell-Lama Act of 1955, named for State Senator MacNeil Mitchell and Assemblyman Alfred Lama, authorized state or city loans covering up to 90 percent of construction cost and repayable over a period of up to fifty years. In addition, the city could grant a tax exemption of up to 50 percent for thirty years.*

Sponsors of some federally funded Title I projects used them to line their own pockets, as in the case of Manhattantown, a project that was to occupy the three-block site between Central Park West and Amsterdam Avenue from 97th to 100th streets. It was stalled for various reasons, and a congressional investigation in 1954 revealed that sponsors of Manhattantown and their business associates were doing well from their slum properties despite the lack of progress in construction. A white knight was needed to save the situation, and William Zeckendorf, the big name in real estate at the time, seemed to fit the description. He had assembled the Turtle Bay area site for the United Nations on the East River, displacing the city's most pungent packing houses. Zeckendorf headed the

---

* Some 138,000 rental and co-op Mitchell-Lama units were built in New York City between 1958 and 1975 at interest rates of 3½, 4½, and 5½ percent (after 1975 it became impossible to float bonds at such low interest rates and no more Mitchell-Lama housing was built). The State Housing Commissioner supervises rents (maintenance payments in the case of co-ops) in Mitchell-Lama projects. From 1958 to 1985, applicants for Mitchell-Lama housing had to show that their income was no more than six or seven times the rent or maintenance charge; the formula was changed in 1985 to seven or eight times the rent or maintenance.

firm of Webb and Knapp, which took over the Manhattantown site at the invitation of Robert Moses and developed it in partnership with the Aluminum Company of America (Alcoa). West Park Apartments, as it was called beginning in July 1957, soon became Park West Village, a complex of twenty-seven hundred middle-income apartments in seven buildings, with open-air parking spaces.

Park West Village, built between 1957 and 1960 from Central Park West to Columbus Avenue (1986 photo; tennis courts in foreground, private, belong to Columbus Racquet Club)

Neighborhood groups had opposed the $37.5 million Manhattantown-Park West Village project, complaining that rentals would be too high. Minorities evicted to make way for the project would have to vacate the area, they said. Similar opposition would attempt to block slum clearance projects elsewhere on the upper West Side.

To the northwest, on a twelve-block site with grassy lawns from 100th Street to 104th between Manhattan and Amsterdam avenues, are the Frederick Douglass Houses, a project originally intended for eighteen hundred families. The number was later increased to 2,462 in twenty-nine buildings, including rehabilitated four-story structures and twenty-story high rises. The Douglass Houses received their first tenants in September 1957. Each family paid $55 per month in rent.

Social critic Jane Jacobs' 1961 book *The Death and Life of Great American Cities* preached the doctrine that life was safer and more pleasant in neighborhood communities of low-rise buildings where people lived in the streets and on their doorsteps rather than in the depersonalized environment of modern high-rise cities. City planners talked about using Title I funds to reconvert a substantial number of upper West Side brownstones from rooming house use to apartments for middle-class living, but the buildings put up in the West Side Urban Renewal Area were all of the sort that Jane Jacobs deplored, and many people, Lewis Mumford among them, shared her view.

The Frederick Douglass Houses, built between 1957 and 1970, replaced tenements above 100th Street (1986 photo)

West Siders were more concerned about the social policies of urban rehabilitation. The original city plan for the urban renewal area, as drawn up by Robert Moses and his Slum Clearance Committee in the mid–1950s, had called for four hundred low-rent public housing units in a mix that would include also high-rent apartments and apartments for middle-income residents.

While nearly $31 million in federal, state, and city contributions were earmarked for West Side urban renewal, planners hoped for some $125 million in private capital for construction and rehabilitation. Full tax-paying apartment buildings were needed for tax revenues that would strengthen the city's economy (middle-income buildings would pay only partial taxes, low-cost housing, little or none), and these would have to be privately financed. James Felt, chairman of the City Planning Commission, expressed the view that it would be economic folly to make the West Side primarily an area of subsidized low-income housing. Felt was the man chiefly responsible for the conception of the West Side Urban Renewal Project. To build low-rent housing in the area was to him as stupid as building such housing in Sutton Place. Renewal plans would stand or fall, it was reasoned in 1961, on the degree to which private enterprise found them attractive and wished to participate.

Prospective builders, however, balked at the idea of increasing the allotment of low-income public housing units. J. Clarence Davies, Jr., chairman of the Housing and Redevelopment Board, said, "The builders' attitude is based on the assumption that upper and middle income persons will not choose to live in close proximity to large numbers of low income minority groups."

By 1961 the plan had been revised. There would be one thousand low-rent public housing units, twenty-eight hundred high-rent apartments, and forty-two hundred middle-income apartments. Puerto Rican leaders insisted that there be a minimum of twenty-five hundred low-income public housing units. Otherwise, they said, there would be a mass removal of low-income groups from the area. Few blacks or Puerto Ricans could afford the new middle-income housing, they said, and there were charges that urban renewal was in reality just a scheme to force blacks and Hispanics to vacate the upper West Side and move to less desirable parts of the city.

Robert Moses resigned in order to head up planning for the 1964–1965 World's Fair, and Jackie Robinson, the baseball star, hailed the proposal for West Side urban renewal as "the first truly integrated project the city ever attempted." Not everybody agreed. In May 1962, a public hearing of the City Planning Commission erupted in a dispute between Jack E. Wood, the housing secretary for the National Association for the Advancement of Colored People (NAACP), and Aramis Gomez, leader of a Puerto Rican group. Wood said that to devise a plan that would provide low-rent housing for every low-income family to be relocated in the project area would be "to give municipal sanction for containment and encourage the development of a community characterized by racial and economic balance." The NAACP did not condone all the city's relocation programs, said Wood, but he pleaded for "the kind of racial and economic balance and integration that complements the open city concept of New York." Gomez charged that the city's method for achieving a balanced community was "to get rid of the Negroes and Puerto Ricans and low income families from the area." He called the project "a massive piece of deception" and "the biggest hoax perpetrated on the neighborhood and the people of New York City."

A 1962 City Planning Commission report on the West Side Urban Renewal Area sought to reassure skeptics: "Old time New York residents," the report said, "still remember a quieter, more leisurely city: clean, attractive, good to look at it, good to live in. That is essentially what the plan seeks to make out of these twenty crowded blocks with their rows of substandard houses and the squalid face of blight. When the plan has been carried out, new plazas will open unaccustomed stretches of sunlight and air. Traffic flow will be improved, trees planted, and attractive new stores will replace rundown shops. New community facilities will serve the neighborhood. Old community facilities—nine schools, two school playgrounds, ten religious structures, two community centers—will stay. There will be large areas of new building in the neighborhood. The good houses of today will still be there. In short, the neighborhood will keep the charm of diversity—the mixture of old and new, big and small, the variety of people and materials and buildings that has always attracted people to city living. It will be spacious, housing as many people as today, but in a far better way. Many of the buildings will be cooperatives, in which occupants will share ownership as well as pride in their neighborhood. There will not be the enormous population turnover of today. It will be, above all, a pleasant place to live."

Private builders were not convinced. Politics dictated that the needs of low- and middle-income residents come first. Even before any land was cleared for high-rise "development" projects, the City Housing Authority had begun converting rundown tenements. In 1963 it took four such buildings at 48–54 West 94th Street, scene of the 1962 brick- and bottle-throwing battle, and converted them into forty new apartments renting for between $43 and $79 per month, including utilities. Mostly, though, the West Side Urban Renewal Area was built up with high-rise apartment buildings.

Some of these buildings were entirely for low-rent tenants, others mixed low-rent tenants with middle-income houses. Community groups sponsored most buildings. The Riverside Neighborhood Association, for example, sponsored the RNA Houses; the Goddard Riverside Community Center, the Goddard Riverside Towers. Trinity House includes an addition to the Trinity School, many of whose faculty but few of whose students live in the low- to middle-income apartments.

A few blocks to the south, in West 84th Street between Amsterdam and Columbus avenues, the city had dealt summarily with the people responsible for the July 6, 1961 riot in that block. It had bulldozed their tenements along with others and was replacing them with school buildings and playgrounds. The Louis D. Brandeis High School of 1965 replaced a 1903 structure in the block. P.S. 9 at 100 West 84th Street was built at about the same time.

Slum clearance was proceeding meanwhile in the Lincoln Square area, where about twenty thousand New Yorkers had been living in tenements west of Broadway in the West 60s. Rehabilitation of fifty-two acres was accomplished largely by razing these tenements, along with a few more substantial structures such as St. Cyprian's Church, the Kennedy Building, the 212th Coast Artillery Armory, and the Lincoln Square Arcade, which had given refuge earlier in the century to financially pinched painters, including a few of the Ashcan School. St. Cyprian's Church, an Episcopalian house of worship with a black congregation, was razed to make way for the new Metropolitan Opera House, part of the Lincoln Center for the Performing Arts that was funded by tax-deductible private contributions, primarily from the Rockefellers. This project, which began

Columbus Avenue buildings transformed the 80s and 90s (1986 photo).

in the 1950s and continued through most of the '60s, attracted new housing and inspired renovation throughout the area.

John D. Rockefeller III took a leading role in sponsoring the arts center superblock, which was opposed by local businessmen whose places of business were in the area slated for demolition. They organized to fight the Lincoln Center project. So did tenement dwellers. There were protests that not enough middle-income housing would be built to accommodate the people displaced when their tenements were razed. Someone recalled that the minister of St. Cyprian's Church had played a key role in averting racial violence in the area half a century earlier and urged that the church be preserved. The West Side Chamber of Commerce demanded that commercial theaters be barred from Lincoln Center because of the effect that they would have on the Times Square theater district. There were objections that using public (Title I) money to subsidize Fordham University's purchase of part of the area for a campus violated the First Amendment and that building on the site of St. Matthew's Roman Catholic Church violated the state constitution. Opponents carried their case all the way to the U.S. Supreme Court, which declined to review it in June 1958. Demolition began in late July 1958 after the vacated tenements had been used as a set for the filming of the Broadway musical *West Side Story*.

Lincoln Center replaced some of the city's worst slums (1984 photo by Susanne Faulkner Stevens courtesy Lincoln Center for the Performing Arts)

Lincoln Center for the Performing Arts occupies four blocks from 62nd Street to 66th between Broadway and Columbus Avenue. Whatever their architectural and acoustic merits (they have always had their share of detractors), the Lincoln Center auditoriums served as a catalyst for change in their immediate neighborhood, which before the Center was built had a similar character to that of the West 40s and 50s today: a warren of tenements interspersed with private houses, most of which had been turned into rooming houses or worse. The area's renaissance is ascribable entirely to the development of Lincoln Center.

In the early 1960s thousands of people moved into the new apartments of nearby Lincoln Towers, a thirty-acre landscaped complex of eight high-rise buildings extending along both sides of West End Avenue from 66th Street to 70th. William Zeckendorf, who, again in partnership with Alcoa, developed this vast middle-class Title I housing project would later rue the fact that his financial backers, Lazard Frères, were too tightfisted to let the buildings have all the quality that he had envisioned, but most tenants have few complaints. Some ten thousand people live in the 3,897 apartments. The buildings are centrally air-conditioned, and the stabilized rents have always included utilities. Tenants of the buildings west of West End Avenue look out on the Hudson River and what remains of the old New York Central railroad yards. A typical apartment was featured in the 1965 film *The Pawnbroker*.

Although at times the West Side might resemble one big urban redevelopment project, some West Siders were still living in the grand manner. At the start of the 1970s, a market research man and his wife had

200 Central Park South, 1964 (1986 photo)

the penthouse at 90 Riverside Drive (at 81st Street), which had its own private swimming pool—a full-sized open air pool that they filled each spring and drained each fall. Even on the East Side there was nothing to match it.

A good deal of West Side hotel and residential construction for the upper middle class went ahead in the 1960s, including the Americana (later the Sheraton Center), a two-thousand-room hotel that opened in September 1962 on Seventh Avenue and 52nd Street. New apartment houses included one at 220 Central Park South, just east of the Gainsborough Studios, which replaced the last brownstones in the block. Under 200 Central Park South was the street's first parking garage. A building at 80 Central Park West was the first new housing to be built on the lower part of that avenue since the 1930s.

Behind the Mayfair Towers, built in 1963 at 15 West 72nd Street, lies the story of the Dakota's sale and its subsequent co-oping. The Clark Foundation had been losing money on the Dakota for years. Louis J. Glickman, a real estate investor, bought the building and its parking lot at the end of 1960 for $4.6 million. He arranged for mortgage financing and permitted tenants to buy individual apartments for a total of $4.8 million, thus making the Dakota a co-op and giving him a $200,000 profit; he promptly sold the parking lot—earlier the site of the Dakota's rose garden, generating plant, and tennis courts—to the Mayfair Corporation for $2 million. Many of the Dakota's larger apartments had been divided into smaller units during the Depression. With the release of the film *Rosemary's Baby* in 1968 the building became widely known. It had a pivotal role in Jack Finney's 1970 novel *Time and Again*, and the tragic shooting of John Lennon there in December 1980 made the Dakota sadly familiar to all the world.

Although Sixth Avenue, officially called the Avenue of the Americas since October 1945 (the eight hundred metal disks representing the nations of the Americas came in October 1960), had been free of its El since April 1939, its first office tower—the forty-eight-story Time and Life Building—did not go up until 1959, when office building construction was picking up all over Manhattan.

Zoning laws played a role in the 1960s building boom. New York's original 1916 zoning code was completely rewritten in 1960 despite opposition from real estate and construction interests. The opponents did force a concession: buildings for which plans were filed before December 1961 would have to adhere not to the new code but to the old, more lenient, code. Developers, rushing to beat the deadline, filed for 150,659 multiple-dwelling units, about five years' worth of housing. The standard zoning that applied from 1961 to the mid–1980s produced straight towers behind open plazas—a departure from the so-called wedding cake style of architecture, if not necessarily an improvement over it. (In 1984 the City Planning Commission would adopt a new upper West Side zoning law mandating a street wall along Broadway of one hundred and twenty feet— twelve or thirteen stories—with setbacks above that level.)

Special bonuses for enlightened land use were granted under the zoning resolution that took effect on December 14, 1961. The chief effect of the new code was to encourage architects to set off their buildings with open plazas. One consequence was a series of towers on the Avenue of the

Americas: the thirty-eight-story Equitable Life Building, the forty-three-story Sperry Rand (later Sperry Corp.) Building, the forty-four-story New York Hilton with 2,200 rooms, the thirty-six-story CBS Building, the forty-five-story J. C. Penney Building, the fifty-story Burlington House, the fifty-one-story McGraw-Hill Building, the fifty-three-story Exxon Building, and the forty-four-story Celanese Building. Until these buildings went up between 1959 and 1974, the area once blighted by the Sixth Avenue El had remained blighted. Only now was the Avenue of the Americas emerging from neglect. It, too, represented an aspect of West Side urban renewal.

The new Time and Life, McGraw-Hill, Exxon, and Celanese Buildings were on land owned by the Rockefeller family, which had eleven acres west of Sixth Avenue in addition to the 11.7 acres of the original Rockefeller Center site. Architectural critics have written at length, rarely in praise, about these ranks of cold monoliths (which acquire more human dimensions in summer when their many trees are in leaf).

Returning to the Lincoln Center area, not all of the land cleared by razing tenements west of Broadway in the 60s was occupied by Lincoln Center and related buildings. Fordham University, the Jesuit institution whose buildings in the Bronx dated in some cases to the 1840s, built a Lincoln Center campus beginning in 1962, when its law school (south building) was completed. Its Leon Lowenstein Center (north building) was completed in 1969.

Also built in 1969, on the north side of Columbus Circle across from Edward Durell Stone's 1965 Huntington Hartford Gallery of Modern Art (later headquarters of the New York City Department of Cultural Affairs), was the Gulf + Western Building, erected on a site once occupied by the American Circle Building. Plans originally called for a thirty-five-story circular apartment tower atop a ten-story office building. The forty-four-story tower (with a subterranean Paramount movie theater) that was finally built has peculiar aerodynamics, creating blasts of air to batter unfortunate pedestrian passersby. Across Broadway and a block north is Skidmore, Owings and Merrill's American Bible Society Building of 1965, which replaced a structure on the southwest corner of Park Avenue and 57th Street.

Upper West Side residential construction continued in the 1970s, some of it in the ongoing West Side Urban Renewal Area effort. Buildings in this latter category—all between 88th and 110th streets and on Columbus or Amsterdam Avenue—include St. Martin's Tower, Columbus Manor, the New Amsterdam Houses, Turin House, Leader House, Heywood Tower, Glenn Gardens, Tower West, Westgate, and the Cathedral Parkway Houses. Some of these, such as Trinity House, Tower West (the scene of an owner-tenant war in the early 1980s), the Lincoln-Amsterdam House, and Westgate, were put up with Mitchell-Lama money. St. Martin's Tower, sponsored by St. Martin's Episcopal Church, was the first middle-income development to be sponsored by a black organization.

The new housing was, in fact, given over largely to low- and

Gulf + Western Bulding at Columbus Circle, 1969 (1986 photo)

middle-income black and Hispanic families. None of the buildings in the West Side Urban Renewal Area was a luxury house for high-income tenants. As had been predicted in 1961, no private builder was yet willing to gamble that upper-middle-class tenants would want to live "in close proximity to large numbers of low income minority groups." So the upper West Side, while it was the most successfully integrated part of the city, racially and economically, was by no means homogenized. It had rich white neighborhoods and poor ethnic neighborhoods with a certain amount of mixing within those neighborhoods.

Aside from the "projects," most of the West Side housing put up in the 1970s consisted of high-rent, co-operative, and condominium apartment buildings. As one critic put it, "After the project developers had come in and raped the upper upper West Side, the fast-buck artists came in to exploit the rest of the lower upper West Side." Most, although not all, 1970s buildings were examples of developers looking for quick and oversized returns on their investments. Mews—unlike the Carnegie Mews, built in 1971 at the northeast corner of Broadway and 56th Street—are generally low-rise stables along a courtyard or alley. That concept was long out of date in the 1970s; now the name of the game was to create the maximum number of rental units (which would later become co-op or condo units) in the minimum amount of space. One Sherman Square, built in 1971 at 201 West 70th Street, has three hundred and seventy-eight units where perhaps a hundred existed before. That a six-story apartment building was erected in 1972 at 23 West 91st Street, just north of the Eldorado, merely indicates that the area was not then attracting money for high-rise construction.

Far more ambitious were the forty-story 1 Lincoln Plaza, completed across from Lincoln Center on the east side of Broadway in 1971, and the thirty-story 30 Lincoln Plaza Tower, completed to the south a few years later at 44 West 62nd Street. Both were put up by Paul Milstein in partnership with his brother Seymour and his father Morris. A former chairman of the City Planning Commission had proposed that a mall be built to link Central Park West with Lincoln Center. Nothing came of that, and a sixty-thousand-square-foot parking lot, owned by the New York Academy of Sciences, sat on the east side of Broadway facing Lincoln Center between 63rd and 64th streets. The Milsteins bought the site in December 1967 and retained Philip Birnbaum to design a building. His plan for 1 Lincoln Plaza, revealed the following June, called for a forty-story structure housing seven hundred apartments of two and a half to six and a half rooms each, with a rooftop swimming pool and cabana club, an underground garage for three hundred cars, and a sunken plaza with shops. The Milsteins got their building, although not without a fight and not exactly as originally designed.

The Gloucester, put up in record time in 1976 at 200 West 79th Street, facing the Lucerne Hotel of 1904, is a high rise with two hundred and seventy-two apartments. A 1977 building is Philip Birnbaum's Nevada Towers (actually just one tower) on the triangular site between Broadway and Amsterdam Avenue at 70th Street, where the Nevada apartments had once stood.

Close to the pier that has since become Manhattan's last remaining passenger ship terminal, the pink concrete Clinton Tower apartment house opened in 1975 at 790 Eleventh Avenue, between 54th and 55th Streets, toward the north end of the Clinton area, which was trying to lose its Hell's Kitchen image. Harbor View Terrace, a New York City Housing Authority project extending from 54th to 56th streets between Tenth and Eleventh avenues, went up in 1977.

New York's theater district, a bit farther south, was seeing a few changes of its own.

IX. The Rialto Revisited

From the 1930s until the '70s, no new legitimate theaters were added to the city's stock. Many existing houses, if they did not become movie theaters, were dark for months—even years—at a time. Theater owners—the Shubert and Nederlander families own most New York theaters, the Jujamcyn Corporation owns a few—either pocket so much money when a hit is on the boards that it makes sense to hold a property through lean times, or the land under the theaters appreciates so much each year that they keep the houses as an investment.

The federally funded American National Theater and Academy, founded in 1943, bought the Theatre Guild's Guild Theater, built in 1925, and renamed it the ANTA Theater in 1950. The 48th Street Theater of 1912 was demolished in 1955 after extensive damage caused by the collapse of its water tank. The National Theater became Billy Rose's Theater in 1959.

The 1960s saw Madison Square Garden razed and replaced by a new Garden seventeen blocks south. And from 1962 to 1968, the development of Lincoln Center in the West 60s ended a more than eighty-year stand by the old Metropolitan Opera House and added new facilities for the performing arts.

Along with Lincoln Center's concert, opera, and ballet theaters were two legitimate theaters, built in the face of opposition from theater owners in the Times Square area. The $10.3 million Vivian Beaumont Theater, seating 1,000 to 1,089, opened in April 1966 as the Forum, and the Mitzi E. Newhouse Theater, seating 280, opened in 1973 as the home of the Lincoln Center Theater Company. Eero Saarinen and Associates designed the building with the collaboration of Jo Mielziner.

Among those who found West Side apartments attractive were actors and musicians. Indeed, no other neighborhood in the world had such a concentration of show people in residence. The Dakota had accepted its first actor tenant in the 1930s: William Henry Pratt, better known as Boris Karloff, moved in during the Depression (his good friend Basil Rathbone lived down the street). Lauren Bacall; José Ferrer and his wife, the singer Rosemary Clooney; Judy Garland, Judy Holliday, Jack Palance, Eric Portman, Robert Ryan, the dancer Gwen Verdon, the opera singer John Brownlee, musicmakers John Lennon and his wife, Yoko Ono; soul singer Roberta Flack, playwrights William Inge and Sidney Kingsley, film director John Frankenheimer, filmmaker Albert Maysles, agent Ted Ashley, and other entertainment figures subsequently lived at various times at the Dakota. While not every co-op building welcomed show business types, the Dakota did not go co-op until late 1961, and by that time it already had many denizens of Hollywood and Broadway as tenants.

In the theater district, a change in zoning regulations permitted construction of theaters in buildings designed primarily for other purposes. Several such theaters—the American Place, Circle-in-the-Square, Uris (later called the Gershwin), and Minskoff—opened in the early 1970s. These new theaters simply exploited special Times Square zoning bonuses that allowed a developer to build more than the normal bulk in return for constructing a legitimate theater.

Off-Broadway houses, including a few on the upper West Side, were giving new choices to theatergoers and, together with television, were creating more opportunities for the city's unending supply of would-be actors, directors, playwrights, stage designers, and the like. Some of this talent found accommodations in the redbrick Manhattan Plaza apartment complex built as a Mitchell-Lama project in 1977. Rising forty-five stories on Ninth Avenue and forty-six on Tenth above what used to be Hell's Kitchen and containing 1,688 units, it extends from 42nd Street north to 43rd between the two avenues. The apartments are reserved entirely for performing artists, who pay no more than 30 percent of their gross incomes for rent, the balance being subsidized by Housing Preservation and Development, a federal agency.

Hotel construction in the early 1980s was concentrated on the East Side (Donald Trump's Grand Hyatt replaced the old Commodore near Grand Central Station, while the Helmsley Palace incorporated the Villard Houses of the mid-1880s on Madison Avenue between 50th and 51st Streets), but the West Side had the new forty-six-story Park Lane at 36 Central Park South, which opened in 1971 with 640 rooms, and in 1982 got a stunning new hotel in the forty-two-story Parker Meridien, which opened with seven hundred rooms in 56th Street between the Avenue of the Americas and Seventh Avenue, replacing the Great Northern Hotel of 1910. The hotel's amusingly narrow 57th Street entrance welcomes visitors—many of them Hollywood types—through a mirror-lined, elaborately ceilinged, five-story passageway to the hotel proper. Owner Jack Parker, an American, employed a French management company owned by Air France. The thirty-two-story, 470-room Novotel opened in 1984 at 52nd Street and Broadway. And the forty-six-story Marriott Marquis, designed by John Portman with 876 rooms, a revolving bar, and glass-bubble elevators, opened in 1985 as part of a Times Square redevelopment program. The hotel's Marquis Theater, operated by the Nederlander organization, has fifteen hundred seats. These do not begin to replace all the seats that were lost when five houses (only three of them still legitimate theaters) were bulldozed out of existence in 1982 to make way for the new hotel: the Astor (built in 1906), the Bijou (1917), the Gaiety (built in 1909 and turned into the Victoria movie theater in 1943 after burlesque was banned by Mayor La Guardia), the Helen Hayes (1911), and the Morosco (1917).

Times Square's Marriott Marquis Hotel displaced some theaters and brought radical change to the Great White Way (photo courtesy Marriott Marquis)

*Community efforts failed to save the Beacon movie palace
(75th Street and Broadway), which went disco
late in 1986 (1986 photo)*

Petitions, rallies led by the likes of Colleen Dewhurst and Jason
Robards, Jr., and sympathetic press attention were for nought in efforts
by the theater community to save the above theaters from being bull-
dozed. Up at 75th Street, there were demonstrations to keep the Beacon
Theater from being turned into a discotheque. Elsewhere on the West
Side, community action was only a little more successful.

X. Community Efforts

Urban renewal development on the West Side was not accomplished without resistance. New Yorkers have a long history of fighting anyone who tries to push them around, stand in their way, or jeopardize the quality of life in their neighborhood. West Siders have been particularly energetic in asserting their rights in what they regard as *their* turf. They have been doing it for a long time.

Riverside Park, designed by Frederick Law Olmsted in 1873, was completed in May 1880 after ten years of lawsuits and design changes. In the spring of 1880 the contractor blocked off cross streets with derricks and timbers, claiming that the city still owed him money. He posted guards at night to prevent people from entering the park, but the public was not to be denied. In the middle of a May night, a crowd broke through the barricade, and from then on Riverside Park was open to the people—a promenade disturbed only by the New York Central tracks along the river's edge.

West Siders today mostly stop short of taking the law into their own hands, although there have been episodes over the years in which tenants have moved into vacant buildings to protest the city's failure to provide low-cost housing or for some other reason. West Siders do find legal ways to control their environment. City planners, developers, and builders must always contend with neighborhood activists—people who know how to bring pressure on a builder and force him to be a good citizen. Pressure can also be brought against individual neighbors.

Community action begins at the block level, even at the individual apartment house level. What may have been the West Side's first block association was formed in the early 1940s in the West 65th Street "park block." A six-story elevator building at 10 West 65th was the only middle-income house in the block. Opposite stood some brownstones subsidized by the Ethical Culture Society and inhabited by some Ethical Culture teachers. Everything else was tenements, housing mainly black and Hispanic families and with some singleroom occupancy. The SROs were a source of some noise and crime, which the people at 10 West wanted to eliminate. They held meetings at the Holy Trinity Lutheran Church at 65th and Central Park West and eventually were able to get their Hispanic neighbors involved. That eliminated a lot of the antagonism that had existed between one side of the street and the other. People began to know each other and to say hello.

"When you see someone at meetings you stop thinking of him as

Spring clean-up is a community effort in West 92nd Street as elsewhere on the West Side
(1986 photo)

an enemy that you're going to rip off," observed one of the block association's veterans more than four decades later. "And nobody wanted noise and crime, whatever their economic situation. What we tried to do was get some of the buildings renovated, get better living quarters, which would attract a different class of tenant. We didn't think it through. We believed in improvement and we didn't want the area to remain a low-income neighborhood. We wanted a mixed-income society, and in the early days we never gave much thought to what would happen to the low-income people who were forced out."

New York has fifty-nine community boards, established in 1977 through a change in the city charter. More than twenty years earlier, in the mid–1950s, Mayor Robert F. Wagner, Jr., appointed a prototype community board as a volunteer advisory committee to Manhattan's borough president. Although the board had no staff, it did have considerable influence. Today's boards, staffed and funded by the city, probably have less power than their shoestring predecessors did. Yet few boards, if any, are as zealous as Community Board 7, at 5 West 63rd Street, which responds to complaints in the area between Central Park and the Hudson from 59th Street to 110th.

Before there was Community Board 7 there were neighborhood groups such as the Citizens Watchdog Committee on Relocation, set up at the time that land was being cleared to build Lincoln Center. An active member of the committee was Rabbi Edward E. Klein, who in 1949 succeeded Stephen Wise as head of the Free Synagogue in West 68th Street, in 1952 cofounded the League of West Side Organizations, and later supported the establishment of Lincoln Center and the adjoining Fordham University campus.

To build Lincoln Center required relocating some five thousand families. There had never been anything like it in the city, and no clear rights had been established for people who had to be moved on such a grand scale. Members of the committee sat down with representatives of the Rockefellers, the Zeckendorfs, and others; they impressed the Lincoln Center people with their responsible approach; and after a while Rabbi Klein was approached by the developers, who said, in effect, "We realize we are a disruptive element in this community. That is unavoidable if the center is to be built. But we want to be a good neighbor." The developers agreed to pay reasonable relocation benefits.

Working with the developers, the Watchdog Committee found ways to make sure that residents of the area to be cleared wound up in accommodations comparable to what they had had in the tenements and rooming houses that were to be razed. Space was available in other tenements in the West 80s and 90s and in the Bronx. A few families were relocated to Brooklyn. Many of the Italian families, living in cold-water flats on and off West End Avenue, could afford better housing and took the opportunity to move into more modern buildings.

Out of the committee grew the Lincoln Square Community Council, organized to make sure that residents of the West Side from 59th

Street to 86th had a voice in how their area was to be developed. Rabbi Klein, chairman of the council, died in July 1985. Two weeks later, Leonard X. Farbman, an electrical and plumbing contractor who had served as chairman of the council's Community Action Planning Program, recalled some of the council's efforts:

"Public money and tax-deductible charitable money cleared the slums to build Lincoln Center. That created an upward acceleration of property values in the area. Builders who came into the area got a free ride. We felt they had obligations to the community. We didn't always succeed, but we made an effort. When Paul Milstein submitted plans for 1 Lincoln Plaza, for example, he wanted it to be several floors higher than the zoning law permitted. The building threatened to overshadow Lincoln Center, and the Lincoln Center people weren't crazy about it, but we were the ones who bore the brunt of the battle. Milstein kept threatening that if he didn't get the extra floors he would go to the Board of Standards and Appeals and plead economic hardship, which he did. When the board ruled in his favor and granted a variance, we went to the Planning Commission, the Department of City Planning, which filed suit in state supreme court against the Board of Standards and Appeals. It was the first time, and I guess the only time, that the city sued one of its own agencies."

Under the provisions of a proposed special zoning code for the district, a builder who installed an arcade of certain dimensions and additional pedestrian walkspace to facilitate the flow of traffic would be permitted a ratio of floor space to lot area of 14.4–2.4 more than was allowed under the 1916 zoning law. The Board of Standards and Appeals granted the Milsteins a ratio of 16.9. And the Milsteins, with financing from Chase Manhattan Bank, began excavating early in 1969, having filed suit against the Buildings Department for refusing to grant them a foundation permit pending the outcome of the suit brought—at the urging of the Lincoln Square Community Council—by the Department of City Planning.

"In the end we got screwed, and the Milsteins got what they wanted," Farbman concluded. "The Board of Standards and Appeals made a motion to which the Zoning Commission had to reply within thirty days, and somehow they didn't reply in time. So because of a legal mix-up the issue never came to trial."

In its early days the council helped tenants obtain money for relocation. Farbman recalled the Nevada Towers of 1977 and its predecessor. "The old Nevada apartment building on the site had degenerated into a singleroom occupancy hotel. The builder wanted to get the tenants out. Some of them were drug dealers and whatnot, but some were perfectly decent people. One of them, an old socialist, came to us and said, 'You've got to do something.' We said to him, 'Basil, you go and organize a tenants' group and we'll back you a hundred percent.' He got up a tenants' committee, we negotiated, and we stopped them from tearing down the old hotel until everybody in it was relocated. Every tenant got something in the neighborhood of $5,000 to $10,000 for moving out. In fact, Basil got $20,000. We had no legal basis to force them to meet our terms. All we could do was stall the project."

The Lincoln Square Community Council concentrated its efforts on keeping its area from being a "gilded ghetto," an enclave of luxury housing that would crowd out elderly and disadvantaged tenants. It obtained a rezoning order to prevent further demolition of brownstone houses. For 1973, it proposed that six hotels in the West 60s and 70s—the Alamac, the Bradford, the Hargrave, the Kimberly, the Riverside Plaza, and the Walton—be acquired and converted to provide a thousand units for the elderly. It proposed that the Phipps Houses, with 346 units, be preserved for low and moderate income families. And it proposed that 560 new units be built: 138 in an extension to the Amsterdam Houses, 187 in a high-rise co-operative, 35 in a combination garage project, and 200 in other combination projects. The Phipps Houses were preserved, and the Kimberly at 73rd Street and Broadway, with 350 units, was acquired for the elderly. (The Kimberly's life as an old people's residence was brief: in the mid–1980s it was turned into a condominium and renamed the Fitzgerald.)

The council-sponsored Mitchell-Lama high-rise co-op is the Lincoln-Amsterdam House on West End Avenue between 64th and 65th streets, finished in 1976. "It took years to get the thing going," says Farbman. "We interviewed a number of builders and picked Starrett Brothers. We had it all set up for a certain budget, and then the city got into some problems and there was a big escalation in construction costs. Starrett Brothers had agreed to a fee of $250,000 but now wanted more. We forced them into an agreement under which we would go out and get competitive bids, and if we were able to do it under the budget they could hold their fee and we would take over the construction. Since I was in the construction business, I was able to find another builder. We got $50,000 back from Starrett Brothers, and we allocated that for improving the Amsterdam Houses playground, across the street from the Fiorello H. La Guardia High School playground. Now we're working with young adults in the neighborhood on basketball and volleyball tournaments and so forth.

"In another case, a builder sent his plans in to the City Planning Commission and wanted an extra story or two, which he could get pretty much by right. We blocked him until he made a deal with us. He contributed $50,000 in cash toward whatever improvements the neighborhood wanted—meaning what the Lincoln Square Community Council and Community Board 7 wanted. The council took $25,000 to renovate a playground, and the other $25,000 was spent on new malls, which basically was good for the builder, too. Out of that grew the idea that if an owner wanted something beyond what he was allowed by right, then he would have to provide what we call amenities. We tried to work out a way for the builders to give something back to the community in return for the free ride they were getting.

2 Lincoln Square, built in 1975, was the subject of controversy (1985 photo)

"When the Mormon Church and 2 Lincoln Square were built in 1975, one of the amenities we insisted on was the passageway through the building from 66th Street to 65th Street, which is a crosstown bus street. We thought it was a terrific idea. It turned out to be an absolute horror because it became a hangout for muggers. Community boards nowadays are coming to realize that this trade-off for amenities generally benefits the builder more than it benefits the community. If you need a plaza or a park then let's do it. Don't give the builder an abatement that lets him have two extra floors when that is more height and bulk than good planning justifies."

There is a growing feeling, in fact, that open plazas are not especially desirable in residential areas, especially when they mean taller buildings, more people, and less light. Residents complain that the benches dotting bare concrete plazas are occupied mostly by people from outside the neighborhood. Storekeepers complain that store windows are more visible when they are not set back away from the street.

A dispute that took more than twenty years to resolve involved moderate-income housing to be built as part of the West Side Urban Renewal Area on the west side of Columbus Avenue between 90th and 91st streets, where Father Henry J. Browne of the Church of St. Gregory took an active role in the community (West 90th Street between Columbus and Amsterdam avenues is today designated as Henry J. Browne Boulevard). In 1962 the Board of Estimate approved the proposal. There ensued a tug-of-war as rival community groups argued bitterly over how much of the housing would be set aside for low-income tenants. Nine years later the city changed its mind and decided to build a public housing project on the site. Opponents carried the case all the way to the Supreme Court, which upheld the city. The Lefrak Organization, however, claimed to have development rights to the site and also brought suit.

Finally, in late May 1985, there was a compromise. The Board of Estimate approved a plan to build two housing developments on the site: one a $6 million federally funded public housing project to be erected by the city housing authority with eighty-seven units for the elderly, the other a Lefrak-built combination of three town houses plus a twenty-one-story tower in which one apartment in five would be subsidized by rents from the other four. Of the 201 units to be built by Lefrak, 80 percent would be rented at the market rate, and 20 percent would be set aside for fifteen years for low- and moderate-income housing.

The contested site included a city-owned lot that served for some years as a depot for stolen cars. Dee Parisi, a bass player whose three children attended P.S. 166 down the block in 89th Street, obtained a $64,000 grant from the city's Department of Housing Preservation and Development in the mid–1970s to landscape the site until such time as housing construction began. She started garden plots for neighborhood schoolchildren, founded the West Side Community Garden, got free manure from the Claremont Riding Academy, expanded the site when more land became available through the razing of some old brownstones in 1981, and

Community gardens, west of Columbus Avenue between 89th Street and 90th (1986 photo, with P.S. 166 in background)

eventually had an area nearly the size of a football field with some 130 members tending garden plots, some of them the size of small studio apartments. Threatened with extinction, the gardens were spared in 1985 by Jerome Kretchmer, developer of a fourteen-story apartment house at the corner of Columbus and 90th Street and six-story condominium town houses in the block. A onetime state assemblyman from the West Side who was Mayor John V. Lindsay's commissioner of environmental protection, Kretchmer agreed to allot 17,800 square feet for a new garden area adjacent to the present gardens. He also contributed $100,000 of the $150,000 that the new gardens were expected to cost. Green beans, lettuce, radishes, spinach, tomatoes, and flowers from the West Side Community Garden will still appear on neighborhood tables, if not from the same plots.

Development often draws protests on the West Side (1985 photo)

"I think he looked on the garden as a way of easing his development," said one of the heads of the Community Garden, "as a way of not having people out here screaming or lying under bulldozers." "The Community Garden became very powerful, with the whole community caring for and about it. We had to be reckoned with," said Parisi. "The developer did more than he thought he ought to be doing, and less than the community thought he should do," said the vice chairman of the City Planning Commission. "But you don't see this kind of balance outside the West Side."

Architectural critics complained in the 1970s that the upper West

Side's new "development" housing was destroying the character of the area, turning much of Manhattan into a depressing imitation of Queens Boulevard. Defenders of the new construction insisted that the chief priority was to relieve pressure on housing prices and to provide accommodations for growing numbers of people—aesthetics be damned. Aside from architectural considerations there were hot debates over the demographic future of the area: should it be built up entirely with federally funded housing for low-income families, be built up with high-rent luxury housing, or be a series of mixed-income neighborhoods? Trinity School spent $150,000 in legal fees to fight the first idea, fearing that it would create a vast slum, as had happened in Detroit and St. Louis.

Although these fears were not realized, some cynics say the West Side Urban Renewal Plan has succeeded only because applicants to many of the new buildings were carefully screened. Some buildings are admittedly jungles in which the racial and socioeconomic mix does not work, but most of the developments have tenants who live harmoniously, not (say the cynics) because they are all God-fearing, law-abiding citizens but because certain would-be tenants did not get through the screening process.

Other cynics would question the power of community action against the deep pockets of developers, individuals with political connections who can afford the best lawyers and can wear down any opposition.

Community Board 7 and other groups remain active on the upper West Side. In recent years Community Board 7 has worked with local police precincts to have drug sellers arrested and convicted. It has been instrumental in obtaining a youth employment grant to help fix up the 86th Street subway station at Broadway. It worked with the developers of the Bromley at Broadway and 83rd Street to keep the scale of the building down. Strictly speaking, a community board has only advisory power to comment on local land use, to suggest budget priorities, and to monitor city services. In fact it has considerable clout. Its access to public officials and to certain information makes it a group of educated and informed lobbyists. The community board can make suggestions to the City Planning Commission. It can push zoning proposals that will limit density of future housing. It can stir up opposition to projects. Other groups can organize tenants and mount delaying efforts.

Beyond that limited degree of community power the fortunes of the West Side are in the hands of city officials and real estate interests. Pressure from voters is what ultimately makes city officials responsive to community interests. New Yorkers know this. They want a voice in what happens to their neighborhoods, and nowhere is their consternation and determination more evident than on the upper West Side.

XI. Life on the West Side

Community boards, preservationists, and other civic-minded groups concern themselves with the qualities that make a neighborhood—and ultimately an entire city—attractive and livable: Is it safe? Is it too densely populated? Is there a good socio-economic balance in the population? How are the neighbors? Is it convenient to transportation facilities? To places of worship? Are affordable services—food stores, dry cleaning establishments, shoe repair shops, restaurants—readily at hand? How far away are theaters and concert halls? Are there good shops in the neighborhood? Is it quiet? Is it clean? Is there plenty of light and fresh, uncontaminated air?

Looking back to the imposing Riverside Drive mansions of his youth, Lewis Mumford noted a drawback to their magnificence:

"But these early settlers had not reckoned with the fact that their handsome Riverside Drive quarters were not sealed against atmospheric pollution. They were soon to find that the fresh winds that blew across the Hudson also blew the fumes and smoke from noisome factories on the Jersey shore, to say nothing of the odors from the long trains of cattle cars that used to pass down to the slaughterhouses in the West Thirties, along the open tracks between Riverside Park and the Hudson . . . I can understand the dejection that grew to desperation when a prosperous family discovered that the grand sweep of the river did not offset the putrid odors and hard west winds."

New York Central freight cars, many of them malodorous open cattle cars, continued to move along the tracks west of Riverside Drive until the West Side Highway was built in the mid–1930s. The tracks thereafter ran under Riverside Park and, south of 60th Street, along Eleventh Avenue and through an open cut. Traffic in and out of what became the Penn-Central yards continued until 1984; two tracks remain in place by virtue of a permanent easement.

The West Side is still first in line when the prevailing wind brings industrial fumes and smoke from New Jersey fires. But if sensitive noses discouraged some people from living on the upper West Side earlier in the century, the upper East Side was for many years an even smellier part of town, which goes a long way toward explaining why much of it was so slow to develop.

Few are left who recall the early 1900s, when Fourth Avenue was known as Pig Alley. Trains running down the avenue's big ditch (completed in 1875 for Commodore Vanderbilt's New York Central) carried

The fragrance of horse droppings once permeated the city (1986 photo)

hogs destined for the slaughterhouses of the East 40s, an area known as Turtle Bay. By 1913, when Grand Central Terminal was completed, most of the tracks had been covered over to create Park Avenue. The abattoirs of Turtle Bay continued to waft their fragrances over much of the East Side until they were razed in the late 1940s to make way for United Nations headquarters. Chicago may have been "Hog Butcher for the World," as Carl Sandburg said, but New York butchered its own.

Although only a few parts of New York ever had the aroma of a stockyard town, the city's air was for years polluted by the pervasive smoke from soft coal burning in thousands of stoves and furnaces. And like every other city, this one for years smelled overwhelmingly of horse droppings. New York at the turn of the century had some 150,000 horses. A healthy horse produces from twenty to twenty-five pounds of manure per day, and in dry weather this manure was pounded by traffic into a dust that blew into trouser cuffs and skirt linings, and onto windowsills, permeating furniture and carpets with an aroma that was impossible to eliminate and difficult even to cover up.

The city echoed to the clip-clop of hooves and the rumble of wagon and carriage wheels. Heavy velvet draperies helped to muffle the sound in the cold-weather months; in summer there was no escape save a retreat to the mountains or seashore. Horsecars continued to operate on Fifth Avenue until 1907, although by that time they had been replaced everywhere else by elevated trains and, later, trolley cars. By the 1890s trolley tracks were being laid up and down many avenues and on major cross streets. Still, farmers grew acres and acres of oats to feed New York's horses; stables, blacksmith shops, and carriage works still occupied a good deal of choice real estate (converted stables are still to be seen by the sharp-eyed observer on West Side and East).

To the din of horsecars, wagons, and carriages there was added in some parts of town the screech and rattle of the elevated trains. The first line began in 1867 on the lower West Side, running on a single track between Battery Place and 30th Street over Greenwich Street and Ninth Avenue. Later Els had three tracks, the center one for express trains. These steam trains, noisy as they were, and despite the ashes, sparks, oil, and cinders that they dropped on pedestrians below, provided much quicker transportation than did the horsecars below.

General Sherman often rode the El downtown to the old theater district at 23rd Street. At 109th Street and Columbus Avenue, the El veered east via what was considered an engineering marvel—a sixty-three-foot high trestle, known as suicide curve, that carried it across 110th Street to Eighth Avenue, where it resumed its south-north course to 155th Street. In 1880 the El carried 60.8 million revenue passengers; horsedrawn surface cars carried 148.6 million. On June 1, 1886, Second and Ninth Avenue El fares dropped to five cents at all hours. Before that, fares had been ten cents except during rush hours (5:30 to 8:30 in the morning, 4:30 to 7:30 in the evening) when they were five cents, but a fare-payer was guaranteed a seat. Third and Sixth Avenue Els halved their fares on October 1, 1886.

By 1890 El ridership was up to 190 million. Electrification came in 1902, and in 1904, when the first New York subway opened, the El carried 286.6 million revenue passengers. On September 11, 1905, a rush-hour Sixth Avenue El going more than three times the regulation nine miles per hour on the 53rd Street curve left the track; the second car plunged to the street below, killing thirteen passengers and seriously injuring forty-eight. But not until 1913 did the subway carry more passengers than the El, whose traffic peaked at 374.3 million revenue passengers in 1921. The Sixth Avenue El continued to operate until December 4, 1938; the Ninth Avenue El ended service south of 155th Street on June 11, 1940.

The rattle of the El interrupted conversations (1947 Arnold Eagle photo courtesy Museum of the City of New York)

Because of the El, Columbus Avenue became the upper West Side's main shopping area, and although the El doomed other avenues to cheap tenement construction, relatively well-off people lived on Columbus despite the noise. Lauren Bacall, growing up on Columbus Avenue in the 1930s, had to learn, as did residents of some other avenues, to pause in a conversation when a train went by and to resume—without missing a beat—after it had passed.

Lewis Mumford, recalling his two months as a seventeen-year-old copyboy for the *Evening Telegram* in 1913, noted that he worked the "lobster trick" (the early-morning shift) and had to be at work at four o'clock in the morning. "The job forced me to get up at two-fifty A.M., make my own breakfast, and catch a Sixth Avenue El to Herald Square; and I could tell, by leaning out the kitchen window and noting whether the train then passing had green or yellow lights—even at that hour they ran at *ten minute intervals!*—how much time I had left for finishing my cocoa. The darkness and loneliness gave a dramatic touch to this journey. It made one feel slightly superior to be abroad alone in the city at that hour, before even the milkman had started on his rounds."

Today, partly because public transit does not operate at such frequent intervals after midnight, New Yorkers tend to feel something other than "slightly superior" if obliged to travel in the small hours of the morning.

People have always berated cities as dangerous places to live. Late in the nineteenth century and even well into the present one, streets from 36th to 59th west of Ninth Avenue all the way to the Hudson constituted a dangerous mixture of tenements and factories. Street gangs began to flourish in the area after the Civil War: some seventeen thousand sailors were robbed in 1870 alone. There were 7,500 licensed grog shops plus many more unlicensed ones, and crime was rampant. New York's Finest patrolled city streets with their billy clubs, and the crime rate elsewhere in town was relatively low, but constables in Hell's Kitchen walked in pairs. Applied earlier to the area farther south, in the 20s and 30s, the term first appeared in print in September 1881,* when a *New York Times* reporter went into the West 40s with a police guide to get the details of a story about a man who had killed his daughter and fatally wounded his hired man while "defending himself from a gang of ruffians." The reporter used the term "Hell's Kitchen" in reference to a single building, but he said the entire section was "probably the lowest and filthiest in the city . . ." According to one story, the term was coined by a veteran policeman as he watched a small riot in West 39th Street with a rookie; the younger man turned to the older one and said, "This place is hell itself." "Hell's mild climate," the veteran replied. "This is hell's kitchen."

Until the El came along in the late 1870s, Ninth Avenue still contained vestiges of the aqueduct that in 1842 carried Croton water to the city's receiving reservoir in what later became Central Park; underground pipes replaced the aqueduct, whose old masonry served to harbor thugs and highwaymen before the El was built.

To say that the city has always had high levels of crime does not

---

*The term "Tenderloin" dates to 1876, when Alexander ("Clubber") Williams became precinct captain of the large area from Madison Square north to 48th Street between Fifth and Ninth avenues. Sometimes called Satan's Circus, it was notorious for prostitution, gambling, white slavery, opium dens, illegal saloons, and criminality. And it was a prime source of graft for Tammany Hall Democrats and their boss, Richard Croker. No more rump steak, Williams told a reporter: henceforth he was going to eat only tenderloin.

make anyone more comfortable about the present situation. New York today is by no means the most crime-ridden American city; it is so regarded only by the misinformed. Still, even though the police department does not release figures comparing one precinct to another, the upper West Side (20th, 23rd, and 24th precincts) of Manhattan may have more arrests for larceny, prostitution, narcotics offenses, and violent crime than does the upper East Side. It also has fewer arrests (and complaints) than some other parts of town.

Former Manhattan District Attorney Frank S. Hogan, that legendary predecessor of Robert Morgenthau, Jr., lived for more than twenty years at 404 Riverside Drive (113th Street) from the 1940s to the 1960s. He saw his neighborhood decline as nearby slum tenements were turned into hotels with a transient trade and as weekly arrests increased. Young, unmarried men account for most crime; single room occupancy hotels have always been havens for criminals; when SROs are converted, crime rates decline.

A community affairs officer at the 20th Precinct House, 120 West 82nd Street, recalled in 1982 that the 20th had once been the largest SRO precinct in the city. He told a West Side weekly newspaper reporter about chasing suspected drug peddlers into the old Endicott Hotel, which had been cut up into single rooms with doors leading from one room to the next. A suspect would lose himself in the maze of rooms and evade the pursuing police. As SROs have become tenanted increasingly with older, less transient guests, cases of violent crime have decreased, the community affairs officer said; police complaints today are more likely to involve noise or—with the influx of young people looking for night life—automobile and pocketbook thefts.

Maybe. And maybe, as some West Side brownstone-dwellers believe, it is safer to live in a small walk-up building, where everyone knows his neighbor, than in a big elevator building with a doorman, where almost any well-dressed stranger can gain entrance—although most people feel safer with the doorman. And while East Siders may be accused of trying to escape from the real world, as reflected by life on the West Side, there do seem to be more muggings and other crimes on the West Side. Fewer than in years past, certainly, but more than many people will tolerate.

All cities have crime. What sets this one apart from most other cities is that few New Yorkers own automobiles and almost no one needs to. Public transportation, including taxis, is entirely adequate. The automobile, in fact, has had far less effect on the profile of New York than on other American cities. In most of the country it has become virtually impossible to live without a car; downtown buildings have been razed to create parking lots, garages, and viaducts. Not so New York, where newcomers soon learn that unless one can afford garage space, owning a car is generally more trouble than it is worth.

New York's West Side has the dubious distinction of being the site of America's first automobile traffic fatality. It occurred on September

Crime has become a major concern throughout the city (1986 photo)

13, 1899, when Henry H. Bliss, a real estate broker, alighted from a southbound trolley at 74th Street and Central Park West, turned to help a lady, and was struck by an electric cab carrying a doctor back from a house call in Harlem. Bliss's head and chest were crushed in the accident.

Parked cars became an even bigger problem than reckless drivers; they clogged city streets, making it difficult to keep pavements clean. In 1955 the city instituted alternate-side-of-the-street parking in a belated effort to alleviate the pressures on street cleaning caused by automobiles. (Contributing to cleaner streets today is the so-called Pooper Scooper law, enacted by the City Council in 1975 after a campaign waged largely by Fran Lee (Mrs. Samuel Weiss), a sixty-five year-old former actress and onetime kindergarten teacher. Dog owners are required by the law to clean up the mess left when they walk their dogs. Peer pressure makes most people cooperate.)

Fifth Avenue's open-air double-decker buses, which had run up and down Riverside Drive, were replaced beginning in 1936 with closed-top "Queen Mary" double-deckers; they finally disappeared altogether beginning in 1948, when New York transit fares doubled to ten cents (matching the fare charged for years on Fifth Avenue buses). All the double-deckers went out of service in 1953 as labor costs made it impractical to employ fare-collectors in addition to drivers.

New York thoroughfares had by then become impossibly congested. First and Second Avenues on the East Side were made one-way in June 1951, but two-way traffic continued on every other avenue until 1954, when Seventh Avenue became one-way southbound and Eighth Avenue became one-way northbound. Traffic on those avenues was suddenly 25 to 40 percent faster. The Fifth Avenue Coach Company claimed it had lost customers on its Seventh and Eighth Avenue routes, and the Transport Workers Union opposed further one-directionalization of thoroughfares. Nevertheless, in 1956 Broadway below 47th Street was made one-way southbound, and in 1957 the Avenue of the Americas became one-way northbound. On April 7 of that year the city's last trolley clanged its way into history, crossing over the Queensboro Bridge from Manhattan to Long Island City and joining the horsecars, steam locomotives, and El trains that had been such familiar parts of New York life in the years before the internal-combustion engine gained supremacy.

West Side piers, meanwhile, were losing traffic. New York's harbor was still the world's most famous gateway, and Manhattan in the 1960s still had the greatest single concentration of general cargo piers designed for deep-draft vessels to be found anywhere, but less and less cargo was moving through Manhattan piers. There were thirty-nine Hudson River piers from 13th Street to the New York Central yards in the West 60s, but their volume was diminishing year by year.

September 3, 1957, saw the *Britannic*, the *Queen Mary*, the *Mauretania*, the *Flandre*, the *Olympia*, the *United States*, and the *Independence* berthed simultaneously in Hudson River terminals. New ships (such as the *Queen Elizabeth 2* in 1969) continued to come into service. Schoolchil-

*When most East Side avenues became one-way, on the West Side only Sixth, Columbus,
and Amsterdam went one-way (1986 photo)*

dren on buses moving down West End Avenue and motorists on the West Side Highway strained to see what ships were in port. New Yorkers tingled with excitement to see the great floating hotels loom above their streets and to imagine what glamorous people were about to embark.

Passenger-ship travel had kept streets humming on the far West Side with longshoremen, truckers, and florists' and fruiterers' deliverymen. Now the luxury liner trade was fading into the sunset. Commercial transatlantic jet flights were inaugurated in October 1958. By the end of 1959 airlines were carrying 63 percent of all traffic across the Atlantic—more than 1.5 million air passengers as compared with 881,894 sea passengers. Most travelers to Europe went east—to Idlewild (later John F. Kennedy) Airport—rather than to a West Side pier. On Monday, April 16, 1984, the *New York Times* published its daily Shipping/Mails column as it had done for decades, listing the arrivals and departures of passenger ships to and from New York piers. Few people noticed when the column failed to appear on Tuesday.

Apart from nearly two hundred Caribbean cruise sailings each year, the career of New York's West Side as a passenger-liner port is about over. New York harbor, however, remains vitally important because piers in Brooklyn, Staten Island, and New Jersey handle cargo that cannot be loaded or unloaded from Hudson River piers because of high costs (due in part to congested streets) and dockside crime.

* * *

Some of the crime is the so-called victimless crime of gambling, which has always flourished in New York and has been perhaps especially active on the West Side. In 1905 the police raided 101 West 77th Street, the address of a better-class tenement at whose door unusual numbers of well-dressed young matrons had been seen alighting from carriages. It turned out to be a betting parlor, or "poolroom," in the slang of that time. The ladies were given a lecture and sent home; the poolroom operators were indicted. Today's West Side has many hundreds of numbers-racket betting parlors masquerading as *botanicas*, stationery stores, variety stores, or other seemingly legitimate establishments.

Prostitution is another all-too-familiar "victimless" crime. In the Jazz Age there was Polly Adler, who later told all in *A House Is Not a Home*. She operated her famous establishment on Riverside Drive, which housed a number of such houses of ill repute. Many West 72nd Street apartments in years past were kept by East Side businessmen for the accommodation of their mistresses. While that may not constitute prostitution, open flesh peddling continues to be part of the West Side scene, not only in the theater district and near the Lincoln Tunnel (where some of the "women" are not women) but on upper Broadway, where the police have arrested streetwalkers in the 80s and 90s in response to complaints from Community Board 7.

While the business is less overt than in the 1960s and '70s days of the Minnesota Strip—so called because of the runaway Midwestern teenagers who were introduced to drugs, to which they often became addicted, and who were pressed into working in peep shows and massage parlors, the call-girl business in New York City is estimated to gross $500 million per year. Women Against Pornography estimates that the city has some twenty-five thousand prostitutes, either in the streets or in apartments, and that more than ninety-five hundred of them are on the West Side. In 1983 police raided two "brothels" in the Carnegie Mews at 211 West 56th Street: one, on the fifth floor, catered to the "pay for pain" trade; the other, on the eighth floor, offered straight prostitution without torture.

The "Mayflower Madam" made headlines a year later. Officers from the Manhattan North Public Morals District made two raids on the night of October 11, 1984. They used sledgehammers just before midnight to enter a small first-story apartment at 307 West 74th Street, where they found three women using a shredding machine to destroy records; an hour later they arrested a young woman in a $300-per-night room at the Parker Meridien Hotel in West 56th Street, where she was entertaining a "John" (actually an undercover cop).

Records found at 307 West 74th Street indicated that the young woman's boss was operating a ring of twenty or thirty call girls that she was advertising in the classified telephone directory as an escort service, using the names Cachet, Elan, and Finesse, each with a different address. Records further indicated that clients were charged $200, $300, and $400 per hour, or $1,150 for an overnight stay. The clients were said to include company presidents, lawyers, physicians, and Arab sheiks.

"Sheila Devlin," who surrendered to District Attorney Robert Morgenthau, Jr., five days later, proved to be Sidney Biddle Barrows, a thirty-two-year-old descendant (on the Barrows side, not the Biddle) of two Pilgrims who arrived at Plymouth in 1620. She was listed in the 1984 Social Register and attended the annual party of the Mayflower Society in March 1984, even though her landlord had been trying to evict her from her West 80th Street apartment for alleged "business use" offenses and excessive "traffic."

Eyebrows were raised at the idea of a "quality" $1 million-a-year call-girl network being run out of the West Side, but Barrows was widely admired for her business acumen. "She's phenomenal," said a sergeant in the Manhattan public morals squad. "The most professional madame we've ever run across." Using the yellow pages and the *Village Voice* to recruit young women, she schooled them to dress and act as if they, like she, had gone to finishing school; she discouraged her girls from using alcohol or drugs; and she forbade them to use condoms, instructed them to kiss clients on the lips, and encouraged them to be "romantic" and "loving."

One of the complaints against "Sheila Devlin" at her West 80th Street address was that street people learned about the prostitutes in the building, knew they carried money, and proceeded to mug several tenants. The police heard these complaints. So did the landlord, who managed to obtain some records relating to her highly prosperous operation. After plea bargaining, Barrows got off with a $5,000 fine; she was permitted to keep more than $150,000 in profits; the names of her three thousand clients were not revealed.

*   *   *

Most New Yorkers shrug off such unpleasantness as long as it does not interfere with their sleep. If they live in a building erected since World War II, peace and quiet may be as elusive as in the days of the El and of cartwheels on cobblestone streets, only now the noise often originates inside the building. Today's apartment houses usually have twelve floors in the same height that once accommodated only ten. Ceilings, in short, are lower, and floors thinner. While postwar European builders installed a concrete floor topped by a layer of sand topped by a layer of cork overlaid, finally, with wood, New York builders lay wood atop concrete and in some cases put fine print in leases requiring tenants to install wall-to-wall carpeting. Walls of new buildings are also thinner, and where old, steel-frame buildings had structural mass that broke up sound and isolated it, sound is easily transmitted through the continuous, monolithic structure of new buildings, 90 percent of which are made of reinforced concrete.

Of course, it was much easier to reduce sound transmission in buildings with large apartments that had entrance halls, foyers, and galleries than it is in buildings with one, two, and three rooms in which long, narrow living rooms are placed side by side, and bathrooms and kitchens are inside rooms instead of being placed on outside walls. And it was easier to muffle sound in an era of thick carpets, upholstered chairs, and heavy draperies instead of oiled teak and plastic window blinds. Yet when all is said and done, the relative noisiness of new buildings is primarily a factor of builders' cutting an inch here and an inch there from flooring, insulation, plaster, and everything else in order to squeeze out one more floor, or one more room per floor, of rentable—or salable—space, thus increasing profits at the expense of tenant tranquility.

Most such postwar building has been on the East Side, not the West. The quality of life on the West Side today is generally better than it was in the days before urban renewal and is far better than it was before subways and buses, before one-way traffic. If drugs and crime remain problems, their severity is probably not what it was. Con games, which flourish primarily in neighborhoods where there are elderly, kindhearted people of means, comprise a growing source of complaints on the upper West Side.

What troubles many about the upper West Side now is that it may become so precious, so trendy, and so expensive as to be unlivable. The worriers have good reason when they fret about the little things in life: the shoe-repair shop, the hardware store, the dry cleaner, the five-and-dime, the hamburger joint, the coffee shop. It is all very well to improve the neighborhood, but who wants to live in a gigantic boutique with plenty of fancy shops but no place to buy a safety pin? Even if one can afford it, who wants to pay fifteen dollars for breakfast?

XII. Magnets for Mavens

Whether or not the West Side is more prominent than the East in terms of pleasures of the flesh, the sensual pleasure of eating has for years been savored more on the West Side. In the Belle Epoque before World War I, when New York's best restaurants were Delmonico's and Louis Sherry's, both on Fifth Avenue in the 40s, the West Side had Shanley's (in the Palmer Building on the west side of Broadway between 43rd and 44th streets) and Rector's.

George Rector, whose hotel and restaurant were on the east side of Broadway between 43rd and 44th streets, used to say that Diamond Jim Brady, the railroad equipment salesman, was the best twenty-five customers he had. Brady, who took the El each morning at 8 o'clock from 86th Street and Columbus Avenue to his Wall Street office, had a lavish expense account. His dinner might begin with two or three dozen Lynnhaven oysters, each six inches long, followed by six crabs, followed by soup—generally green turtle soup, generally two bowls of it. Six or seven lobsters, two whole canvasback ducks, and two portions of terrapin would pave the way for a sirloin steak with vegetables. Then came the dessert platter. Brady ate everything on it and topped it off with a two-pound box of candy.

Free lunch was still the rule at saloons. Brady's father ran one such establishment on the lower West Side, which is perhaps where Jim developed his appetite, exercised not only at Rector's but also at Shanley's lobster palace on Longacre Square, George Considine's Metropole restaurant-bar on the southwest corner of 42nd Street and Broadway, Louis Bustanoby's Café des Beaux Arts at Sixth Avenue and 40th Street, and other West Side eateries.

Farther uptown, at 66th Street and Columbus Avenue, was Tom Healy's Golden Glade Café with three large dining rooms plus several smaller ones for private parties. Specialties of the house included game birds such as Egyptian quail, French partridge, English grouse, mallard, redheaded duck, and the canvasback that was then ubiquitous. An orchestra drowned out the roar of the El. Patrons included the painter Winslow Homer, who had opened a studio nearby in 1906. In 1913, at the time of the famous Armory Show, Homer and other leading artists threw a beefsteak dinner for their friends and enemies in the press. They decided that Healey's presented the proper bohemian setting, and it was to Healey's that everyone repaired. Waitresses sang and danced, everyone else did the same, and the bill for some forty-five people came to $234.

Desserts may have included Horton's ice cream, produced on Columbus Avenue at 74th Street and served on transatlantic liners and fine dining cars. There were figures of Liberty and Columbia molded of Horton's ice cream at both President Cleveland's and President Harrison's inaugural balls (1885 and 1889, respectively). The brand is now history, but the name remains on the building at 302 Columbus Avenue.

The best free lunch in town (it included lobster salad) was said to be at the Hotel Lucerne, 79th Street at Amsterdam Avenue, where the actor James O'Neill, father of Eugene, kept an apartment. Today's West Side has nothing to compare, either with the restaurants of "Diamond Jim" Brady's day or with Lutece, the Four Seasons, the Quilted Giraffe, and other top East Side restaurants. What the West Side *does* have is good sources of food such as Barney Greengrass, Murray's, Zabar's, Fairway, Citarella's fish store—and people who appreciate them.

The West Side's favorite fish store, on Broadway at 75th Street, moved into larger quarters in 1986 (1986 photo)

West Siders are *feinschmeckers* from way back. When *Fortune* magazine compared typical East Siders (the Xs) and West Siders (the Ys) in 1939, it found the most "startling difference" to be in "the item of food." "The Ys may spend as much as $2100 a year on food, or $300 more than the Xs, and they get a great deal for their money. Their success is compounded of two chief factors: their freedom from gastronomic snobbery, and Mrs. Y's remarkably interested, expert, selective marketing. By comparison with her, Mrs. X on the other side of town is an amateur. Mrs. X usually chooses the nearest Gristede's or Daniel Reeves chain store and telephones her order to it, probably from her bed, where she is lounging over her breakfast tray. The food in her house is almost triumphantly mediocre and dull, because she neither knows nor cares much about the fine art of good domestic cooking, which can make such delicious use of inexpensive and unusual materials. For every Mrs. X who is clever and original about food, there are many others who serve to guests (extrabudgetary items charged to entertaining) what they hope will be impressive because it is expensive—squab broilers, baby lamb, turkey, filet mignon. Ivy Leaguers regard food as either of two possible extremes: ostentation or mere subsistence. People who regard it with consistent enjoyment are like Mrs. Y on the West Side.

"She goes to market in person to select meat, fresh fruit and vegetables at good quality stores on Columbus and Amsterdam Avenues, seldom in chain stores. She knows that one store has the best butter, another the best veal. She knows that a poultry dealer like Frankenthaler at 386 Amsterdam Avenue has the finest fresh-killed poultry in New York, worth its high price. When she buys beef she avoids ordinary Western packing-house killed (the chain store grade), rather preferring the prime New York City-dressed, heavy, aged beef, which is the most expensive and the best. Or for cheap beef there is kosher meat, also city-dressed."

In 1905 most of Columbus Avenue (the stretch between 68th and 81st streets was an exception) existed primarily to supply residents of Broadway and Central Park West with coal, lumber, ice, flour, bread, beer, vegetables, fruit, and meat. Frankenthaler (same family as the painter, Helen) is long gone, as are most of the area's kosher butchers and delicatessens. One deli survives only in the name Hellman's mayonnaise. Richard Hellman, a German-born entrepreneur, opened a delicatessen in 1905 at 490 Columbus Avenue and kept a large blue-ribboned jar of his wife's mayonnaise on his countertop. By 1912 Hellman's mayonnaise was a favorite throughout the neighborhood. Although supermarkets have replaced grocery stores, West Siders are still food mavens. Merchants know it and are there to meet the demand—some of which originates across Central Park on the East Side.

Oldest of the well-known West Side food establishments is Barney Greengrass the Sturgeon King. Barney himself, who died in 1956, came from Russia and opened a store in 1908 at 1403 Fifth Avenue, near 115th Street, specializing in lox and whitefish. He soon moved to 113th Street and St. Nicholas Avenue, in the heart of Harlem, and remained there until 1929, when he relocated to 541 Amsterdam Avenue, opposite the Belnord, north of 86th Street. The store remains much as it did in 1929—an old-fashioned, full-service grocery store-*cum*-restaurant (sawdust on the floor when it rains) whose focus is on smoked fish. Loyal customers overlook the tacky simulated-wood Formica tables and gold leatherette chairs of the small dining area (jam-packed on Sunday mornings) to indulge in silky sable, moist whitefish, white kippered salmon, borscht

Some kosher butchers remain (1985 photo)

(made in the kitchen downstairs), bagels, and scrambled eggs with nova and onions.

The likes of Al Jolson, the Marx Brothers, Alfred Hitchcock, Franklin D. Roosevelt, Marilyn Monroe, and Irving Berlin (who had two quarts of borscht and a supply of nova delivered each Tuesday and Friday until he was ninety-six) made the name Barney Greengrass famous in earlier decades. Today's customers include actors Dustin Hoffman and Robert Wagner, designer Calvin Klein, violinist Itzhak Perlman, the heads of major record companies, and leading political figures.

Barney's son Moe and Moe's wife, Shirley, who ran the operation after 1956, remain active, but their son Gary, still in his twenties, now calls the shots. An older son, Barney, is in Wall Street. Both sons were graduated from the Ramaz School in East 85th Street and from New York University.

"Nova Scotia salmon is our biggest item," Gary Greengrass says. "Eastern nova is the top of the line. The best salmon come from the Gaspé Peninsula or near the Faröe Islands, between Iceland and Scotland. Salmon caught on a hook generally beats salmon that is netted. Eastern nova is milder than the Western, which is called Nova Scotia but actually comes from the Pacific. All salmon has salt in it. The Eastern is higher in oil and fat content so we're able to put it into a second brine, which takes out a little more of the salty taste. Smoking salmon is a two-step process. The fish is first dry-cured in brown sugar and salt. Then it is placed in a brine before the smoking begins. It is smoked for eighteen hours before it is ready to eat.

"Scotch salmon is a good salmon, probably one of the best, but when somebody comes in and asks for Scotch salmon I know it's their first time. We like a five-to six-pound side of salmon. Scotch salmon range only from maybe one pound to three and a half pounds. It's too lean, not fatty enough. You cut two slices and the whole fish is gone. Also there's a problem getting it fresh. The salmon we get is freshly smoked in the New York smokehouses. Some of them deal with us and not with some of our competitors. It's a personal relationship. You deal with the same people for more than fifty years and they give you the cream. We pay top dollar and we get the best that's available."

A politician coined the slogan "Barney Greengrass the Sturgeon King" in the 1930s. After Barney died in 1956, Groucho Marx said, "[He] may not have ruled any kingdoms or written any great symphonies, but he did a monumental job with sturgeon."

"We have never sold river sturgeon," says Gary Greengrass, "only lake sturgeon. A fish runs anywhere from ten or twelve pounds to forty pounds. And today it's expensive. It used to come from the Great Lakes, but now those lakes are so polluted we get all our sturgeon from Canadian lakes. And they're getting scarce. Lake sturgeon will probably become extinct in our lifetime, I'm afraid. We're known as Barney Greengrass the Sturgeon King. I only hope we don't have to change that."

The Greengrass store, with its Art Deco cheese counter, began as

Three generations of Greengrass sturgeon kings: Barney (in portrait on wall), Moe (at right), and Gary (1985 photo)

a one-stop store in the days before supermarkets. It still stocks certain staples for customers who order by phone and want to order everything at once. "And if we don't have an item we'll send out for it," says Gary Greengrass. "It's a personal service." In smoked fish, which represents more than 50 percent of sales, Greengrass competes on the basis of quality, not price. On items such as Twining's tea he may have the lowest prices in town.

A relatively recent arrival on the West Side food scene is the Fairway Market at 2127 Broadway (west side between 74th and 75th streets). The name goes back half a century, to a Fairway grocery store on the site that was owned and operated by Nathan Glickberg, who later turned it into a supermarket. When D'Agostino Brothers opened a much larger supermarket next door, Glickberg sold the business to two men who promptly ruined it and sold it to someone else. But Glickberg held onto the original lease on the property. In the early 1970s, his grandson Howard was in Wall Street, the stock market was doing poorly, and there seemed to be an opportunity in the fact that people were rediscovering the virtues of fresh produce. A store featuring produce had opened on Central Avenue in Yonkers and was thriving. A former Carvel stand on Long Island had been turned into the Fruit Tree and was enjoying great success. Korean greengrocers, most of them professional men who had emigrated with their families but were unable to practice in America, were prospering, some on the upper West Side. So Howard Glickberg, in partnership with his brothers-in-law Harold Seybert and David Sneddon, launched Fairway into the produce business in 1975. Occupying only 3,700 square feet, it now serves an estimated thirty thousand customers per week—customers such as restaurant critic Gael Greene, artist Milton Glaser, filmmaker Albert Maysles, and actors Ralph Bellamy, Elliott Gould, Mariel Hemingway, Celeste Holm, Anne Jackson (and her husband, Eli Wallach), Angela Lansbury, and Tony Randall.

"We caught it at the right time," says Seybert, whose store now does more business on a Saturday than it did in a week when it first opened. "People were getting tired of supermarket produce. They were going back to fresh. And the neighborhood helped. The West Side is a beacon for the country. What happens happens here first. It's such a bright community, so alive, so alert. We had the right thing at the right time. We gave the people value and we haven't changed one iota from our original concept, except that we've updated the merchandise. We had deli and cheese along with produce from the start, but where we started with thirty different varieties of cheese we now have three hundred, because cheese is a big thing."

Fairway's Steven Jenkins, who manages the cheese department, travels to Europe each year to visit farms and select cheeses. The only American member of the eight hundred-year-old French Guilde des Fromagers (master cheesemongers), he knows dairy farms the way wine experts know grape regions. Fairway also sells cold cuts, belly lox, Gaspé salmon, whitefish, chubs, smoked Scottish mackerel, sturgeon, and other

Fairway, on Broadway north of 74th Street, is the city's biggest purveyor of fresh produce
(1985 photo)

delicacies. It has a good assortment of coffees and nuts at remarkably low prices. It has dairy cases full of imported butters, creamy yogurts, and the like. Its bakery department features Russian black bread, Lithuanian whole wheat bread, French rolls, slim baguettes, and bagels.

Two-thirds of Fairway's business remains in produce, including such ethnic items as okra, collards, and mustard greens, imported green beans, Chinese cabbage (*bok choy*), Japanese white radish (*daikon*), and Japanese mushrooms such as *shiitake* and *enoki*. The store's buyer is at Hunts Point market in the Bronx (the largest produce terminal in the country) every evening at six o'clock, when trucks are being unloaded. He and two or three assistants buy through the night, not getting home until seven in the morning. In addition, Fairway buys direct from three farmers in Long Island and Pennsylvania, guaranteeing them a profit even at times of glut when prices at the Hunts Point market are depressed.

In the spring Fairway gets fresh local strawberries delivered seven days a week (the store is open seven days) when other stores are selling California berries. "These strawberries were picked a few hours ago," Seybert said one afternoon in late June. "You've only got a few more days. You're not going to get them at any other store. Or maybe Balducci's (in Greenwich Village) will have them at five dollars a box." In late summer, Fairway gets local sweet corn delivered seven days a week at prices that beat those charged by the farmers' markets set up in various Manhattan locations.

"This stuff is labor-intensive," says Seybert, who had a wholesale tomato business in New Jersey employing his brother-in-law David Sneddon before joining his brother-in-law Howard Glickberg, "but there is always a decent margin on produce."

Fairway buys apples direct from farmers, obtaining certain grades and varieties that do not ordinarily come into New York. Not just Baldwins and Jonathans and Northern Spies, says Seybert, but "good Red Delicious in the season. I pay as much to get them direct as I would pay thirdhand in the market, because I want them. We still cater to people who cook. They're the people who come here. I can't sell quiche. A good cook makes quiche so fast that if she wants it she makes it herself. I've tried many times to sell different kinds of quiche, without success. As opposed to Zabar's, which sells a lot of quiche because it's a prepared [food] type store."

Zabar's does tend to specialize in ready-to-eat food (the true meaning of the word delicatessen). This includes lobster, shrimp and crab-meat salad (three hundred pounds of each per week), chopped liver (also three hundred pounds per week), and caviar. Although nearly half its business is now in pots and pans, blenders, coffee-makers, grinders, mixers, processors—all of the hardware associated with food preparation—it is the nonpareil among New York delicacy shops. Fortnum and Mason has been in London's Piccadilly since 1707, Paris has had its Fauchon *épicerie* in the Place de la Madeleine since 1886. New York's closest equivalent, Zabar's, is much younger. Louis Zabar and his wife, Lillian, came to New York from Russia in the 1930s and opened a kosher delicatessen in Brooklyn. They moved to the west side of Broadway between 80th and 81st streets before World War II. But when Louis died of cancer in 1951 Zabar's was by no means the gastronomic wonderland it later became. It was merely one of five self-service food stores operated under various names on Broadway at 110th, 96th, 92nd, and 91st streets in addition to the store between 80th and 81st. Louis Zabar's three sons, who inherited valuable parcels of West Side real estate, were hardly prepared to take over the food business. Saul, twenty-two, was about to enter medical school; Stanley was eighteen; Eli, seven. Saul, doing his best to keep the business going while Stanley went to college and law school, sold all the stores except the one between 80th and 81st streets.

Designed by Elliott Schneider in 1966, this shopping bag is known all over town

Smoked fish and pickled herring had been specialties right from the start, and the flagship store began emphasizing gourmet items as early as 1962, but it was Murray Klein who turned Zabar's into **Zabar's**. A refugee from Russia who arrived almost penniless in 1950, Klein met Louis Zabar before he died and worked briefly as a bottle sorter at his 110th Street store. Later he worked as assistant manager of the 96th Street store, became manager, remained for ten years, and then quit to join a partner in the five-and-dime housewares business. After three years he got a call from Stanley Zabar. Could Klein come back and manage the store?

The store was almost bankrupt, Klein recalled later, and the Zabar brothers were ready to sell it for $50,000. Klein, who was made a partner in 1967, turned it around with merchandising savvy. From selling coffee beans and a few cheeses along with smoked and pickled fish, Zabar's added more and more specialties, phasing out the rest of the business by 1968 to concentrate on smoked fish, coffee beans from more than a dozen countries, and cheeses almost beyond counting—delicacies not to be found elsewhere except perhaps at much higher prices. Klein also added kitchen tools. When Bloomingdale's complained that Zabar's was selling Cuisinarts too low, Cuisinart refused to supply Zabar's. That led to a Cuisinart War, which was followed by a Beluga Caviar War with Macy's Cellar, which led to price wars between Macy's and Zabar's over Amaretti macaroons, Dijon mustard, Lindt chocolate bars, and even smoked salmon. Zabar's thrived on the publicity that such controversy generated, and by 1972 the store was doing so well that Stanley Zabar gave up his law practice to handle Zabar's paperwork and finances. He also handles meat, while his son David handles fish (Zabar's sells half a ton of smoked salmon per week in its busy season). Saul is the coffee buyer (Zabar's sells ten thousand pounds of coffee per week, roasted on the premises). Eli, the youngest Zabar brother, split with the others in the 1970s to open a Madison Avenue delicatessen, E.A.T., with his wife, Abbie.

In 1977 Zabar's purchased the entire four-story pseudo-English half-timbered building in which it had leased space for nearly forty years, and began to expand from its original 2,500-square-foot size. By 1980 the store was doing $12 million worth of business per year. By 1981 it was doing $15 million. In 1985, with nine thousand square feet and 160 employees (not counting its agents abroad), Zabar's did an amazing $25 million, nearly $5 million of it in cheese. Boursault, Boursin, Fropain des Mages, gorgonzola, umpteen kinds of goat cheese, locatelli romano, pecorino romano—Zabar's carries nearly four hundred varieties and sells ten tons per week.

When the movie producer Dino de Laurentis opened his DDL Food Show in the Endicott two blocks east of Zabar's in 1980, he announced that he was going to teach Americans how to eat. Says Murray Klein, "You don't teach Americans how to eat. You learn from them. To be in business you learn from the people you do business with. De Laurentis knows movies but he doesn't know food. He made one of the most beautiful stores there is, and it was like a beautiful woman who says, 'Don't touch me, don't come near me.' People came, they looked, but when they compared what they found with Zabar's they saw we gave them the best quality, the biggest variety, the best price. DDL attracted customers from the East Side who wound up coming to Zabar's. We increased our business more than 10 percent after they opened up." When DDL converted from a food store to a restaurant in 1985, Klein purchased their refrigerated display cases and similar items, most of them Italian-made, paying $3,000 for equipment that had cost something like $200,000.

It is hard to conceive of a West Side without Zabar's, and it is hard to believe that a store doing $25 million worth of business per year could disappear. So even though Murray Klein is retiring, and even though its ownership is likely to change, there will almost certainly be a Zabar's in the West Side's future. Along with the take-out fried chicken, sweet potato pie, and other soul food items that meet a demand in the northern reaches of the area, smoked salmon, beluga caviar, pickled herring, gorgonzola, sushi, crabmeat salad, fresh-roasted coffee beans, borscht, sweet-and-sour pork, and egg rolls will continue to find a ready market. And as tastes continue to bridge ethnic lines, good food should help to lower the barriers that have always divided the various population groups that make up the West Side.

XIII. Cerebral New York

"The chief glory of every people arises from its authors," wrote Doctor Johnson in his famous dictionary. While some may question the applicability of his statement to modern America, there can be no disputing the fact that New York has for more than a century and a half been a center of literary pursuits and publishing. And if many of the city's publishers have in recent years moved out of high-rent midtown offices to more reasonably priced quarters near Union and Madison Squares, the upper West Side has become the residential center of New York's intellectuals and literati.

Years ago the hub of the literary life, the capital of Bohemia, was Greenwich Village. Low rents and the companionship of fellow writers provided the initial attraction, but as they became successful most of these literary types moved elsewhere—uptown, to Brooklyn, to Europe. By 1929, when the young critic Lionel Trilling first took an apartment in the Village to signal his "solidarity with the intellectual life," most of the old-timers had left. James Agee arrived in 1932, Mary McCarthy a few years later, Anais Nin in 1940, Tennessee Williams in 1941, James Baldwin in 1942, Richard Wright in 1945, William Styron in 1947, Edward Albee at about the same time, Michael Harrington in 1949. Most stayed for only a few years. E.E. Cummings, Mark Van Doren, William Rose Benet (with his wife, novelist Elinor Wylie), and Joseph Wood Krutch remained until the late 1950s or early '60s.

Chelsea is another New York area with long literary associations. Clement Clark Moore, the biblical and classical scholar now remembered for his 1823 poem, "A Visit from St. Nicholas," inherited much of Chelsea from a seafaring grandfather (the estate stretched from 14th to 27th Street and from Seventh Avenue to the Hudson River). The Chelsea Hotel in West 23rd Street has been home in the more than one hundred years of its existence to the likes of William Dean Howells, O. Henry, Mark Twain, Edgar Lee Masters, Thomas Wolfe, Dylan Thomas, Brendan Behan, Tennessee Williams, Arthur Miller, and Yevgeni Yevtushenko. Stephen Crane lived in Chelsea at the end of the century, Edwin Arlington Robinson a few years later, literary historian Van Wyck Brooks from 1909 to 1911, poet Wallace Stevens from 1909 to 1916, Sherwood Anderson late in 1918. Malcolm Cowley lived in Chelsea in the early 1930s, "Beat" novelist Jack Kerouac crashed in a loft there in 1951, playwright Le Roi Jones arrived late in 1958.

The Tenderloin area from 23rd Street to 32nd between Sixth and

Seventh avenues, slightly to the east of what purists call the true Chelsea, attracted James Weldon Johnson, the Florida lawyer and songwriter ("Lift Every Voice and Sing," written with his brother John Rosamond and published in 1899, was called the black national anthem). Johnson arrived with his brother in 1901, soon gave up songwriting to further his education, and became a poet and essayist. His *Autobiography of an Ex-Colored Man* was published in 1912 (although he did not acknowledge authorship until 1927).

Edgar Allan Poe wrote "The Raven" in West 84th Street (1986 photo)

Many writers continue to make their homes in the Village, and some still live in Chelsea. But, as Susan Edmiston and Linda D. Cirino wrote in their 1976 book *Literary New York*, "If New York has anything approaching a literary center today, it is the upper West Side."

The observation has gained validity since then. Dozens of prominent (if not necessarily glorious) writers have moved to the upper West Side, which has never been Bohemian but which today has, in addition to many writers, the world's heaviest concentration of actors, musicians, playwrights, composers, and sundry intellectuals, not to mention those with pretensions in such directions—people who might once have disdained the bourgeois ambiance of large apartment houses as compared with the walk-up charms of older neighborhoods but who now often have children to raise. They also have the wherewithal to indulge themselves in the creature comforts of elevators and, sometimes, even doormen.

To date the West Side's literary career to the summer of 1844 may be stretching a point. That is when Edgar Allan Poe lived in a Bloomingdale Village farmhouse between Amsterdam Avenue and the Bloomingdale Road (now Broadway); street signs on 84th Street eastward from Riverside Drive today commemorate that brief and distant summer. While it may fit the poetic image of starving genius to say that Poe and his wife lived in a garret under the eaves of the house, it must be added that the poet enjoyed a spacious study on the floor below as he worked to finish "The Raven."

William Dean Howells, who moved to New York in 1888 after a distinguished twenty-two-year career as *Atlantic Monthly* editor and novelist in Boston, lived initially at the Chelsea Hotel but later came to prefer the area of West 57th Street as he reveled in the success of his 1889 novel *A Hazard of New Fortunes*. He was no doubt familiar with Theodore Dreiser, who lived at 6 West 102nd Street in 1899 while writing his first novel, *Sister Carrie*; its heroine, living in the sparsely settled area of 78th Street near Amsterdam Avenue, could see the Hudson River and the tops of trees in Central Park from her third-floor apartment, which consisted of six rooms and a bath and cost $35 a month. Dreiser later lived at the Ansonia, on Broadway and 73rd Street. Called the dean of American letters, Howells conducted The Easy Chair column in *Harper's* magazine from 1900 until his death in 1920 at age eighty-three and lived on the southern edge of the fast-growing upper West Side, taking apartments at the nine-story Dalhousie, at 48 Central Park South (later torn down to make way for the St. Moritz Hotel) and at 40 Central Park South (razed in the late 1930s for a high-rise apartment building). It is doubtful that Howells knew Gertrude Stein, who returned from a trip to Europe with her brother Leo in the winter of 1902 and stayed with three friends in a wooden West 100th Street house overlooking the Hudson. Her first novel, which discussed a lesbian affair, was begun in that apartment but remained unpublished until after her death, when it came out under the title *Things As They Are*.

Ellen Glasgow, the Richmond-born novelist who made her reputation at age forty with her 1913 novel *Virginia*, wrote that work at 1 West 85th Street, where she lived from 1911 to 1916 in an apartment overlooking Central Park. Her poet friend Sara Teasdale, who came to New York and married Ernst Filsinger in 1914, had her book *Rivers to the Sea* published in 1915 while living in West 23rd Street. Two years later she and her husband moved to the old Beresford at 211 Central Park West, a few blocks south from Glasgow.

Louis Untermeyer was another upper West Side literary type, working in the Village on the *Masses* in 1916 while living the bourgeois life at 310 West 100th Street, where he entertained Vachel Lindsay, Robert Frost, Amy Lowell, and (from downtown) Edna St. Vincent Millay, to whom he served "fine sandwiches and very good Viennese pastries"; cheese and beer sufficed when others of the Village crowd came uptown to visit.

Growing up on the West Side in the early years of the century were Dorothy Rothschild (later Dorothy Parker), whose family had a private house at 57 West 68th Street, and Lillian Hellman, who arrived in New York from New Orleans in 1911 at age five and lived on the West Side. Parker (still Dorothy Rothschild then) went to work on the editorial staff of Conde Nast's *Vogue* in 1916, earning $10 a week and paying $8 for her room and two meals a day at a boarding house at 103rd Street and Broadway. Anais Nin, born in Paris early in 1903, came to New York with her mother and brother in 1914 (the father had abandoned his family) and lived until 1919 on the first floor of a rooming house at 158 West 75th Street, beginning a diary that would become a major literary work.

Nathanael West was the son of a contractor who wanted his son to attend the progressive P.S. 81 in 119th Street between Seventh and St. Nicholas avenues. He built an apartment house one block from the school and took an apartment for his family. When West (still Nathan W. Weinstein then) was fourteen, he moved with his family in 1917 to Tenth Avenue and 59th Street, close to DeWitt Clinton High School, where the young man's classmates included Lionel Trilling and Countee Cullen. (West did so badly that he got into Brown only by altering the transcript of his grades.)

Edna Ferber, who had been churning out novels and magazine stories since age twenty-four, lived at the old Majestic from 1920 to 1921. She was thirty-seven when she moved into an apartment in the Prasada at 50 Central Park West in 1923. When she established her reputation the following year with her novel *So Big*, winning a Pulitzer Prize, she was emboldened to take a five-year lease on a larger apartment in the same building with eight windows looking out on the park.

F. Scott Fitzgerald and his wife, Zelda, were kicked out of the Biltmore Hotel in the late 1920s for being too "disruptive" and took a large apartment at 38 Central Park South, close enough to the Plaza Hotel for room service to send over an occasional meal. H. L. Mencken, Dorothy Parker, and Edmund ("Bunny") Wilson were among those who attended the lavish parties thrown by the Fitzgeralds.

When the Century apartment house opened in 1929 at 25 Central Park West, one of the tenants was Marc Connelly, a onetime *New York Morning Telegraph* theatrical reporter who eight years earlier had collaborated with George S. Kaufman to write the hit comedy *Dulcy* and had gone on to coauthor a series of Broadway and Hollywood successes. It was at the Century that Connelly put the finishing touches on his play *The Green Pastures*, which opened at the Mansfield Theater in February 1930 and ran for 640 performances.

The tabloids in 1929 reported the murder-suicide of Harry Crosby, who killed a woman companion and then himself at the Café des Artistes in 67th Street. Crosby was publisher of the Black Sun Press in Paris. His wife, Caresse, was attending the theater in the company of Hart Crane, the poet, when news came of what might be called the West Side's first literary scandal.

Fannie Hurst moved into the Hotel des Artistes in 1932 and occupied a vast triplex there until her death in 1968. And while 1932 was a terrible year for most Americans, it was the year that Herman Wouk's family moved from the Bronx to a fifteen-story apartment house at 845 West End Avenue, on the corner of 101st Street. Young Wouk was seventeen and awed by the luxury of it all. The heroine of his 1955 novel *Marjorie Morningstar* lived in the Eldorado at 300 Central Park West, but it was the building at 101st Street and West End, Wouk later said, that "furnished the milieu, the story and the characters."

J. D. Salinger was living at 390 Riverside Drive in 1934 when, at age fifteen, he began writing. His fictional Glass family lived at the Alamac Hotel on Broadway at 71st Street before moving to an apartment building at 110th Street and Riverside Drive modeled on the one at 111th Street in which Salinger grew up and from which he attended public school.

While census figures suggest that the upper West Side lost about ten thousand residents in the 1930s, upwardly mobile Jewish families of eastern European background continued to move into the area; the Jewish population actually increased by 6.6 percent. In the decade that followed, thousands of refugees from Nazi Germany, many of them Jewish, found homes in the upper West Side. Only 300,000 Jews were able to leave Germany, and less than half of them arrived in the United States, but most of those landed in New York. By 1941, according to one observer, 24 percent of the city's refugees—Jewish and non-Jewish—were living on Central Park West or West End Avenue. Another 28 percent lived in Washington Heights, and smaller percentages were in the west Bronx, Jackson Heights, and Forest Hills. The Eclair, a West 72nd Street coffeehouse, became a social gathering place for West Side refugees, providing employment as well as refreshment for émigrés eager to find compatriots who spoke their own language.

The refugees were not, of course, all intellectuals or creative types, but enough of them were to make a significant contribution to the growth of the West Side as an intellectual center. Only those with some means were able to live on Central Park West or West End Avenue. The others found apartments, often cramped, in side-street buildings. Many attended a mass rally held in 1943 at Madison Square Garden, then on Eighth Avenue between 49th and 50th streets, to honor victims of what would later be called the Holocaust; Kurt Weill, who gave a concert with Lotte Lenya that year at Hunter College, composed the music for the rally.

Sinclair Lewis, the Minnesota-born novelist whose 1935 novel *It Can't Happen Here* had described a future Fascist takeover of the United States, was divorced from Dorothy Thompson in 1942; the following year he took a duplex at the Eldorado. "I have taken a gaudy flat," he wrote to a friend (Edmiston and Cirino quoted the letter), "a cross between Elizabeth Arden's Beauty Salon and the horse-stables at Ringling Circus Winter Headquarters: 29 floors up in the air and commanding a fair view of the Orkney Isles on the West, of Girard Avenue South on the North and West." Lewis was evidently unaware of the difference between a flat and a duplex. His upper floor had a huge living room, dining room, and sitting room with fireplace, his lower floor, a study and several bedrooms, all with terra cotta tile floors, bleached woodwork, pale gray walls, and furniture upholstered in dull green, beige, and yellow.

Riverside Drive, the upper West Side's other great boulevard, was Saul Bellow's choice when he came to New York to be visiting lecturer at New York University. He took an apartment at 333 Riverside Drive in a house later owned by Duke Ellington, one of the fine turn-of-the-century limestone-trimmed brick houses that still line the block between 105th and 106th streets. As Edmiston and Cirino wrote, "It was only in the fifties that the West Side began to be viewed as a place for writers and intellectuals to live."

Bellow's 1956 novella *Seize the Day* was set in the Hotel Gloriana, a fictionalized Ansonia described as being "like a baroque palace from Prague or Munich enlarged a hundred times, with towers, domes, huge swells and bubbles of metal gone green from exposure, iron fretwork and festoons." Of the elderly people who lived from the West 70s to the 90s Bellow said, "Unless the weather is too cold or too wet they fill the benches about the tiny railed parks and along the subway gratings from Verdi Square to Columbia University, they crowd the shops and cafeterias, the dime stores, the tea-rooms, the bakeries, the beauty parlors, the reading rooms and club rooms." Later, in 1970, Bellow's Arthur Sammler would survey the planet that lay beyond his window curtain: "Brownstones, balustrades, bay windows, wrought-iron. Like stamps in an album—the dun rose of buildings canceled by the heavy black of grilles, of corrugated rainspouts . . . Such was Sammler's eastward view, a soft asphalt belly rising, in which lay steaming sewer navels. Spalled sidewalks with clusters of ash cans. Brownstones. The yellow brick of elevator buildings like his own. Little copses of television antennas. Westward the Hudson came between Sammler and the great Spry industries of New Jersey. These flashed their electric message through the intervening night. SPRY."

In the fall of 1960 Norman Mailer, who had been living in Perry Street in the Village with his second wife, Adele, moved with her and their baby daughter into a twelfth floor apartment at 250 West 94th Street; the novelist Harold L. ("Doc") Humes, who had helped to start the *Paris Review* with George Plimpton, Peter Matthiessen, John Train, and friends in 1953, lived on the eleventh floor. Plimpton, Humes, poet Allen Ginsberg, critic C. Wright Mills, critic Norman Podhoretz, actor Tony Franciosa, and writer Barbara Probst Solomon were among those present at a birthday party for a friend given by Mailer at 94th Street on Saturday evening, November 19. Toward dawn on Sunday morning, after most of the guests had left, an intoxicated Mailer stabbed his intoxicated wife in the dining room in front of five or six people, puncturing her cardiac sac. A surgeon saved Adele Mailer's life; her husband was said by an examining physician (quoted by Peter Manso) to be "having an acute paranoid breakdown with delusional thinking" and to be "both homicidal and suicidal."

Mailer was arraigned on a charge of felonious assault and spent seventeen days in the Bellevue psychiatric ward. Within a few years he had married two other women, seriatim, and never again lived on the upper West Side.

Norman Podhoretz, who had left the party before the stabbing incident, became editor-in-chief of the American Jewish Committee's monthly magazine *Commentary* in 1960 and began a long career in that position. He had joined the magazine in 1955 and had written the first serious essay on Mailer in 1958. The two Normans became quite close in the aftermath of the episode as Mailer turned to Podhoretz for guidance. Podhoretz and his wife, Midge Decter, lived at 105th Street and West End Avenue and were part of the West Side literary scene for many years until they moved to the upper East Side in the mid–1980s.

At the time of the nearly four-month-long New York newspaper strike that ended Hearst's *Daily Mirror* in the spring of 1963, Robert Lowell, the eminent poet, was living with his wife, novelist Elizabeth Hardwick, in one of the great duplexes at 15 West 67th Street ("the last gasp of true Nineteenth-Century Capitalistic Gothic," Lowell called it). The Lowells may not have been *Mirror* readers but they missed the *Times* and *Herald-Tribune*, which carried literate book reviews. So did Jason Epstein, a Random House editor, and his wife, Barbara, who lived in an apartment exactly like the Lowells a few buildings down the street. Over dinner in the Epstein apartment early in 1963 the idea for an independent book review was conceived. From that evolved the *New York Review of Books*, an intellectual biweekly whose first issue was laid out on the Lowells' dining room table and whose writers and editors were among the first to oppose the Vietnam War. (Lowell and Hardwick, who had married in 1949, were divorced in 1972; Lowell thereupon married Caroline Blackwood and moved to England. On September 12, 1977, he returned to New York from Ireland, where he had been visiting Caroline and their son, Robert Sheridan. Coming into the city from Kennedy Airport by taxi, he suffered what the newspapers called a heart attack and had the driver stop at 17 West 67th Street. His ex-wife, Elizabeth, was summoned and took Lowell to Roosevelt Hospital, where he was pronounced dead.)

More recent upper West Side authors have included Jeff Greenfield, who grew up at West End Avenue and 106th Street in the 1940s and early '50s and returned in 1968 to Riverside Drive and 72nd Street; Erica Jong, who grew up in the area and has lived at 20 West 77th Street; Letty Pogrebin, of 33 West 67th Street; Irving Howe and Susan Sontag, who have lived on Riverside Drive; Alfred Kazin, who has lived on West End Avenue; Nora Ephron, of the Apthorp; Murray Kempton, who lived on West End before moving in with Barbara Epstein in West 67th Street; playwright Jack Gelber (his landmark work *The Connection* was produced in 1959), who has lived on West End Avenue in the 90s; Joseph Heller, who has kept an apartment in West 80th Street; and Isaac Bashevis Singer, who has lived on the West Side for more than forty years, most of them at the Belnord in West 86th Street.

The West Side YMCA at 5 West 63rd Street has been the scene of the Writer's Voice, a program launched in 1981 by Jason Shinder, a writer and editor who has organized workshops taught by professional authors and has arranged readings by James Baldwin, Saul Bellow, Kenneth Koch, Kurt Vonnegut, and others, some of whom attracted such large audiences that the events had to be held in the nearby Little Theater of the Ethical Culture Society, which holds about a thousand people. Emerging writers read their works at the McGinn/Cazale Theater (Second Stage) at 2162 Broadway (76th Street) in evening programs arranged by a group that calls itself Writer Nights.

For writers affluent enough to afford it, the upper West Side has become New York City's preeminent place of residence. This is not to suggest that anything like London's legendary Bloomsbury group has blossomed there, although some West Side writers do socialize and give each other support and inspiration. Most, especially those with families, prefer the section simply as a matter of practicality, of spacious quarters at relatively sane prices. Others like its proximity to parks, superior food stores, theaters, concert halls, and good schools.

XIV. One Giant Campus

The upper West Side is home to many of the city's institutions of higher learning—Columbia University with Barnard and Teachers College, Union Theological Seminary, Fordham University's College at Lincoln Center, Fordham School of Law, some other Fordham graduate schools, New York Institute of Technology, and John Jay College of Criminal Justice. Columbia, the largest of these institutions, is on Morningside Heights, although some Barnard women have in recent years been quartered in the old Lucerne Hotel at Amsterdam Avenue and 79th Street. Enrollment at Fordham's College at Lincoln Center (CLC) declined in the fall of 1985 to just under 2,400, down from nearly 3,300 in the late 1970s; a new dormitory, to be built by 1987, is expected to reverse this decline. Meanwhile some Fordham undergraduates are quartered in the Empire Hotel opposite Lincoln Center.

Some of the city's best secondary schools are also to be found on the upper West Side. Most of the tonier private schools—Allen Stevenson, Birch Wathen, Brearley, Browning, Buckley, Chapin, Dalton, Nightingale-Bamford, St. Bernard's, Spence—are on the East Side, but the most academically prestigious schools—Collegiate and Trinity—are on the West Side, which also has the Anglo-American, Bank Street, Calhoun, Columbia Grammar and Prep, McBurney, Professional Children's, Rhodes, St. Hilda's and St. Hugh's, and Walden schools.

The oldest school in the city is either Collegiate or Trinity; they have contesting claims. Collegiate dates to 1638 and possibly even to 1628; Trinity dates to 1709. But in the years of the American Revolution, during which New York was occupied by British troops, Collegiate closed down while Trinity, operated by Loyalists, remained open. Trinity has therefore been in continuous operation since 1709, whereas Collegiate's history contains a hiatus of about nine years. Both began as church schools for poor children, Collegiate having been founded at Nieuw Amsterdam by the first minister of the Dutch Reformed Church in America, the Reverend Jonas Michaelius. Michaelius wrote a letter on August 11, 1628, describing his efforts to teach catechism to Indian children in a town that then had only a few hundred settlers; this has been used as evidence to support the contention that Collegiate antedates Boston Latin School, founded in 1635 and generally considered to be the nation's oldest secondary school.

Collegiate, once coeducational but an all-boys' school since the fall of 1893 (it is now the only nonreligious single-sex school on the West Side), moved to its present location, 241 West 77th Street at West End

Trinity School has been in West 91st Street since 1895 (1985 photo)

Avenue, in 1892; Trinity moved to its present location, 139 West 91st Street, in 1895. Trinity was actually the Charity School of Trinity Parish and was commonly called the Free School until 1838, when it began to charge tuition and became the Trinity School. Church funds had supported it in its early years, and it was supported by the city and state for some years until 1838, when it became an all-boys' school. A physician left his estate to the school in the 1790s, and when Trinity finally gained the use of the funds nearly a century later, after fourteen or fifteen changes of venue, it was able to move into the building at 91st Street—its first real schoolhouse since Trinity Churchyard in the eighteenth century. Enrollment increased by 85 to 90 percent. Trinity founded a school for girls, St. Agatha's, in 1898; it lost about $60,000 per year for ten years in the 1930s and was sold in 1941. Girls were admitted to Trinity once again beginning in 1971, when they were taken first into the ninth grade, then the tenth, and so forth. Later, Trinity began admitting girls into its kindergarten, then its first grade, and so on; it became totally coeducational only in 1986.

Modern annexes were added to both Collegiate and Trinity in 1968 and 1969, respectively, and in the late 1970s Collegiate acquired the twelve-story West End Plaza apartment hotel contiguous to its 78th Street building, giving itself a new main entrance on West End Avenue plus a reception area and new dining room-kitchen space. Collegiate and Trinity today have thoroughly modern facilities. Collegiate has about 540 students, Trinity about 850, up from no more than 350 before World War II, when high school tuition was $350 (versus $8,000 in 1986).

Collegiate alumni include William Randolph Hearst, Jr., class of '27; actor Douglas Fairbanks, Jr., '27; Chemical Bank chairman Donald C. Platten, '35; playwright George Axelrod, '40; real estate developer William Zeckendorf, Jr., '48; movie director Peter Bogdanovich, '57; and actor John Rubinstein, '64.

Trinity likes to claim that its alumni include Edward H. Harriman, who actually left school at age fourteen (in 1862) to become a broker's clerk in Wall Street. Humphrey Bogart, son of a physician with a house in 103rd Street between Broadway and West End Avenue, was at Trinity beginning in the third or fourth grade and would have been in the class of 1917 had he not been sent to Andover for his senior year (he quit before Christmas, 1916 and never finished high school. Trinity classmates remember him as a sissy who never participated in anything; his best subject was religion). Although Trinity graduates tend to be lawyers, doctors, businessmen, clergymen, and educators, recent students include Truman Capote, '42; *Psychology Today* editor Jack C. Horn, '43; writer James Fixx, '50; former *Boston Globe* editor Michael C. Janeway, '58; *New York Times* foreign editor Warren Hoge, '59, and *Times* reporter Steven Crist, '74; grain merchant Paul Fribourg, '72 (who is also claimed by Collegiate) and his two brothers; and John McEnroe, '77, who commuted from Douglaston, in Queens (as did his brother Mark), and who set up a scholarship at Trinity. McEnroe each year takes Trinity students to the West Side Tennis Club at Forest Hills and sees that they have lessons.

The Anglo-American School, incorporated in 1980 when English-man Paul Beresford-Hill became headmaster, is at once the newest of West Side schools and one of the oldest. It occupies the 18 West 89th Street building of the former Franklin School, founded in 1872 as the Sachs Collegiate Institute. Julius Sachs of the banking family (Goldman, Sachs had its beginnings in 1869) returned from Heidelberg with the traditional dueling scar on his cheek, determined to create a German-style *Gymnasium*. Graduates of his institution included Herbert H. Lehman, who became governor of New York State and one of its more distinguished U.S. senators; Henry Morgenthau, Jr., who became secretary of the treasury; and Walter Lippmann, who became a prominent journalist and political theorist. When Sachs was succeeded by a new headmaster in 1912 the school renamed itself Franklin (after Benjamin). Franklin graduates include the writer Truman Capote (who went to Trinity to repeat his senior year but got most of his education at Franklin), the Broadway producer Harold Prince, and the artist Roy Lichtenstein (who lived as a boy at 175 West 93rd Street). Today's Anglo-American School has about three hundred students from kindergarten through high school.

The West 90s in the early 1960s had become downright dangerous. The boys of Trinity School, whose dress code required them to wear blazers bearing the Trinity emblem, were often beaten up, both on the East Side and when they came across Central Park and changed buses outside the Endicott Hotel at 81st Street; the emblem was making the boys targets for hoodlums and drug addicts, so the school adjusted its dress code to permit high schoolers to wear plain blue blazers. Trinity elected to stay put after some efforts to find new locations. So did other good schools in the West 90s.

One of those schools is Columbia Grammar School at 5 West 93rd Street. It was founded in 1764 to prepare students for Columbia University, which began as King's College in a room of the Trinity School in 1754. Columbia Grammar moved into its present building in 93rd Street in 1907. It began accepting girls in the early 1930s in its kindergarten and lowest grades, its headmaster joined with a female member of the staff in 1937 to found the Leonard School for Girls in some brownstones in West 94th Street, and the two schools merged in 1956. The upper West Side at the time was in a state of shocking decline. Only the announcement of an urban renewal program for the area persuaded the school's trustees not to move, and there were some anxious years before the renewal program made the West 90s a safe and pleasant neighborhood once again. Columbia Grammar's trustees and headmaster looked far and wide for a new location in the late 1950s; they found nothing that would compare to its 93rd–94th Street site in terms of breadth, access to public transportation, and proximity to Central Park. When the pace of West Side Urban Renewal Area construction began to increase in 1962, and the neighborhood started to improve, pressure to move the school abated and applications increased. Columbia Grammar and Prep now has nearly six hundred students. Its new annex, completed in the late summer of 1985 and containing a new gymnasium in addition to a classroom complex, is across the street from its main building and runs through to 92nd. Columbia Grammar and Prep alumni include Clarence Day, '92, who wrote *Life with Father*; the songwriter Lorenz Hart, '14; the tennis player Frank Shields, '28 (who spent his senior year at a Connecticut boarding school); former RCA head Robert Sarnoff, '35; the Nobel physicist Murray Gell-Mann, '44; and concert pianist Gary Graffman, '46.

The Walden School, a few blocks south of Columbia Grammar at 281 Central Park West (1 West 88th Street), dates to 1914, when Margaret Naumburg and Claire H. Raphael founded the Children's School, a nursery school in East 60th Street. Inspired by Thoreau, they took the name Walden in 1917 and moved their progressive school to a couple of brownstones in West 68th Street near Central Park. There it remained until 1933, when it acquired the old Progressive Club building on Central Park West at 88th Street. Applicants were (and still are) given Rorschach tests. Faculty members in the early years were required to have knowledge of, or training in, psychology, psychotherapy, or counseling. Lewis Mumford (history), William Zorach (art), and Louis Untermeyer (English) taught at Walden, whose graduates include historian Barbara Wertheim (later Barbara Tuchman) (class of '29), music critic Edward Downes (also '29), actor-director Mike Nichols ('48), and actor Matthew Broderick ('80). Most schools put on plays; Walden students perform in plays written by fellow students. The school places considerable emphasis on music, dance, drama, art, and handiwork. It now has ample facilities for such pursuits.

The bodies of Andrew Goodman, a seventeen-year-old Walden graduate, and two other teen-aged civil rights workers were found at Philadelphia, Mississippi, in early August 1964. The Goodman family (whose Growe Construction Company had built many Central Park West apartment houses) raised money for a memorial to young Andrew. The Andrew Goodman Building at 2 West 88th Street, built in 1973, now houses the school, whose enrollment shrank by a third to about three hundred in the early 1980s. In 1983 Walden's trustees sold air rights over the old corner building to a condominium developer for nearly $6 million. The developer, who also acquired surplus space within the old building, agreed to assume the school's capital debt of $2.5 million and to provide the school with at least twenty-two thousand square feet of renovated space in the new building that was to rise above the neoclassical base of the old Progress Club. Walden has said that its very survival depends on its being able to build the condominium tower, but opposition by neighbors and preservationists to a high-rise building has kept the project tied up in litigation; the old building continues, meanwhile, to house Walden's cafeteria and some of its art rooms.

Founded the same year as Walden is the Professional Children's School (PCS), now at 132 West 60th Street. Mrs. Franklin W. Robinson and Deaconess Jane Harris Hall, who started PCS, had gone backstage at the Broadway hit *Daddy Long-Legs* and discovered five young actors playing poker instead of studying. The women recognized the need for stage children to have some formal education, and the original students were all performing onstage as actors, comedians, dancers, jugglers, musicians, and singers. Ruby Keeler was in the class of 1924. PCS today has coeducational classes for two hundred children in grades 4 through 12; its student body, including one hundred and sixty high schoolers, embraces not only stage actors, dancers, singers, and musicians but also film and television performers and young athletes training for the Olympics. About 40 percent study dance, some of them at the School of American Ballet. About 20 percent are working actors or models.

Two years older than Walden and the Professional Children's School is the Rhodes School, founded in 1912 in a private house in West 54th Street. That building was sold in 1979 to the United States Trust Company, and the school moved in January 1980 to 212 West 83rd Street. Rhodes has close to two hundred students in grades 6 through 12.

The Calhoun School has since 1975 been at 433 West End Avenue in a building whose big curved window strangely (and ironically, given the usual attitude of educators to television) resembles a giant televison screen. Calhoun was founded in 1896 as the Jacobi School for Girls. Laura Jacobi, whose students were mostly from families of wealth and social position, found a successor in Mary Edwards Calhoun, a onetime Horace Mann School teacher who had been associate head of another school for girls. Miss Calhoun joined the school as headmistress in 1916, added a course in economics, emphasized the biological and physical sciences, and in 1923 moved the school from 158–160 West 80th Street to 309 West 92nd Street, where it remained until 1975. Jacobi became Calhoun in 1924; coeducational since the early 1970s, it has about 440 students from prekindergarten through twelfth grade.

The McBurney School was founded in September 1916 to educate the sons of YMCA employees throughout the city. The West Side Y was then at 318 West 57th Street, and the school began with thirty-five students and seven teachers; by 1919 there were 105 students taking courses that included occupations, economic geography, physiology, and machine work. Students were encouraged to prepare for college and to attend Saturday morning spelling classes ("The business world holds no place for poor spellers"). When the West Side Y moved to 5 West 63rd Street in late March 1929, McBurney moved with it, occupying sixteen rooms, including two laboratories with new equipment. J. D. Salinger attended McBurney in the West Side Y for a while. Among its alumni the school lists songwriter Johnny Marks of "Rudolph the Red-Nosed Reindeer" fame (class of '27); physician-writer Lewis Thomas, '29; writer Martin Mayer, '43 (who grew up on the West Side but has lived on the East River for nearly forty years); Pulitzer prize-winning journalist Haynes Johnson, '48, of the *Washington Post*; historian Roderick Nash, '56; classical pianist Richard Goode, '59; actors Henry ("The Fonz") Winkler, '63, and Richard Thomas, '69; and financier Felix Rohatyn, '44, of Lazard Freres, chairman of the Municipal Assistance Corporation, who is credited by some with having saved New York from bankruptcy in 1975.

In 1957, after twenty-seven years at 5 West 63rd Street, McBurney moved to an adjoining YMCA building at 15 West, where two other schools had held classes. Enrollment reached a peak of 463 in the 1968–69 school year but, like some other private schools, declined with the changing economics and demographics (and rising tuitions) of the 1970s. It accepted young women for the first time in 1973 and by the fall of 1985 had an enrollment of 226 in grades seven through twelve. The school separated from the YMCA and became an independent institution in July 1983. In November 1985, McBurney announced plans to merge with Carnegie Hill, a private elementary school with an enrollment of eighty-five; to sell Carnegie Hill's building at 12 East 96th Street; to move out of the YMCA building into new quarters at 60th Street and West End Avenue; and to expand into a school that went from nursery through twelfth grade. McBurney is now at 20 West End Avenue in a four-story building (built in 1949 as a warehouse) with forty thousand square feet—more than twice the space occupied at the West Side Y. Although the location, opposite the Penn Central rail yards, seemed a desolate one at the time of the move, school officials believe that this area may be poised for bold new development.

Bank Street School, at 610 West 112th Street, is physically close to St. Hilda's and St. Hugh's, operated by nuns of the Episcopal Church at 619 West 114th, but philosophically far removed. (A Bank Street parent has called St. H. and St. H. "an urban version of a military academy.") Launched in 1919 in Greenwich Village as the Bureau of Educational Experiment, Bank Street grew under the leadership of the late Lucy Sprague Mitchell, wife of a Columbia economist and herself a former University of California dean. Bureau teachers worked with progressive schools in the Village to study children and learn more about how to develop programs based on how they really behave rather than on how educators in times past wanted them to behave. In order to be able to grant master degrees in teaching, the bureau became the Bank Street College in the early 1950s. Its children's classrooms became so crowded that the school moved uptown to 112th Street in 1970 and now has about 450 children from prekindergarten through the eighth grade. St. Hilda's and St. Hugh's has close to five hundred from prekindergarten through twelfth grade. Bank Street has what it calls a good ethnic mix. It starts off with a very small infant program for children under age three. A summer program and a number of after-school programs supplement the regular curriculum.

The West Side has a number of Montessori schools for children aged two and a half and up, although only one, St. Michael's at 225 West 99th Street, goes through the sixth grade. St. Michael's, housed in a church but unaffiliated with any religious group, was founded in 1964. Enrollment varies from year to year; it is usually between 110 and 125. The teachings of the late Maria Montessori are variously interpreted by different Montessori school educators. By Bank Street and Walden standards the Montessori schools tend to be overly "structured," imposing certain ways of doing things on their pupils. Montessori educators, like those at St. Hilda's and St. Hugh's, tend to view Bank Street and Walden practices as too permissive.

The growth of the above-named private schools at a time when the West Side, like the rest of Manhattan, was losing population (and most especially school-age population) is, unhappily, a commentary on the decline of the city's public schools that began in the 1960s if not earlier.

The High School for the Performing Arts and the High School of Music and Art are both in the Fiorello H. La Guardia High School near Lincoln Center. Those aside, the upper West Side has two regular public high schools: Martin Luther King at 122 Amsterdam Avenue (just north of Fiorello H. La Guardia between 64th and 65th streets), with about 2,150 students, and Louis D. Brandeis (formerly the High School of Commerce) at 151 West 84th Street, with about 3,200. Enrollment in the alternative West Side High School at 140 West 102nd Street is roughly 560.

District 3 of the Board of Education, headquartered in the Emily Dickinson School (P.S. 75) at 300 West 96th Street, does not administer the high schools but does have responsibility for two junior highs (grades seven through nine) and two intermediate schools (grades six through eight) as well as eighteen elementary schools (kindergarten through sixth grade). The junior highs are Joan of Arc (118) at 154 West 93rd Street and Booker T. Washington (54) at 103 West 107th Street; the intermediate schools are William J. O'Shea (44) at 100 West 77th Street and Wadleigh (88) at 215 West 112th Street. District 3 covers the area between 59th and 122nd streets. In 1958 the district, then number 8, extended south to 52nd Street and north only to 110th. Its schools had 23,000 students; today there are fewer than 11,000. This decline in numbers came about partly because of the nationwide "baby bust," which slowed the rate at which the population was reproducing; partly because West Side slum clearance projects reduced overall population in the district; and partly because gentrification (read "higher housing costs") has encouraged occupancy by singles and unmarried couples rather than by families with children. Political pressure from the Hispanic community, abandoning an Intellectually Gifted Children (IGC) program, and instituting bilingual education have also helped to balloon enrollments in private schools at the expense of those in neighborhood public schools, which no longer even begin to reflect the ethnic mix of their neighborhoods.

Two-thirds of District 3 elementary schools have scores below 50 percent in citywide reading tests. P.S. 87 (the William T. Sherman School at 160 West 78th Street) was no better than the rest when Naomi Hill became principal in June 1980. Now 73.3 percent of the pupils read at or above grade levels. Apartment hunters with children look for addresses in the P.S. 87 neighborhood. The school has doubled its student body to 794 and quadrupled the number of its kindergarten classes to eight. Credit for this outstanding record goes to an involved and supportive parent group, skillful teachers, and special programs, including one aimed at the brightest students, another in computer literacy, and a third consisting of after-

Martin Luther King, Jr. High School, Amsterdam Avenue near Lincoln Center (1985 photo)

school activities. But most of the credit belongs to the school's principal. Naomi Hill attracted the teachers, instituted the special programs, and has made P.S. 87 a model for elementary schools not only in New York City but also in the state and nation.

P.S. 84 schoolchildren, 32 West 92nd Street (1985 photo)

Aside from P.S. 87, with its remarkably well integrated student body, West Side public schools are now overwhelmingly Hispanic and black (P.S. 9, at 100 West 84th Street, is about 52 percent Hispanic, 40 percent black, 4.61 percent Oriental, and less than 3 percent white; P.S. 191, at 210 West 61st Street, and P.S. 145, at 150 West 105th, have only slightly larger white minorities). Until the late 1960s the public school curriculum included an Intellectually Gifted Children program, which played a role in keeping many white families from moving out of the city. Minority leaders complained that this program amounted to virtual segregation of white children from black and Hispanic children. They prevailed, and the program was discontinued. New York City's Hispanic community, which has resisted assimilation for fear of losing its native language and culture yet cannot afford to educate its children in that culture, has used political muscle to make public schools teach Spanish culture and tradition as well as Spanish language, thus preparing its children for life in the Hispanic community if not in the larger world.

Operating under a consent decree by whose terms it conforms to a 1974 Supreme Court decision, *Lau* v. *Nichols*, New York State schools employ bilingual teaching. The case involved a San Francisco woman, Kam Wai Lau, whose son Kinney was learning nothing in school because he spoke only Chinese. The court ruled unanimously that schools must offer language-minority children special attention, either giving them intensive courses in English so that they can understand what is going on in class or teaching them in their native languages. Relieved of the language handicap, children gain pride and confidence. American schools today are teaching in Albanian, Arabic, Cambodian, Cantonese, Choctaw, Creole (Haitian), Italian, Khmer (Cambodian), Lao, Spanish, Tagalog (Fillipino), Tigrinya (Ethiopian), and Vietnamese. Bilingual education is often simply education in a language other than English and is, depending on one's point of view, a blessing or a curse.

As more and more white families withdrew their children from public schools, private school enrollments swelled. Not so Catholic parochial school enrollments. Several West Side parochial schools have, in fact, closed since 1970. St. Paul the Apostle in 59th Street west of Columbus Avenue closed in 1974; Holy Trinity at 282 West 83rd Street closed at the end of 1979 (its building was leased to the Rhodes School); Power Memorial Academy, a high school owned and operated by the Congregation of Christian Brothers at 161 West 61st Street, closed in June 1984 because it would have cost too much to make the building safe. (Basketball star Lew Alcindor—later Kareem Abdul-Jabbar—played for the Power Memorial team in the 1960s.) Of the two remaining upper West Side parochial high schools, one (Cathedral Prep Seminary at 555 West End Avenue) is strictly for boys planning to enter the priesthood. Tuition is $850. Notre Dame Convent School, 170 West 79th Street, opened in 1894 and is owned and operated by the Sisters of St. Ursula. Alumnae include Corazon Cojuangco, class of 1949, who later became Corazon C. Aquino and was elected president of the Philippines early in 1986. Tuition is $1900 and is subsidized, as are tuitions at Cathedral Prep and at all Catholic parochial schools. The four parochial schools on the upper West Side are strictly neighborhood schools with grades extending from first or kindergarten through junior high. All of these schools have been renovated, or enlarged, or both over the years. Tuitions range from $300 to $850, although families from outside the parish may be asked to pay slightly more; where applications exceed openings, preference is generally given to children of parishioners.

Although a majority of the enrollment at Catholic parochial schools citywide today is Hispanic, instruction at all of these schools is entirely in English. This is true also of the nonparochial Cathedral School, on the close of the Cathedral of St. John the Divine at 110th Street and Amsterdam Avenue, and the Second Presbyterian Church's Alexander Robertson School at 3 West 95th Street. Cathedral has 150 students from prekindergarten to eighth grade; tuitions in the mid-1980s ranged from $4,800 to $6,495 with 51 percent of pupils receiving financial aid. Tuition at Alexander Robertson, which runs from kindergarten through sixth grade, was $3,200; little financial aid was available.

The affluent minority among New York's Jewish community has always funded its own schools for the education of young people in the Hebrew language and in Jewish culture and traditions. Enrollment at Jewish schools on the upper West Side in the mid-1980s totaled about twenty-eight hundred, with another sixteen hundred or so attending after-school or weekend classes at supplementary schools. Three of the four Jewish elementary schools are orthodox, as is the Chofetz Chaim Mesivta high school at 346 West 89th Street (in the old Isaac L. Rice mansion on Riverside Drive, which also houses one of the elementary schools, the Chofetz Chaim Yeshiva). Abraham Joshua Heschel Day School, for Conservative Jews, is at 270 West 89th Street. Rodeph Sholom Day School is at 10 West 84th Street. Manhattan Day School (Yeshiva Ohr Torah) is at 310 West 75th Street, off West End Avenue. Founded in 1943 for the children of German refugees, Manhattan Day has close to four hundred students from nursery school through eighth grade. Tuition at a good Jewish day school in the 1950s was $35 per month, $315 per year; thirty years later it ranged from $2,540 per year (grades one through three at Manhattan Day School) to $6,400 (sixth grade at Rodeph Sholom). These tuitions are substantially lower than those at nonsectarian private schools, and scholarship aid is available to families who need it.

Supplementary Jewish schools on the West Side include Rodeph Sholom at 7 West 83rd Street, which has Reform classes for high school and special education students. The Stephen Wise Free Synagogue at 30 West 68th Street and Habonim at 44 West 66th Street also offer Reform high school classes. The Lincoln Square Synagogue and Gustav Stern Hebrew High School at 200 Amsterdam Avenue have orthodox classes for nursery school and kindergarten children, high school students, and special-education students. Shearith Israel at 8 West 70th Street holds orthodox kindergarten and high school sessions. The Society for the Advancement of Judaism at 15 West 86th Street has Reform and Conservative kindergarten and high school classes. The West Side Jewish Community Nursery School at 131 West 86th Street offers prekindergarten and kindergarten classes for children of Conservative families.

In the polyglot world of New York's upper West Side, there are many fewer children than in generations past. As co-ops, condominiums, and superexpensive rental buildings crowd out older buildings and make the upper West Side affordable only for Yuppies and rich retirees, the number of school-age children will inevitably decline. West Side schools today are at once the community's pride and its shame, a source of hope, despair, and, sometimes, friction.

XV. Where Euterpe Hangs Out

Euterpe, the Greek muse of music, has long made the West Side her New York headquarters. Nearly a century has elapsed since the first Metropolitan Opera House and then Carnegie Hall were built on the West Side. Lincoln Center for the Performing Arts came in the 1960s, and today the whole world looks to Manhattan's West Side for remarkable performances and exciting talent. With the notable exceptions of Hunter College's Assembly Hall and the 92nd Street Y's Kaufman Concert Hall, every important New York auditorium is on the West Side. And now that the Mannes College of Music has moved to West 85th Street and the High School of Music and Art to West 65th, so is every important music school.

West Siders have for years been accustomed to hearing voice students practicing arias and to instrumentalists playing scales. The Hotel Majestic of 1894 was home at various times to Enrico Caruso, Lillian Russell, the American soprano Lillian Nordica, the Italian baritone Antonio Scotti, the Austrian soprano Marcella Sembrich, the operatic manager Maurice Grau, and the German tenor Johann Andreas Dippel, who was joint director of the Met with Giulio Gatti-Casazza from 1908 to 1910. Gustav Mahler and his wife had an eleventh-floor suite with two grand pianos at the old Hotel Majestic in 1909 (he was writing his Tenth—and final—Symphony while serving as conductor of both the Philharmonic and the Metropolitan Opera).

The Ansonia, virtually soundproof because of its heavy fireproof construction, attracted Leopold Auer, Feodor Chaliapin, Mischa Elman, Geraldine Farrar, Gatti-Casazza, Herbert Janssen, Lauritz Melchior, Yehudi Menuhin, Ezio Pinza, Lily Pons, Tito Schipa, Friedrich Schorr, Igor Stravinsky, Arturo Toscanini, and other prominent musical figures. The Hotel des Artistes also had its share of musical tenants, including the sopranos Emma Calve and Margarete Matzenauer, the baritone Lawrence Tibbett, and the songwriter E. Y. ("Yip") Harburg. The musicians made such a racket that they were eventually banned. George Gershwin, a relative of Harburg, applied for an apartment and was turned down.

When 15 West 67th Street opened in the fall of 1902, one of the original tenants was Edwin T. Rice, a lawyer and enthusiastic amateur cellist who invited scores of musicians to his home over the years for chamber music sessions. Rice's daughter Helen, barely one year old when her father took the apartment with its two-story living room, played the violin in one of her father's musical evenings as early as age fourteen. She inherited the apartment and went on to become secretary of the Amateur Chamber Music Players, who numbered writer Catherine Drinker Bowen among the original members, which she cofounded in that apartment in March 1947. Hundreds of musicians participated in her musical evenings at the high-ceilinged apartment in West 67th Street. She died there in April 1980 after seventy-seven years at the same address.

Peter Nitze, a New York lawyer, investor, and son of the diplomat Paul Nitze, has lived for some years in the seventeen-room apartment built for Edward S. Clark in the Dakota. For a musical evening in his drawing room, Nitze has had four pianists perform at once on four concert pianos.

The Sherman Square Studios at 160 West 73rd Street was built in 1929 by Tillion and Tillion with soundproof studios designed specifically for professional musicians. Bela Bartók was living at 309 West 57th Street when he died in September 1945. In the 1960s a fifteen-story apartment house at 685 West End Avenue, corner of 93rd Street, attracted young musicians who found that they could practice without having to fear pounding on the walls and complaints from unappreciative neighbors. Jaime Laredo, a young Bolivian violinist, took a fifth-floor apartment with his wife, Ruth, a pianist, and were often accompanied by Peter Serkin, a young pianist, and other instrumentalists. Philip Lorenz, a German-born pianist, lived on the ground floor with his Chilean wife, Gina Bronstein, also a pianist.

The Chalfonte Hotel at 200 West 70th Street had many musician tenants in the mid–1980s. In various apartments at 175 Riverside Drive lived the pianists Vladimir Ashkenazy and Emanuel Ax, several members of the Juilliard School faculty, the violinist Itzhak Perlman, the cellist Nathaniel Rosen, and the violinist Pinchas Zuckerman with his wife, flutist Eugenia Zuckerman.

On October 22, 1883, the Metropolitan Opera House opened with a performance of Gounod's *Faust* sung in Italian with the Swedish soprano Christine Nilsson as Marguerite. The 3,700-seat Met, between Broadway and Seventh Avenue at 39th Street, succeeded the smaller, twenty-nine-year-old Academy of Music in Irving Place. Carnegie Hall (originally Music Hall) opened on May 5, 1891, nearly a mile north of the Met, at the southeast corner of 57th Street and Seventh Avenue. It was built with private contributions, 90 percent of them from steel magnate Andrew Carnegie (who earned $4.3 million that year). Walter Damrosch, director of the New York Oratorio Society, had persuaded Tchaikovsky to come from Russia to conduct the opening concert, which was heard by a packed house of three thousand plus a few hundred standees.

The New York Philharmonic, which had given its first concert on December 7, 1842, adopted Carnegie's Music Hall as its home in 1893 and remained there for nearly seventy years. But after Carnegie's death in 1919 there was no angel to make up the yearly deficit. In 1925 the hall was acquired by Robert E. Simon, a New York real estate developer whose name survives on P.S. 165 at 234 West 109th Street (Simon lived a few blocks away at 404 Riverside Drive). The terms of the sale prevented Simon from demolishing the hall or using it for anything less than an auditorium before 1930.

Simon inaugurated a series of free daily noontime organ recitals, which continued for some months during the Depression. But studio rentals declined sharply, and Simon was tempted to turn the hall into a movie theater. To cut his losses, he made many of the studios into rental apartments and opened a street-floor art gallery to serve the many artists who lived and worked in the building. Simon died suddenly in September 1935, whereupon his son Robert E., Jr., took over. Benny Goodman and His Orchestra gave the first Carnegie Hall jazz concert on January 16, 1938, with guest performers including Count Basie and members of the Basie and Duke Ellington bands. Pianist Jess Stacy played "Sing, Sing, Sing." In most of the years under Robert, Jr., Carnegie Hall turned a profit, often in the neighborhood of $100,000 per year. (Mrs. Robert E. Simon, Sr., continued to live in a large apartment at 404 Riverside Drive with her housekeeper, whose son also lived in the apartment. Mrs. Simon's daughter grew up in the apartment and was later married, as was the housekeeper's son. Both subsequently were divorced and married each other, which placed Mrs. Simon and her housekeeper in an interesting new relationship.)

Carnegie Hall ticket stubs

The City Center of Music and Drama at 131 West 55th Street, another auditorium for the West Side, came into being as the "people's theater" on December 11, 1943, with cultural entertainment at popular prices.

Artur Rodzinski conducted the opening night gala, and the performers included baritone Lawrence Tibbett. Mayor La Guardia had persuaded the city to take over a masonic temple, built in 1924 by the Ancient Arabic Order of the Nobles of the Mystic Shrine (the Shriners), that was about to be sold for taxes. Its main theater seated 2,745. Despite World War II, the center's administration created the New York City Opera and New York City Symphony, both in 1944. The New York City Theater Company followed in 1947 and the New York City Ballet in 1948.

When the City Ballet and Opera moved in 1966 to the new New York State Theater in Lincoln Center, the City Center Theater survived for a decade with performances by other dance, light opera, and theater companies, including the Moscow Art Theater, the Comédie Française, the D'Oyly Carte Company, and Marcel Marceau. The 55th Street Dance Theater Foundation, created in 1976 to take over the City Center's administration, has given it new life with regular appearances by such companies as the Alvin Ailey American Dance Theater, the Joffrey Ballet, Jennifer Muller and The Works, the Murray Louis, Alwin Nikolais, Merce Cunningham, and Paul Taylor dance companies, the Grands Ballets Canadiens, and the Dance Theater of Harlem.

In the mid-1980s the developer Ian Bruce Eichner acquired City Center's air rights in order to build a seventy-two-story tower and, in order to win approval from the Board of Estimate, agreed to spend $5.5 million on renovating, modernizing, and expanding the Center's stage and backstage areas. He also agreed to contribute $3 million each to the City Opera and the City Ballet, which perform at Lincoln Center.

Just over half a mile from the City Center is the Lincoln Center for the Performing Arts, which has brought the West Side to full flower as the world capital of music. On September 23, 1962, the New York Philharmonic gave its first concert at Philharmonic Hall. The 2,658-seat, $19.7 million concert hall designed by Max Abramovitz was part of the complex of eight buildings then nearing completion between Amsterdam and Columbus avenues from 62nd to 66th streets. Philharmonic Hall was beautiful but it did not sound right, much to the distress of Leonard Bernstein, who lived nearby at the Dakota. Acoustical engineers tinkered with it, and in 1965 the hall's seating capacity was expanded to 2,836. Still, acoustical engineers continued to make adjustments. The auditorium was renamed Avery Fisher Hall on September 20, 1973, in honor of the pioneer in high-fidelity components who had begun a business in 1937 and sold it in 1969 for $31 million, a large portion of which he contributed to making Philharmonic Hall sound the way a great concert hall should. Not until its reopening on October 19, 1976, after repeated guttings and redesigns, did the new hall, now with 2,742 seats, have acoustics to rival those of Carnegie Hall. That house remained a viable auditorium despite efforts to demolish it (only the strenuous efforts of Isaac Stern and other music lovers saved Carnegie Hall from the wrecking ball and clamshell).

The new Metropolitan Opera House, which opened on September 16, 1966, is the largest and most expensive building in Lincoln Center.

The old Met, which it replaced, was razed in 1967 and supplanted by a new office tower for the garment district. Wallace K. Harrison, brother-in-law of Abby Rockefeller, designed Lincoln Center's $46.9 million opera house. The 3,788-seat house (slightly larger than the old Met) opened with the world premiere of *Antony and Cleopatra*, with music by Samuel Barber and with Leontyne Price as Cleopatra. The opera was a disaster, the new Metropolitan Opera House a mixed success.

Metropolitan Opera House at Lincoln Center, 1966 (1986 photo)

The $19.5 million New York State Theater, funded initially by the state and city to serve as part of the 1964 New York World's Fair, opened on April 23, 1964. Philip Johnson was the architect for the new home of the New York City Ballet and New York City Opera. (It is also used by the Joffrey Ballet and other groups.) Like Philharmonic Hall, the State Theater had abominable acoustics, so another $5.3 million—$4.5 million of it private money—was spent for reconstruction; the hall reopened on September 7, 1982, with 2,792 seats.

Lincoln Center's Damrosch Park, with its Guggenheim Band Shell, opened on May 22, 1969 with open-air seating capacity for between 2,500 and 3,500. Old-time residents of the nearby Phipps Houses recalled the days when the famous conductor Walter Damrosch used to come into the area looking for talented children and encouraging youngsters to take music lessons and practice. Alice Tully Hall, in the same building as the Juilliard School, opened on September 11, 1969, to serve as the home of the Chamber Music Society of Lincoln Center. The hall seats 1,096.

Since 1978, West Side auditoriums have included the Merkin Concert Hall, which began as a "four walls" rental facility in the Abraham Goodman House at 129 West 67th Street. It leased about thirty-five evenings in its first season and presented four concerts. The hall was thereafter named after its chief benefactors, Hermann and Ursula Merkin, and presented five series—twenty concerts in total—in its first regular season, 1981–1982, beginning a career as the one major New York chamber hall to feature young American artists and works by emerging American composers. Additional series are now given under outside auspices; these include An die Musik, St. Luke's Chamber Ensemble, Pro Musicis, and For the Love of Music. Merkin Hall now presents some 270 concerts each year to audiences that total more than 55,000.

Both the Juilliard School and the High School of Music and Art were for years on Claremont Avenue at 135th Street. Juilliard had its beginnings in 1905, when Frank Damrosch and James Loeb founded the Institute of Musical Art. The name Juilliard is that of a French-born textile merchant, Augustus D. Juilliard, who started a New York firm in 1874, amassed a fortune, and died in 1919 at age eighty-three, leaving a large sum of money and a will stipulating that income from the Juilliard Musical Foundation be used to further music in America. The Juilliard Graduate School was founded in 1924, the Foundation's trustees took over the Institute of Musical Art in 1926, and in 1946 the two schools were combined under the name Juilliard School of Music.

In 1968 Juilliard moved into a handsome new $29.5 million building, designed largely by Pietro Belluschi, immediately to the north of Lincoln Center between 65th and 66th streets. A bridge over 65th Street connects the structure with a plaza behind Avery Fisher Hall. The school, which includes Alice Tully Hall in its structure, has an orchestra- and chorus-rehearsal room; fifteen major studios for ballet, modern dance, opera, and drama; three organ studios; eighty-four practice rooms; twenty-seven classrooms and ensemble studios; and thirty private instructional studios. Juilliard's theater, which opened on October 26, 1969, seats 1,026; its Paul Recital Hall 278; its drama workshop 266. Juilliard has just over nine hundred college and postgraduate students from forty-eight states and forty countries, plus more than three hundred precollege students, some as young as six. Except for about seventy in dance and a similar number in theater, the college students all major in music or voice/opera. Juilliard graduates include pianist Van Cliburn, conductor James Levine, pianist-composer Henry Mancini, trumpeter Wynton Marsalis, violinist Itzhak Perlman, soprano Leontyne Price, and soprano Shirley Verrett.

Close to Juilliard is another combination of two schools, although the High School of Music and Art and the High School of the Performing Arts have always been administered as one school. After nearly two decades of construction, the Fiorello H. La Guardia High School opened in September 1984 to house the two schools on Amsterdam Avenue and between 64th Street and 65th. La Guardia would have been finished much earlier had it not been for New York's fiscal crisis in the mid–

*The Japanese-born violinist Midori taking instruction from her Juilliard teacher
Dorothy DeLay (1985 photo)*

1970s. Intended to cost $30 million, it has thus far cost closer to $100 million and has been plagued from the start by design and construction flaws.

Of the twenty-six hundred students at La Guardia, about six hundred are in the School of Performing Arts, founded in 1936 and located for years in the theater district at 120 West 46th Street. The other two thousand are in the School of Music and Art, created in 1936 by Mayor La Guardia and located until 1984 at Convent Avenue and 135th Street, close to City College (CCNY).

The Mannes College of Music, after sixty-four years in East 74th Street, moved in February 1984 to 150 West 85th Street, a handsome red-brick building put up in 1926. Mezzo-soprano Frederica von Stade, concert pianists Murray Perahia, Richard Goode, and Eugene Istomin, conductor Julius Rudel, and Opera Orchestra of New York conductor Eve Queler all attended Mannes.

New York street musicians are often Juilliard or Mannes students (1985 photo)

In addition to these schools is the Bloomingdale House of Music in West 108th Street; numerous beyond listing are individual West Side voice coaches, instrumental teachers, ballet schools, music copyists, and all the ancillary services essential to the city's thriving concert music, opera, and dance world. And coexisting with the world of classical music, opera, and ballet is another world of music, largely self-taught, in which blacks of the West Side have been outstanding.

A stone's throw from La Guardia High School is Thelonius

Sphere Monk Circle in the Amsterdam Houses (the Sphere in the Circle confuses the uninitiated; it was, of course, Monk's middle name). Monk grew up in a ground-floor apartment at 243 West 63rd Street, in one of the old Phipps houses, close to where Reisenweber's restaurant, famed for its original Dixieland jazz band, introduced New York's first cover charge about 1916. A neighbor recalls that when Monk was a youngster in the 1920s he picked up piano-playing simply because there was a piano in the house. "We used to holler at him to shut up," she recollects. "We didn't none of us know he was that good. And in those days they were very strict. If you played loud music and all like that after a certain hour they'd get in touch with you and let you know you couldn't do that." Then, in the 1950s and '60s, the pioneer of bop was visited by his patroness, the Rothschild heiress Baroness Panonica de Koenigswarter (whose family had helped to finance New York's first subway) and by Dizzy Gillespie and others in the music world. People in the block began to realize who Thelonius Monk was.

The Duke owned a Riverside Drive house just south of the street that now bears his name (1986 photo)

Duke Ellington Boulevard, as West 106th Street is now labeled, got its name in December 1977. Edward Kennedy Ellington was a Washingtonian who moved to New York in the early 1920s, started his own band in 1923, and went on to write such pieces as "Mood Indigo," "Sophisticated Lady," "Do Nothin' Till You Hear From Me," and "Don't Get Around Much Anymore." At the time of his death in May 1974 he owned

333 Riverside Drive, one of the classic Beaux Arts houses between 105th and 106th streets.

The Duke no doubt conducted his band on occasion in renditions of "Tea for Two," written by Vincent Youmans. Youmans was born on September 27, 1898, at the northwest corner of 61st Street and Central Park West (a plaque on the wall of the Mayflower Hotel attests to this) and grew up to write music for such Broadway hits as *No, No Nanette* (1925). His songs include "I Want to Be Happy," "The Carioca," and "Great Day."

Richard Rodgers, four years younger than Youmans, grew up on the West Side and wrote the annual varsity show in his freshman year at Columbia. Shortly afterward he met Lorenz Hart, a recent Columbia graduate who, like Rodgers, had attended DeWitt Clinton High School, and at seventeen he teamed up with Hart to write "Any Old Place With You" for Lew Fields's 1919 musical *A Lonely Romeo*. But it was the Rodgers and Hart classics "Manhattan" and "Sentimental Me," written for the Theatre Guild's *Garrick Gaieties* of 1925, that made the pair famous. Before Hart died late in 1943, Rodgers had gone on to collaborate with Oscar Hammerstein II on *Oklahoma*.

Rodgers and Youmans were just two of many musicians who have lived and worked on the West Side, a part of town where people do more than just whistle and tap their feet. The violinist Mischa Elman lived at 101 Central Park West in the late 1940s, and in the 1950s Alan Jay Lerner lived at the Beresford, 211 Central Park West, while writing the lyrics for the Broadway musical *My Fair Lady*. Other Beresford tenants have included the violinist Isaac Stern, the operatic diva and impresario Beverly Sills, and Sheldon Harnick, lyricist for *Fiddler on the Roof* and other Broadway musicals of the 1960s. Burton Lane, who has lived at the Majestic, was writing for Broadway in the early 1930s, wrote the music for *Finian's Rainbow* (1947) and *On a Clear Day You Can See Forever* (1965), and is well known for such songs as "The Lady's in Love with You," "Everything I Have Is Yours," and "How About You?" Harold Arlen (*né* Hyman Arluck), who lived at the San Remo until his death there in April 1986, at age eighty-one, was twenty-four when he wrote the music for the *Nine-Fifteen Revue* of 1930 to begin a career in which he would compose the music for *The Wizard of Oz* and Broadway's *Bloomer Girl* and *House of Flowers*, becoming famous as well for such songs as "Let's Fall in Love," "Blues in the Night," "That Old Black Magic," "One for My Baby," and "Ac-cent-tchu-ate the Positive." The world will never stop dancing to songs by West Side New Yorkers.

A less pleasant aspect of the West Side music scene is noise pollution. Moving up any West Side avenue, on foot or in whatever vehicle, one crosses a street and is suddenly aware of transistor radios playing at noise levels calculated to be heard a block away. Article 1403.3–3.01 of the city's noise control code is all too rarely enforced. Hi-fi speakers too often disturb the peace of apartment dwellers. Requests to turn down the volume are never welcome and have led to violence. At the Belleclaire in early February 1983, the building's porter played reggae music long after midnight, flooding the air shaft with his amplified cacophony. Tenants had trouble sleeping, there were complaints, and the porter wound up killing his wife, two other tenants, and the manager. "WEST SIDE RAMPAGE" screamed the *New York Post*.

To conclude this chapter on a happier note, West Side block parties often feature entertainment by top-drawer instrumentalists; the Lincoln Center Library for the Performing Arts is a treasure trove of recordings, manuscripts, and musical lore; and Symphony Space, near the Thalia Theater on the west side of Broadway at 95th Street, gives exposure to musicians of every persuasion.

Whether music hath charms enough to soothe tenants who receive the savage rent and maintenance and common carrying-charge bills in the West Side's newest buildings is quite another matter.

XVI. The Latest Thing

As demand went up in the 1970s and '80s for housing at almost any cost, tax abatements encouraged developers to renovate older New York buildings, and market incentives encouraged builders to erect new luxury apartment buildings, many of them on the upper West Side, each with a story all its own.

The Harkness, a condominium on West 62nd Street with 293 apartments, incorporated the Broadway site of the short-lived Harkness Theater for Dance, named for its patron Rebekah Harkness, who was married to a member of the Harkness Standard Oil family, which had contributed funds to build Columbia-Presbyterian Hospital's Harkness Pavilion.

Le Premier was erected in 1982 by the Trump Organization across from the new Parker-Meridien Hotel in West 56th Street. A mixed condominium with commercial space, including a health club, on its first nine floors, Le Premier has two two-bedroom apartments on each of its higher floors. The Museum Tower, a condominium at 15 West 53rd Street above the Museum of Modern Art, opened in 1984 with manned elevators, teakwood floors, and microwave ovens—all the luxury that money could buy. A one-bedroom apartment with 1,164 square feet was offered for $350,000, a two-bedroom apartment with 1,917 square feet for $770,000. Columbus House, across from the Museum of Natural History south of 79th Street, was built with an exterior of brick in a color and style similar to that used in the museum. A two-bedroom apartment (1,304 square feet) was offered for $303,400, a two-bedroom duplex (1,246 square feet) for $317,810.

Many choice parcels of West Side property are owned by the American Broadcasting Company, which pays the city more in property taxes than anyone else in the area. When Capital Cities Communications bought American Broadcasting in 1985 some people suggested that ABC's West Side landholdings were part of its attraction. Along with all its other buildings in West 66th and 67th streets, ABC occupies the first six floors of 48 West 67th Street, built next to the old St. Nicholas Arena that was acquired by ABC in the early 1960s and supplemented thereafter with modern adjacent facilities.

The Montana, a twin-towered rent-stabilized apartment building with 156 units, is at Broadway and 87th Street. Its form echoes some Central Park West towers of the early 1930s, its name, that of a luxury Park Avenue apartment house built in 1913 (on a site once occupied by the Steinway piano factory) and pulled down to make way for the Seagram Building of 1958. The Montana of 1984, reflecting the life-styles of a new

The Montana on Broadway at 87th Street, 1984 (1985 photo)

era, offered tenants the use of a community room stocked with personal computers. Rents ranged from $1,260 per month for a studio to $3,600 per month for a three-bedroom flat. A 1,300-square-foot third-floor flat with two bedrooms, a dining room, a living room, two baths, and a kitchen with a window overlooking Broadway rented for $2,625 per month—$2 per square foot. The Columbia, in 96th Street, a condominium with 303 units, was a Zeckendorf project completed in 1982. The land had been assembled in the late 1960s for an Alexander's department store, opposition to the store arose, Alexander's canceled its plans, and the Zeckendorf interests finally got hold of the site.

A new generation of luxury West Side apartment buildings, many of them condominiums, opened in 1985.

The Park Belvedere, in West 79th Street across from the Museum of Natural History, has a facade of brick and granite and a lobby of rosewood paneling and marble. By March 1985, only three of the building's 154 units remained unsold. One-bedroom apartments started at $199,000; two-bedrooms at $385,000; three-bedrooms at $550,000; the penthouse sold for $1.4 million. Arthur Zeckendorf, the principal developer, was quoted as saying, "We achieved the highest prices in the history of the West Side."

When the U.S. economy took a nose dive in 1982, Manhattan residential construction dropped to its lowest point since World War II. Only 1,812 units were completed. The number jumped to 2,558 in 1983 and to 3,952 in 1984. Another 4,500 were scheduled for completion in 1985, and the same number for 1986, as developers laid foundations in a rush to beat a November 29, 1985, deadline. After the end of November, benefits under a property-tax abatement program would be greatly reduced everywhere south of 96th Street except on the lower East Side. Three years of construction were compressed into two years, and while the lion's share of building (fifty-four projects, 6,211 units) was done on the upper East Side, sixteen projects (3,515 units) were on the West Side, where rents had increased fivefold in five years and property values were appreciating by 20 percent per year. Outside of a few rental buildings, all of the new construction was of high-priced condominium units.

One of the rental buildings is Tower 67, a forty-eight-story tower* at 145 West 67th Street, on the east side of Amsterdam Avenue. Designed by Philip Birnbaum and Associates, its 450 units are mostly one- and two-bedroom apartments renting for between $1,440 and $3,550 per month. The only studios, thirty-three units on the lower floors, are for elderly low-income tenants chosen by lottery from among existing residents of the Community Board 7 district. The builders, Amir and Eskandar Manocherian, did not have a soft spot for old folks with little means.

---

*Tower 67 and Park South Tower in West 60th Street were approved for construction under the R10 zoning law of 1980. This law was changed in 1984: under R10a, buildings with the density of Tower 67 and Park South Tower are not permitted. New York, however, has weaker zoning laws than do most major cities; developers all too often obtain variances that make a mockery of the laws, which are not strictly enforced.

The Columbia on Broadway at 96th Street, 1982 (1986 photo)

The block on which they built had once been condemned by the city to make way for a public garage; when Manocherian Brothers purchased the land from the city at public auction in 1980 it was a condition of the sale that they provide a certain amount of subsidized housing.

Except for Tower 67, Park South Tower, and a few other buildings, all of the new buildings were built as condominiums. Amir Manocherian, whose rents at Tower 67 average $30 per square foot on an annual basis, told the press, "When I bought the land it wasn't cheap, but if I had to buy it today the only thing I could have built would be condominiums for sale at $400 to $500 a square foot."

Princeton House, under construction on Broadway at 95th Street (1986 photo)

West Side condominiums finished in 1986 included Metropolitan Tower, a sixty-six-story mixed office-and-residential building at 146 West 57th Street. The developer, who claimed a height equivalent to a seventy-eight-story structure, was Harry Macklowe.* He offered tenants valet parking for their cars and a service to shine shoes left outside apartment doors overnight.

*Macklowe had paid $2 million to settle a civil suit brought by the city in connection with the illegal demolition on the night of January 7, 1985, of the Hotel Lenox, an SRO hotel at 143–151 West 44th Street, and three small adjoining buildings. A moratorium on such demolition was to take effect the next day. Criminal indictments were handed down against Macklowe's vice president for construction and against the contractor who did the actual demolition, but criminal intent could not be shown in Macklowe's case. He had bought property zoned for commercial office construction but was prevented from building on it until 1987.

Metropolitan Tower, 57th Street east of Seventh Avenue, 1986 (1986 photo)

The Copley, a twenty-eight-story condominium with 162 units (studios, one-, two-, and three-bedroom apartments, some with formal dining rooms), is on the site of the A&P supermarket that stood until late July 1985 at the northeast corner of Broadway and 68th Street. The Bel Canto, just north of the Regency Theater on Broadway between 67th and 68th streets, is a twenty-seven-story building with a three-story glass-enclosed plaza and three to four condo apartments per floor (studios went for $171,200 and up, one-bedroom units for $191,000 and up, two-bedroom units from $485,600, three-bedroom units from $485,600, duplex penthouses from $775,000). The Bromley, a twenty-three-story structure with 306 condo units, rises above Loew's 84th Street Six movie theater on the east side of Broadway. Studios were offered at $200,000 and up, a duplex penthouse for $1.2 million. New West, a twenty-two-story building with 175 condo units, is on the southwest corner of 90th Street and Broadway, replacing a supermarket. Another building, the Savannah, was replacing the New Yorker Theater and bookstore—meccas for years of the upper West Side intelligentsia (high rents forced the bookstore to close a few years earlier). Princeton House, at the northeast corner of 95th Street and Broaday, is a seventeen-story building with about two hundred condo units.

Projected for completion between 1987 and 1990 are a number of other West Side apartment buildings. Cityspire, a seventy-two-story tower in West 56th Street, is the second-tallest concrete building in North America. Its developer, Bruce Jay Eichner, retained Chicago architect Helmut Jahn of Murphy/Jahn to design the building, which backs up on the brand-new Metropolitan Tower in West 57th Street and has three hundred and fifty-five condominium apartments on its top forty-five floors plus more than 300,000 square feet of office space on lower floors. Eichner's $3 million gift to the New York City Opera and Ballet gained him air rights which permitted him to add twenty-six stories atop the thirty-four permitted under the zoning law. A $5.5 million gift to renovate the neighboring City Center won him another twelve stories. Four members of the Board of Estimate, including the City Council president, the city comptroller, and the vice-chairman of the City Planning Commission, opposed the building on grounds that it was too big. Eichner agreed to give up 12,000 square feet (leaving him with 733,000). His building won approval by a vote of seven to four.

"We tortured our own zoning to make the tower one of the biggest buildings in mid-town, when there is no need for it," said the vice-chairman of the Planning Commission. "This building is totally out of scale, and now the developers have gotten the message that they can break existing zoning to allow larger and larger buildings."

The Jacob Javits Convention Center that opened in April 1986 in the West 30s replaced the Coliseum at Columbus Circle. In a complex on the Coliseum Site, Boston Properties will erect two towers—one thirty-seven stories high, the other seventy-two—designed by architect Moshe Safdie. His plan, approved even before the one for Cityspire, provides for offices (including a new headquarters for Salomon, Inc., which helped back Boston Properties' Mortimer Zuckerman), a curved retail galleria, two hundred and seventy condominium apartments, and two hundred and twenty-five hotel rooms.

Preservationists, alarmed at the spate of high rises that were so radically changing the face of the upper West Side, formed Landmark West! A not-for-profit company, it was incorporated in 1986 after noting that only 293 buildings on the upper West Side were protected by the Landmarks Preservation Commission; the upper East Side had fourteen hundred such buildings. Landmarks West! is not without its opponents. Some say that landmarking is not a legitimate zoning tool. Others maintain that the upper West Side is already such a hodgepodge of large and small buildings that the time for preservation, if it ever existed, has passed.

Still, most people take comfort in the fact that Central Park West, West End Avenue, and Riverside Drive were built up in the 1920s with solid buildings of at least medium density. Never mind that they were built with exploited, non-union labor. If there had still been many blocks of walk-up buildings on those thoroughfares after World War II, the upper West Side would probably have gone the way of First and Second avenues.

* * *

None of the high-rise upper West Side buildings of the 1960s, '70s, or '80s occupies a site anywhere near so mouth-watering as the vast tract that must be every developer's ultimate dream of West Side riches: the 76.4-acre (14.3 acres of which are underwater) Penn Central Railroad yards between 59th and 72nd Streets.

In 1962 the Amalgamated Lithographers Union, Local 1, announced plans for a $240 million Litho City complex of fifteen buildings to be built on this site north and west of the Lincoln Towers complex then being put up by William Zeckendorf, Jr. Litho City's six thousand units would house 24,500 tenants. Opposition came from the Citizens Union, the American Institute of Architects, local residents, and others concerned with the high density of population that such a project would bring. Plans for the ten-block project were dropped early in 1966, the union charging that the railroad had obstructed the plan, the railroad replying that the union had failed to deliver a performance bond. The New York Central merged with the Pennsylvania early in 1968, the resulting Penn-Central went bankrupt in 1970, and no other rail company took over its freight business. Largely because its rail freight transportation system had virtually collapsed and truck transport alone was too expensive, New York lost hundreds of thousands of jobs in the next few years, forcing more and more blacks and Hispanics onto welfare rolls, although the area south of 59th Street was still an important manufacturing center. The upper West Side rail yards fell into disrepair after that; one abandoned pier was partially reclaimed as a summer resort for members of the gay community, but most of the rail yards began to be taken over by rats, derelicts, and prostitutes.

Real estate developers continued to eye the property and envision a shining new waterfront minicity. In 1975 the bankrupt railroad let one developer, Donald Trump, buy an option on the property. Trump and his advisers devised a scheme for a shopping center, marina, park, parking spaces, and housing for twenty thousand families. But the land was zoned for industrial use, not residential. Community Board 7 pressed Trump for concessions, delaying any progress toward obtaining a zoning variance that would permit housing construction.

Penn Central Yards, projected site of Donald Trump's Television City (1980 photo by Andrew Singer, courtesy Mr. Singer)

In March 1980, after Trump's option had expired, the parking garage magnate Abraham Hirschfeld acquired an option, most of which he sold in September 1980 to Francisco Macri, Argentina's largest real estate developer. Macri backed an entity called Lincoln West Associates (owned 65 percent by Macri, 35 percent by Hirschfeld and his family), which announced plans in January 1981 to build over a period of ten years a $1 billion residential, commercial, and recreational development that would include a thirteen-block extension of Riverside Park, a waterfront promenade, and other public space. Lincoln West Associates proposed to provide $2 million for an additional entrance to the 72nd Street-Broadway subway station (later raised to an offer of $29.5 million for rebuilding the station) and claimed that it would build a cultural amphitheater. Lincoln West's eight towers, each thirty-three to thirty-nine stories tall, would contain 4,850 luxury condominium units. The towers would line the west side of a boulevard whose east side would have low-and medium-rise buildings. The architect was Jordan Gruzen, who had earlier designed Litho City and Donald Trump's project.

Critics observed that prices for studio apartments would begin at $150,000, that a moat would separate this "Miami on the Hudson" from neighboring riffraff, that the high-rise buildings would obstruct the light and block the views of existing residential structures, that Lincoln West's environmental impact would be devastating, and that what was really needed for the site was a trailer-on-flatcar (TOFC) rail freight terminal that would create additional jobs in Manhattan's rapidly vanishing factory districts. After Lincoln West Associates' option on the site expired there was further deterioration of rail facilities; beginning in 1984 the Ringling Brothers and Barnum & Bailey circus train stopped in yards in Queens, not in the West Side yards from which its elephants had so often trudged to one Madison Square Garden or the other. Elephants or no, the Penn-Central yards circus went on.

Donald Trump reentered the picture at the end of 1984, paying $95 million to acquire a controlling interest in the site. On March 28, 1985, he showed some members of Community Board 7 a preliminary design for his Lincoln West project to be built on the site. The concept, developed by Helmut Jahn before he undertook the Cityspire, included three clusters of super-high-rise residential towers—sixty-one stories at 61st Street, sixty-five at 65th, and seventy-two at 72nd—with 6,600 apartments, two fifteen-story buildings for back-office commercial space, and a six-story elevated deck to provide three levels for shopping malls and parking space for six thousand cars.

On November 18, 1985, Trump unveiled final plans for Television City, an even more grandiose project for the Penn-Central rail yards than the one he had shown Community Board 7. The National Broadcasting Company's lease in the RCA Building would expire in 1989 and, because the studios had been designed for radio, not TV, the company had held talks with Trump about constructing a vast new studio complex. Jahn's designs for Television City called for a sixty-five-story office tower at 59th Street, six seventy-six-story apartment towers, and a one-hundred-and-fifty-story needle that would rise 1,670 feet above West 66th Street.

This colossal triangular needle, if it were ever built (the elevator ride to the top floor would take twenty minutes, said critics), would be the world's tallest building, a monument—like so many buildings—to one man's colossal ego. Its top hundred floors would contain 2,500 of the 7,900 new luxury condominiums projected for the seven residential buildings—all to be set on a huge landscaped platform that would include more than forty acres of parks, with waterfalls, promenades, enclosed atriums, shops, restaurants, and parking space for 8,500 cars.

Partly because Trump's minicity would bring 20,000 new residents into the area—to say nothing of 40,000 employees—his proposal ran into strong opposition from the start. There are large doubts that such a project could ever survive the scrutiny of the City Planning Commission, the Department of Environmental Protection, and the Board of Estimate, all of which would have a voice under terms of the Uniform Land Use Review Procedure.

Television City and other new housing—actual and projected— have revived concerns about overbuilding in the West 60s. Even Trump's earlier (1985) plan had provided for population density 50 percent greater than that approved by the Board of Estimate in 1982 on a proposal submitted by Lincoln West Associates, which had provided for a $100 million amenities package. Trump argued that the $100 million package of amenities was feasible only if a higher population density was permitted.

As for the argument that permitting construction of buildings over the railroad yards would make it impossible ever to use the site for a trailer-on-flatcar (TOFC) terminal, there is considerable doubt whether there is enough freight volume to justify building such a terminal. Besides, the Port Authority, the city, and the state have agreed to build a TOFC terminal on the Harlem River. Why is it necessary to build one on the upper West Side?

The rail yards controversy illustrates the changing nature of the upper West Side. Architecture critic Paul Goldberger, who had reservations about Television City ("Living 120 or 130 or 140 stories up in the air is fine stuff for fairy tales, but it has little appeal in real life"), had written in the *New York Times* about Trump's Lincoln West project, "The project has stimulated considerable debate on the upper West Side, for it has forced the neighborhood to face what for many of its residents is a troubling fact—that theirs is a well-to-do part of Manhattan whose primary role in the overall city has increasingly come to be the providing of luxury housing. The Upper West Side is less and less a mixed-use area, it is less and less a part of town notable for its mix of incomes, and it is certainly no longer an industrial quarter."

But the rich, the not-so-rich, and the "underclass" still live in proximity on the upper West Side. A fascinating diversity, some call it; others view it with alarm. Can low-income families, most of them minority groups living in subsidized housing, coexist peacefully with (mostly white) young urban professionals, retired erstwhile suburbanites, and other prosperous occupants of expensive West Side apartments? Why not? Harmonious heterogeneity is easily to be found in many other cities here and abroad. People of different races, faiths, ages, tastes, and degrees of wealth can live together amicably and generally do. Despite occasional outbursts of violence, they have been doing it on the upper West Side for more than a century. Political realities make it unlikely that the West Side's poor will be crowded out anytime soon by the rich, or vice versa. Economic realities, at the same time, suggest that more and more of the area's older buildings will be upgraded to luxury levels—"gentrified" in the slang of the day.

XVII. Gentrification

While new construction was beginning to revitalize the West Side at the start of the 1960s, run-down blocks were being reborn through enterprising efforts that rehabilitated older buildings for use as residences, shops, and restaurants.

New York property tax laws favored the entrepreneur who carried out renovations.* Many of the entrepreneurs who renovated West Side brownstones were individuals—architects, lawyers, media people—who saw opportunities to improve their family living conditions by moving to the West Side, often into tree-lined blocks that contained dilapidated rooming houses and shabby transient hotels in addition to brownstones in need of work. There was no lack of individuals willing to buy down-at-the-heel West Side houses. In 1967 an estimated one hundred brownstones in the West 60s, 70s, and 80s changed hands at an average price of about $40,000—half the going price on the East Side. Another $40,000 or $50,000 per house was generally required for repairs.

When his East Side landlord announced that his rent was about to rise from $800 to $1,000 per month, the late Henry Rothblatt, a prominent criminal lawyer, bought a four-story limestone American-basement house at 232 West End Avenue, near 70th Street. He paid $75,000 for it and spent another $60,000 on remodeling. "My landlord did me a favor by forcing me out of the East Side," Rothblatt told a reporter. "I have been getting offers for the building but I have no interest in selling." Most brownstone buyers kept the two lower floors for their own use, turned the two or three upper floors into apartments, and in many cases worked with other buyers to upgrade the neighborhood by pressing for the demolition or renovation of crime-breeding single room occupancy hotels and rooming houses.

An old building that produced comparatively little rental income could, after some renovation, become a gold mine for a landlord. Of course, even a run-down building could be a gold mine for a rent-gouging West Side landlord, many of whom took advantage of Puerto Rican immigrants new to the neighborhood. Such landlords refused to sell their

*The J–51 tax incentive program, enacted by the state legislature in 1955 and renewed thereafter with modifications, provided for tax abatement over a period of time (typically twelve to fifteen years) after which rents could be raised automatically to market levels. The subsequent 421a tax abatement program, enacted in 1971, provided for ten years of tax exemption with rents to be stabilized thereafter. (As buildings began to emerge from tax exemption in 1984, 421a was amended to allow owners of larger buildings to raise rents of vacated apartments to market levels—"vacancy decontrol" in the language of real estate.)

Renovated houses in 88th Street west of Columbus (1986 photo)

This house at 232 West End Avenue, bought for $75,000, was renovated in the 1960s (1986 photo)

old buildings unless they were paid well not only for their real estate but also for the value of their rooming houses as going businesses. Another obstacle to gentrification was governmental foot-dragging; when row houses did become available in the West Side Urban Renewal Area, the Federal Housing Authority made it difficult for middle-income families to buy them. The agency cited the problems of the area as a whole. It undervalued the brownstones. It would insure only a small part of the mortgages. Some people managed, nevertheless, to find their dreamhouses on the West Side.

As for large apartment houses and residential hotels, older buildings were infinitely more desirable to many would-be West Side residents than most newly built housing, and while certain of these older buildings were lofts in inconvenient locations, some were solid structures in almost idyllic spots. Consider the Williams Residence, formerly the Hotel Marcy, at 720 West End Avenue (northeast corner of 95th Street). A fifteen-story structure with a roof garden, the 1920s-vintage hotel was acquired in 1969 by the Salvation Army and converted into the Edgar and Lyndon Perkins Williams Residence with singles, doubles, and a few suites, many with kitchenettes, for just over four hundred men and women aged fifty-five and older. The Residence offers guests their own dining room, lunch counter, barber, hairdresser, music practice rooms, recreation facilities, and weekly movies. Another building, put up in 1895 at 495 West End Avenue (southwest corner of 84th Street) to house German consulate personnel (it has been called the Hohenzollern), had degenerated into single room occupancy. New owners gutted it, renovated it, and reopened it late in 1971 with fifteen apartments per floor—studios and one-bedroom units plus five combination units. Philip Hubert's Sevillia Hotel of 1893 in West 58th Street had fallen by the mid–1970s into a mostly residential and decidedly seedy hotel called the Park Wald. Gutted and renovated, it reopened in late 1977 as a rental apartment house, the Central Park Mews. Another rental house, renovated at about the same time, is the Astor Apartments on Broadway between 75th and 76th streets. The Piano Factory, which opened in 1979 at 46th Street and Tenth Avenue, represents the conversion of an 1870s establishment that made piano actions into a complex of forty-nine apartments—simplexes, duplexes, undivided lofts, garden apartments, and penthouses—grouped round a central courtyard.

The Endicott, built in 1889 at 101 West 81st Street, was in the heart of the upper West Side area that was gaining favor in the 1970s. The six-story building, extending along the west side of Columbus Avenue to 82nd Street, had long since declined from its onetime elegance to become largely a single room occupancy structure harboring criminal elements (in 1972 alone four murders were committed in the Endicott). Rehabilitation began in 1979 and the Endicott was converted into co-operative apartments atop handsome shops, contributing to the new, upscale spirit of the neighborhood.

What remained of Henry J. Hardenbergh's West 73rd Street row-houses of the 1880s were over a period of time divided for the most part into single-occupancy apartments, ten to a building. In the 1980s some of these houses were being restored to their former elegance, not as private houses but at least as buildings with no more than five floor-through apartments each. (Basements of the houses still contained pipes that were once connected to the Dakota's heating plant, which supplied heat not only to the Dakota but also to buildings from the north side of 70th Street to the south side of 74th Street.)

Another gentrified structure is the Schuyler Arms, a 1903-vintage seven-story apartment house with an entrance court at 305 West 98th Street. Reclaimed from decrepitude, it was given amenities that include a glass-walled outside elevator, and turned into a co-operative in 1981. The Central condominium, which opened in 1983 at 250 West 88th Street, is the onetime Central Hotel given an elegant face-lift. Now a seven-story-*cum*-penthouse gem with fifteen-foot ceilings, the Central has a marble-floored lobby; its penthouse units are partially glass-roofed.

Many of the larger conversions have been of buildings little more than fifty years old. The Opera, a co-operative apartment building that opened in 1980 at Broadway and 76th Street, had originally been the Manhattan Towers Hotel of 1930 vintage. The Parc Vendome in West 57th Street, another 1930 building, reopened under the same name in 1981 as a condominium. Prices began at $94,000 for a studio, $165,000 for a one-bedroom apartment. Prospective purchasers were promised the right to reserve private dining and banquet rooms, and the refurbished building had a private library and card room, a billiard room, a backgammon room, and a music room with grand piano. The Pythian Arms, built as a lodge hall in 1927 at 135 West 70th Street, was converted to residential use and opened in 1982 as a condominium with eighty-four units, including duplexes of one and two bedrooms, maisonettes, and penthouses.

The Spencer Arms at 140 West 69th Street, a 1906-vintage twelve-story building with limestone ornamentation and bay windows, was renovated in 1983 and renamed the Lincoln Plaza Hotel. Its old rooftop servants' quarters were turned into duplex apartments.

More affordable was the Vancouver, a thirty-three-unit co-op at 314 West 94th Street. It opened in 1985 with small (750 square feet) one-bedroom apartments at $119,000, two-bedroom apartments (963 square feet) at $225,000. Much of the lobby's original marble work was retained in the rehabilitation of the building, which has oak floors, terra cotta kitchen tiling, exposed brick walls in many apartments, and large Thermopane windows.

Two single-family residences built in 1899 at 327–329 West 108th Street were transformed in 1984 into The Cloisters at Riverside with twenty-four co-ops. Jesuits had purchased the two five-story houses in the 1930s, combined them, and installed stained-glass windows; a society of Assumptionist monks later acquired the property; the modern renovators, who added sixth-story penthouses, left intact the stained-glass windows, the Dutch landscapes painted on paneling by a monk, a handcarved doorway, the ornate moldings of the fireplaces, and the cloistered garden in the

The Schuyler Arms, built in the first decade of the century at 305 West 98th Street, is now an elegant co-op with an exposed elevator (1986 photo)

The Vancouver, at 315 West 94th Street, is a co-op created from a run-down building
(1986 photo)

rear. A 1,088-square-foot one-bedroom apartment was offered in 1985 at $220,000, a 1,191-square-foot two-bedroom at $260,000. Even older is the old Asssociation Residence for Women (later the Association Nursing Home) on the east side of Amsterdam Avenue between 103rd and 104th Streets. Closed in 1974, severely damaged by fire in 1977, and designated a landmark in 1983, its conversion for use as a 450-bed youth hostel has been approved. American Youth Hostels (AYH) has cheap lodgings for members all over the country but none in New York, which has about 20,000 members and, more pertinent, is the gateway to America for most foreign visitors, including many who cannot afford hotels. The original structure cost $100,000 in the early 1880s, and a $100,000 wing was added in 1907; the AYH facility, originally expected to cost about $10 million, will probably have cost more like $14 million by the time it opens in 1988. Plans call for inclusion of a community theater and a commercial restaurant.

On Amsterdam between 103rd Street and 104th, a century-old home for indigent women that is slated to become a youth hostel (1986 photo)

Projects such as these are among the reasons why so much of the upper West Side's Hispanic population is being displaced. The 1980 census showed 41,232 Hispanics living on the West Side between 59th and 110th streets; they represented 20 percent of the population in the area. The 1990 census will show a considerably smaller number and a lower percentage as gentrification prices residents out of the market, as more rent-controlled tenants are bought out by developers, as the *barrio* is pushed farther and farther north.

West 94th Street houses between West End and Riverside Drive, renovated (1986 photo)

Farther south, the 42nd Street Development Project has begun to gentrify the Clinton area, once called Hell's Kitchen. The Marriot Marquis Hotel, for which five theaters were razed, symbolizes a transformation that will include four new Times Square office towers, renovations to nine theaters, and a renovated Times Square subway station. In anticipation of the plan, which would add some 4.1 million square feet of new office space to the area, landlords began trying to buy out long-standing tenants, most of them low-income ethnics. Merchants in the Clinton area looked at what was happening to their counterparts on the upper West Side and joined the opposition to "progress." They wondered if they would share the fate of a Columbus Avenue and 76th Street pizza store owner. The man had sold pizza from his tiny shop for twenty-two years, paying as little as $50 in rent per month. As the income of neighborhood residents moved up, so did the pizza man's rent—to $325 per month, to $2,000 per month. When the landlord told him his next lease would be in the neighborhood of $8,000, the pizza man decided to close up shop. "After all this time, I'm not gonna work for the landlord," he was quoted as saying. Many other merchants felt the same way.

Probably no residential tenant on the West Side, or anywhere else in the city, pays $8,000 per month in rent as such; calculating the monthly income that could be earned on more than a million dollars, however, and adding a substantial monthly maintenance on top of that, more than a few West Siders are in effect paying very close to $8,000 per month just for the roofs over their heads. Some of those roofs cover venerable buildings that have been renovated to make luxurious apartments, their woodburning fireplaces, marble mantels, and high ceilings left intact but equipped now with such modern devices as whirlpool baths, microwave ovens, and trash compactors.

"Cities are best when they are a mix of the old and the new," the director of the Twentieth Century Fund, Murray J. Rossant, has said (he was quoted in the *New York Times* July 14, 1985). Reconversion and rehabilitation efforts will multiply as more and more people perceive the upper West Side as a desirable place to live. They will be called elitist. And they will help to preserve the mix of old and new. But who are the people who have with the wherewithal to live in this gentrified new West Side?

XVIII. Who Can Afford It?

Once upon a time, Manhattan was where an ambitious young man or woman could live cheaply, take a starting job that paid very little, and begin a career.

In 1939, when young people could still live on $20 per week, hundreds of thousands of New Yorkers were living in Manhattan on $5,000 per year or less. That was possible even for a couple with a child. Apartments of one or two rooms at swank London Terrace in West 23rd Street rented for $42.50 to $80 per month. A larger place in an older building could be had for less than $100.

Fortune magazine in 1939 drew a scathing comparison between what it considered two prototypical upper-income ($18,000 per year in those days) New York families, one living on the East Side, the other on the West Side. What made the comparison so remarkable is that the magazine was edited by WASPs (to use the acronym not yet coined at that time), primarily for WASPs, and yet it came down very hard on the standards and pretensions of WASPs.

"There are upwards of 18,000 reported people in New York with incomes of $10,000 to $25,000," said *Fortune*. "Within this income classification live two fairly distinct groups, differentiated by the extent of their compulsion to be stylish as well as metropolitan. Geographically, the division is marked by Fifth Avenue and Central Park. Many West Siders are not much interested in style necessarily as society interprets it; and many of them are interested in culture. The East Siders are less concerned with culture but have, on the other hand, a social pattern to which they feel they must adhere, even when they have no social pretensions . . ."

Fortune then presented the "sad case of Mr. and Mrs. X," their prototypical East Siders whose food values we noted in Chapter 12:

"They have an income of $18,000—Mr. X's salary plus unearned income on about $100,000 of joint inherited capital. The trouble with the X family . . . is that their unearned income fluctuates. Their capital, which is invested in conservative holdings, used to yield about $5,000 but now yields only $3,000 for familiar reasons. The Xs are in their thirties and have two children. The focus of their compulsion is to be stylish. The district of Manhattan in which they live extends from Fifth Avenue eastward to the East River and from 54th Street northward to 96th, an area of some 1,000 acres. Within this district live families ranging all the way from the tenement class to the richest people in New York and rents vary accordingly from under $50 to over $650 per room per year. At apartments whose rents fit the Xs' budget the rates run from $350 to $400 per room per year. The Xs feel that the normal comforts of life entitle them to at least three bedrooms, one for Mr. and Mrs. X, one for the older child, and one for the baby and the nurse. Also they need a living room, a dining room, a kitchen and a maid's room, which brings the total up to what the real-estate people call a seven-room and three-bath apartment (a layout that commands the upper range of possible prices).

"A poorer family without the Xs' compulsion to conform (perhaps near by in this very neighborhood) would know how to make out with fewer rooms, eating in a dinette or at one end of the living room, putting two kids in one bedroom, but the Xs feel that their income and 'position' entitle them to rudimentary conveniences of space and they find that the least they can obtain these for is $2500 a year. An apartment higher up in the building, however, with better light and air, costs $3000 and this is what they take. It is probable that this apartment will have eight rooms instead of seven, since in most buildings of this character the suites were designed on the theory that the tenants would use two servants and were therefore equipped with two maids' rooms. . . . The Xs can afford only one maid and the second servant's room is therefore superfluous . . . Maids' rooms in New York apartments are wretched little boxes about six feet by twelve with baths too short to recline in . . . "

Fortune's Mrs. X, it turned out, did not have a job and therefore had no compelling need for either a nurse or a maid. And Mr. X simply could not afford to be seen in a $65 ready-made suit from Brooks Brothers, Tripler, or Saks Fifth Avenue; he paid $80 to $90 for a tailor-made suit. Virtually everything the Xs did was motivated, according to *Fortune*, by their need to keep up appearances. As a result, they failed each year to live within their income.

Contrasting the life-styles of the East Side Xs and the West Side Ys, *Fortune* arrived at the table shown on the following page.

Like the property prices and rents in a Monopoly game, the numbers look hopelessly out-of-date (although a typical co-operative apartment buyer as recently as early 1969 had an average income of $19,500, according to a survey by the real estate firm of Sulzberger-Rolfe). Income taxes now bite far more deeply into earnings; prices generally are much higher (a hard-cover novel in 1939 sold for $2.50 and the new Pocket Book paperbacks introduced that year sold for twenty-five cents); medical insurance, if not paid for by one's employer, costs far more than anyone budgeted for doctors in 1939 (and only an idiot or an indigent would dare not carry health insurance today); dentists charge the moon; private school tuitions are much higher, and public schools have long since ceased to be a viable option in most Manhattan neighborhoods; carfare, once an insignificant factor, is twenty times its 1939 level.

What does it cost to live today as the Xs and Ys lived in 1939? A minimum of $90,000—five times the 1939 level—would be a fair guess, although many would place the figure far higher (and a few would insist that they can get by on $75,000). The president of the Real Estate Board

$18,000 per year, couple, two children

	EAST SIDE Xs	WEST SIDE Ys
RENT:	$3,000	$2,000
FOOD:	1,800	2,100
NURSE:	900	0
MAID:	900	720
UTILITIES, TELEPHONE:	350	265
LAUNDRY, DRY CLEANING:	500	500
LIQUOR:	350	300
FLOWERS:	100	100
CLOTHES AND SUNDRY:	2,000	1,500
CASH BY MAN AT BUSINESS:	1,200	1,000
WIFE'S POCKET MONEY:	300	300
GIFTS, TIPS:	200	250
SCHOOLS, NURSERY, PRIVATE:	400	250
EXTRA EDUCATION:	100	200
LIFE INSURANCE, SAVINGS:	1,800	1,800
INCOME TAXES:	1,800	1,800
MEDICAL, DENTAL:	300	200
CHARITY:	100	400
SUMMER VACATION:	1,500	1,000
ENTERTAINMENT:	400	600
BOOKS, READING MATTER:	75	75
MOVING:	200	0
HOBBY:	0	250
DECORATING:	500	0
WINTER TRIP:	500	0
AUTOMOBILE:	300	0
TOTAL:	19,575	15,610

deficit: 1,575

surplus: 2,390
(permitting for nurse,
winter trip,
moving and decorating,
major illness,
automobile,
or extra savings)

of New York, Richard M. Rosan, was quoted early in 1985 as saying, "Middle income in New York means $80,000 a year—it's hard to believe but it's true."

A 1984 Chemical Bank study concluded that only 12 percent of all households could afford a new average-priced ($200,000 at the time) one-bedroom condominium or co-operative apartment, and could afford it only if they were willing to spend 45 percent of an annual income of

$50,000 per year on housing expenses. Of New York's 2.8 million housing units, only 800,000 are owner-occupied condominiums or co-ops. Median rental in the 1.2 million rent-regulated apartments was $330 per month in early 1985 (Mitchell-Lama apartments, for which there are five-year waiting lists, averaged $58 to $85 per room in rent or maintenance); there is no good figure on the median rental of the 800,000 unregulated rental apartments, but most renters, whatever their rent, pay more than the traditionally prudent 25 percent of their incomes on housing. In 1983, more than 59 percent of New York tenants paid in excess of 25 percent of their gross income on rent (utilities not included), and about one-third paid more than 40 percent.

Onetime slum areas in the West 90s are now chic (1985 photo)

Runzheimer International, a Rochester, Wisconsin, management consultant firm, surveyed housing costs in 1984 and found that a family of four with an annual income of $30,000 could not hope to find a house in New York or Westchester. As for a rental apartment in a good building in a good section of town such as the upper West Side of Manhattan, a two-bedroom, 1½-bath apartment of fourteen hundred square feet rented for $2,555 in Manhattan as compared with $1,005 in San Francisco, $1,000 in Boston, $995 in Chicago, $590 in Atlanta, and $450 in Houston. (Other living costs did not vary much from one city to another, according to the study.) To afford a market-rate apartment in Manhattan consuming 40 percent of its annual income, a family would need an income of $72,845, the study concluded.

Said *Fortune* magazine in 1939: "You cannot buy New York. To live successfully and excitingly in New York City it is necessary to use your wits to some extent. You may not have to use them as hard as the $20-a-week people do, but if you don't use them at all the city rushes past you, absorbing all your hard-earned thousands of dollars and yielding up little in return. . . . But it can be done if there is no social pattern to conform to, as best illustrated on the West Side of Manhattan which the Ivy Leaguers shun."

People moving into high-priced West Side apartments in the 1980s were themselves, of course, conforming to a social pattern—that of their peers, of a more enlightened generation that was rejecting some of the prejudices of earlier times. No longer was it necessary for a proper New Yorker to have an East Side address. The West Side had once again become socially acceptable.

It was also socially acceptable for a married woman to have a job, even one that paid better than her husband's—although old prejudices were often still strong enough that such a situation could cause marital strains, enlightened generation or not. For most families, indeed, it was a virtual necessity to have two incomes in order to pay the cost of life in Manhattan in the 1980s. Yet even with two incomes, few families today can afford sleep-in help, automobiles, or lengthy vacations. While West Siders may still allocate their funds in subtly different ways from East Siders, most people have to make compromises to live anywhere in Manhattan.

On the other hand, hardly anybody in 1939 lived as well as the Xs and Ys did. And most West Siders today get along one way or another on less than half the $80,000 annual income suggested by the Real Estate Board of New York man as the criterion for "middle income." How long the West Side will remain affordable for moderate-income people is, however, something no one can predict.

Rental apartments in new buildings in the mid–1980s were going for as much as $3 per square foot and even more ($1,400 per month for a small 450-square-foot studio). Condominiums sold for $211 per square foot and up ($95,000 for a 450-square-foot studio). But relatively few of the new buildings were being put up as rental housing. Most of the new luxury houses were condominiums, a new concept for New Yorkers (the law allowing condominium ownership in the city dates only from 1964; no Manhattan condominiums were built until the 1970s) and one relatively new to the United States, although it goes back at least to sixth century B.C. Rome. Condominium ownership gained popularity in western Europe through the housing shortages following World Wars I and II. A condominium is an apartment building whose occupants own their own apartments as evidenced by recordable deeds on their dwelling units. Owners may sell, rent, mortgage, or exchange without consulting anyone else in the building.

Co-operative apartments, pioneered in New York by Philip Hubert in the 1880s, remained relatively uncommon until 1926, when the idea

Young professionals find the West Side a good neighborhood in which to raise children
(1985 photo)

was given a boost by the New York State Housing Act of that year. The boom in co-op apartment construction came in the 1950s, and many rental apartment buildings were also converted to co-operative ownership at that time. More went co-op after the Lindsay administration limited rent increases in 1969.

As rents increase, tenants sometimes strike

A co-op owner does not actually own his apartment. He owns stock in a nonprofit corporation that owns and runs the building. The percentage of stock he owns depends on the size and location of his apartment (stock representing those on higher floors are worth more), but he is a part owner of his building, whereas the condominium occupant owns only his own apartment. The co-op participant agrees to pay a monthly maintenance fee representing his proportionate share of the upkeep on the property, including taxes and payments on the mortgage (which are deductible at least in part from his taxable income even after the 1986 tax reform). Some co-ops are financed privately, some publicly; some are financed at more favorable rates than others. Many variables determine how good a deal any particular co-op is, but all co-op buildings have one thing in common: apartments, and the shares that represent them, may be sold only with the approval of the other co-op owners.

Co-op ownership has a cachet in New York that condominium ownership has never had. Anyone can buy a condominium and can finance it the same way as a house. A prospective co-op shareholder, by contrast, must be approved by existing shareholders in the building and may not even be permitted to finance his purchase. These shareholders have a financial interest to protect: if half (or more) of the members of the co-op were to default, the other half (or less) would have the responsibility of maintaining the building—paying its taxes, meeting its mortgage payments, keeping up the staff. Theoretically, the entire burden of maintenance could devolve upon a handful of co-op owners. Anyone who buys a co-op these days is generally required to pay at least half in cash and to meet stringent requirements with regard to his or her financial condition. Co-op owners may and do reject prospective buyers for reasons other than financial; discrimination for reasons of race, religion, or life-style is often concealed behind stated objections based on the applicant's financial position.

Rental buildings are more and more being converted to co-op or condo ownership

A lady from Dubuque, accustomed to having a deed to prove ownership of her house, may be more comfortable with the concept of a condominium, but New Yorkers, for whom buying and selling stock is a familiar experience, have generally accepted the risks of co-op ownership and have tended to look askance at condominiums, which have connotations of Florida retirement communities. Laws in many other states have discouraged co-op ownership. In New York, Stephen Birmingham wrote in *Life at the Dakota*, "To own a 'co-op' is sophisticated and chic; to own a 'condo' is not."

This attitude may have changed. Certainly it did not persuade many developers to build co-ops rather than condos in the 1980s. Most of the new apartment houses are condominiums, with units offered at prices that in most other parts of America will buy substantial houses with spacious lawns, gardens, garages—even boat moorings, tennis courts, and swimming pools.

XIX. How High the Moon?

New Yorkers never used to talk much about real estate prices. Suburbanites did. Visitors from California did. They went on and on about the rising cost of land, about buying and selling their houses, about property and building costs. New Yorkers lived in apartments, not houses, and most were rental tenants, not owners. So while the talk at dinner parties may generally have been no less mundane than the conversation level at Dubuque dinner parties—who was seen with whose husband or wife, whose son or daughter was kicked out of school, who was about to lose his or her job—it did not deal with how much who just got for his apartment or had to pay for a new one.

Then, in the late 1950s, New York cocktail party chatter began to get as single-minded as the talk everywhere else. Conversations about the new show at the Met, the possible merger downtown, the terrific restaurant that opened last week, the scandal at the private school were drowned out by announcements that this or that building was "going co-op," or that so-and-so had just sold his or her apartment for $100,000, $300,000, $800,000, $1,200,000 (all these being the prices paid for one particular apartment). Monetary values of New York real estate have increased steadily over the years, with only a few reversals. Rising values have made fortunes for developers, for landlords, and—more recently—for owners of co-operative apartments. The upward spiral has been going on for well over a century.

Miller's New York As It Is, or Stranger's Guide-Book, published in 1866, spoke in what now seems archaic language but with the same air of wonder heard today:

"If we glance prospectively, how shall we venture to limit its progressive march in opulence and greatness? In less than half a century hence, it will doubtless double its present numerical importance. As illustrations of the enormous increase in the value of real estate, it may be mentioned that a lot on the northwest corner of Chambers Street and Broadway was purchased by a gentleman who died in 1858, for $1000. Its present value is now estimated at no less a sum than $125,000.

"The lots lately sold at auction, by Ludlow & Co., under the direction of the executors of Judge Jay, were a part of the fifteen acres bought by the late John Jay, at $500 per acre. One lot out of said purchased, situated on Broadway, we are informed has been sold within the past month for $80,000. Fabulous as is the advance from $500 per acre to $80,000 per lot, it is fully justified, as the present owner—who is now

"Your building, too?" As the supply of rental apartments dwindles, West Siders have decisions to make (1985 photo)

erecting a store on the lot—has refused a rent of $16,000 per year for the same.

"A little more than two centuries since, the entire site of this noble city was purchased of the Indians for what was equivalent to the nominal sum of twenty-four dollars. Now the total amount of its assessed property is ten and a half million dollars. If such vast accessions of wealth have characterized the history of the past, who shall compute the constantly augmenting resources of its onward course?"

The outbreak of the Civil War five years earlier had brought housing construction to a standstill, and demand soon far outstripped supply. Brownstones on Fifth and Madison avenues rented for $320 to $500 per month in 1865, twice as much as before the war. Working-class houses that had rented for $40 to $50 per month in 1860 went for $58 to $83, and, the *New York Times* reported, tenants "have to go a-begging to get them for that."

In 1873, there was a financial panic in Europe. European investors withdrew capital from America, the Wall Street banking house Jay Cooke and Company failed on September 18, and by the end of the year some five thousand business firms had gone belly up. Millions of Americans were driven to depend on private charities, and tens of thousands came close to starvation despite the prevalence of soup kitchens. In the economic depression that continued through most of the decade, New York real estate values declined. Well-located brownstones in good condition cost about $60,000 in 1876, down from at least $85,000 in 1873. Wages had dropped 30 percent and, with them, the market for houses. When the economy turned down again beginning in late 1892, there was another drop in property values and rents; they remained depressed until 1897, when a decade of prosperity began.

New York housing prices in the present century have tended to move with the Dow Jones Industrial Average. When the air went out of Wall Street's balloon in 1929, property values fell. So did rents. A one-bedroom apartment at the Osborne on West 57th Street rented for $125 per month in 1929 and for $75 a couple of years later. Wages and salaries also collapsed in the general deflation. The average U.S. wage dropped to $17 per week in 1932, down from $28 in 1929. The Dow Jones average bottomed out at 41.22 on July 28, 1932 (down from its high of 381.17 on September 3, 1929). A lawyer in 1933 typically earned $4,218 per year, a physician $3,382, a public school teacher $1,227. Sleep-in domestic servants could be had for less than $25 per month. A new Pontiac sold for $585, a Stetson hat for $5. Eggs were twenty-nine cents a dozen, milk was ten cents a quart, bread five cents for a twenty-ounce loaf, sirloin steak twenty-nine cents a pound. And while wages and prices were slightly higher in New York than in some other places, money was tight in the big city, too.

Large New York apartments sat vacant or rented cheap in the 1930s. Fannie Hurst, who ground out serialized novels for the women's magazines, moved in 1932 into the Hotel des Artistes in West 67th Street and lived there for three dozen years in a triplex with thirty-foot ceilings. Most people were not so lucky.

Co-op tenants in the Great Depression—and some of the better apartment houses on both sides of Central Park were co-operatives—found themselves unable to pay their monthly maintenance charges. Real estate operators in many cases took over the properties and made them rental houses; not until the 1950s (Wall Street's Dow Jones Average finally reached its 1929 high again on November 23, 1954) would the buildings again become co-ops.

In 1947, a five-bedroom New York apartment rented, typically, for $110 per month. A four-bedroom duplex co-operative in the East 60s near Park Avenue, with a two-story living room and a woodburning fireplace in its sixteen- by twenty-one-foot library, sold for $8,250; monthly maintenance was below $250. An eight-room co-op on Fifth Avenue in the 70s with three bedrooms, a thirty- by seventeen-foot living room, and a view of Central Park sold for $7,434, with monthly maintenance payments of less than $300. Prices on the West Side were even lower. Newcomers to the city could still find comfortable one- and two-bedroom apartments on both sides of Central Park renting at less than $100 per month.

Many prominent New Yorkers preferred the West Side. West Side buildings remained rental houses far longer than did comparable East Side buildings. Perhaps the first to go co-op was the Hampshire House at 150 Central Park South. It had been purchased in November 1945 by a Chicago hotel man for $3,235,000 and was converted to co-operative ownership in 1948. An unfurnished studio with bath sold for $5,100, a luxuriously furnished duplex with three bedrooms, two living rooms, dressing room, terrace, and kitchen sold for $39,900; monthly maintenance charges ranged from $110.50 to $948.

The Majestic at the southwest corner of Central Park West and 72nd Street went co-op in August 1957. Three months earlier, on May 2, the building's lobby had been the scene of a shooting: mobster Frank Costello, who lived with his wife in a penthouse at the Majestic, was grazed in the head by a bullet from a .32 caliber pistol fired by Vincent ("The Chin") Gigante, who escaped. Costello, not badly hurt, grabbed a cab and raced to the emergency room of Roosevelt Hospital. Police went through his pockets and found a slip showing more than $1 million in winnings from his gambling casinos. Earlier Majestic tenants had included Meyer Lansky and Charles ("Lucky") Luciano.

The Dakota, directly north of the Majestic and New York's oldest prestige apartment house, went co-op at the end of 1961, when its tenants included C. D. Jackson (one of the few Jews to rise to the heights in Henry Luce's Time, Inc., empire); stage designer Jo Mielziner; and actress Lauren Bacall, whose husband, Humphrey Bogart, had died nearly five years before and who had only recently moved into the building. There were also a few rent-controlled tenants left over from World War II. Rents at the Dakota had risen only slightly since 1884, when the building opened.

More and more West Side buildings are going the way of East Side buildings
(1986 photo)

A ten-room apartment still went for $500 per month; a tenant with seventeen rooms plus six bathrooms and eight working fireplaces paid $650.

Dakota tenants at the end of 1961 could buy seven rooms with two baths and three fireplaces for about $45,000, although Lauren Bacall paid $53,340 for her apartment overlooking Central Park. Even prices such as those were beyond the means of some tenants; they moved out, and the Dakota, for the first time in its history, advertised for buyers. One fairly large apartment went for only $5,000, whereupon its owner divided it and sold off half of it for $55,000. Someone else bought an apartment for $10,000 and sold its antique mahogany and marble mantelpiece for $35,000.

For most people, these Central Park West houses are mere castles in air. From left, Oliver Cromwell, Dakota, Mayfair Towers, Langham, San Remo, Kenilworth (1986 photo)

While many Dakota co-op owners doubled and tripled their investments, rising maintenance costs forced some others to move out. The Dakota was designated a landmark in 1969; maintenance charges rose 42 percent in the next three years. When a new co-operative board took over in 1971 after a bitter battle, it negotiated a new mortgage at a higher interest rate, thus increasing the tax-deductible share of each tenant's monthly maintenance from 30 to 50 percent. But in the next eight years, partly because the old building needed so much work, at least one tenant's monthly maintenance rose from $800 to $1,700. Not everybody could afford such rates. Still, prices kept going up. A ten-room, four-bath apartment sold for $115,000 in 1977; a seven-room, two-and-a-half-bath apartment sold the following year for $120,000, and an eight-room, three-bath place went for $150,000. By the mid–1980s, such apartments were fetching well over $1 million.

When 173–175 Riverside Drive went co-op in 1969, a three-bedroom-and-dining-room apartment sold for as little as $14,000. Fifteen years later that apartment had a market value roughly forty times greater. (Monthly maintenance charges also climbed steeply, of course.) The same story, with variations, could be heard all over town.

The San Remo at 145 Central Park West went co-op in 1972; although the tenant of an eight-room apartment who was paying about $800 per month in rent could buy the apartment typically for a mere $30,000, the monthly maintenance was almost the same as what had been charged in rent. In a dozen years that maintenance doubled despite installation of self-service elevators and other measures to reduce the staff.

The Beresford, on Central Park West between 81st and 82nd, where a three-bedroom apartment can cost upwards of $1 million (1986 photo)

Wall Street's Dow Jones Average bottomed out on December 9, 1974, at $570.01, down from $1003.16 late in 1972. Co-op prices also collapsed. The triplex of the late Fannie Hurst at the Hotel des Artistes sold in 1974 for only $170,000. New York at the time was in sorry financial shape, and 1975 brought a fiscal crisis. Essential services such as police protection were curtailed. Central Park was in a state of desuetude. Many saw little hope for the city's prospects, and more people left for the suburbs.

Real estate prices recovered with a vengeance as the city regained its fiscal health. Consider the case of a now-prominent financial expert who bought a duplex at the Beresford on Central Park West for about $110,000 in 1971 (monthly maintenance about $700) and had neighbors who included Margaret Mead. He got $140,000 for it when he left in 1977 to take a job with the Carter administration in Washington; he returned to New York in 1981 to find that his old apartment had just been resold for $1.1 million. The bright, sunny duplex, facing south with views of the Hudson River, the Museum of Natural History, and much of Central Park, had a graciously proportioned living room, three large bedrooms, two maids' rooms, a good-sized kitchen, and a big dining room. The market value for such apartments in 1981 was over $1 million.

In the 1980s thousands of Manhattanites, East Side and West, were living in co-operative apartments whose market value had increased ten, twenty, and even fifty times from their original cost. The Eldorado on Central Park West did not go co-op until 1981, when tenants were able to buy enormous two-bedroom-*cum*-dining-room apartments for as little as $75,000. Within a scant three years such apartments had more than quintupled in value, and although the monthly maintenance had climbed above $1,100, the shares held by co-op owners had appreciated enormously. Tuesday Weld, the actress, paid $420,000 for a park view apartment at the Eldorado, many of whose residents—"insiders" at the time of the conversion—could hardly have met the requirements set for new buyers: that they put up at least half the purchase price in cash, and that their annual maintenance charges and the carrying costs of their loans on any outstanding part of the purchase price total no more than one-quarter of their income before taxes.

The prudent rule of thumb that housing expense should not account for more than one-quarter of one's aftertax income had long since become an impossible budgeting measure for many New Yorkers. Forgetting the carrying charges on money borrowed to help pay for a co-op, merely to pay $1,100 in monthly maintenance by the old rule would require an annual income of $50,000 after taxes; many New York couples, even with two incomes, were paying 40 percent of their aftertax income for housing in the 1980s, leaving themselves pinched for all the pleasures for which people generally choose to live in cities. Vacations became few and far between. To have children under such circumstances was becoming an impossible dream.

Relatively few New Yorkers are ever in the market for two- and three-bedroom apartments, much less anything larger. The average household in all five boroughs consists of 1.9 persons; in Manhattan it is 1.5 persons, the second-lowest figure for any county in the United States

The Eldorado, on Central Park West between 90th Street and 91st, went co-op only in 1981 (1986 photo)

(only Hawaii's Kalawao County, which serves as a leper colony on the island of Molokai, has a smaller average household).

Still, many New Yorkers in the mid–1980s occupied fairly large apartments. Thousands of apartment owners, East Side and West, had acquired their co-ops at bargain prices and now found themselves virtual millionaires, at least on paper. There was a catch of course: if they were to realize their gains, where could they move? Rental apartments with two and three bedrooms in desirable locations were almost nonexistent; what few there were often rented at $2,000 to $3,000 per month. To comfortably afford $3,000 per month in rent, said the *Wall Street Journal* in May 1986, "a tenant would need an annual income approaching $130,000." Yet $3,000 was about what many co-op owners were paying when they counted the income that they were giving up on the capital invested in their apartments.

West Siders flock to Central Park's Sheep Meadow, which lost its sheep in 1934
(1986 photo)

More thousands of New Yorkers who were not lucky, or foresighted, enough to be tenants in a building before it went co-op (or to have inherited a family house in the suburbs that could be sold to raise the purchase price of a co-op or condominium in the city) found themselves out in the cold. Appalled at the high cost of Manhattan housing, they looked disconsolately for quarters not only in New York's traditional bedroom boroughs of Brooklyn and Queens (the Bronx, once so heavily Jewish, was now primarily Hispanic) but also in Richmond (Staten Island) and even in Hoboken and Jersey City. Some blamed the high prices of Manhattan co-operatives on rent controls, which were said to have discouraged rental construction except for luxury units at impossible rent levels.

When rent controls first took effect in 1943, the vacancy rate in

New York housing was 5 percent. Rent controls were supposed to expire when the rate once again reached 5 percent; by 1985 it had fallen to 2 percent. And if it was 2 percent for the city as a whole, it was no doubt under 1 percent for Manhattan's favored middle-class residential areas, even though expensive luxury buildings—condominiums, co-ops, and rental structures—might have vacancy rates above 5 percent.

The 1971 Rent Stabilization Act, under which fair, market rent levels for apartments were established, permitted landlords to raise rents by 7 percent per year until they had reached those levels. By the mid–1980s rents for apartments in some older buildings approximated the rents being asked by landlords of new buildings.

The West Side life-style grows trendier by the day (1986 photo)

Opponents of rent control and rent stabilization claim that banks balk at loaning money for construction of buildings whose earnings will be limited by law, hence the slow growth of housing in New York and the actual abandonment of some apartment house properties. Supporters of the law point out that cities without rent controls have also experienced housing abandonment. Rent control laws do not apply to co-ops and condominiums. The laws do not pose a problem to people with substantial incomes, but for the poor they have no doubt been a factor in making it almost impossible to find affordable rental housing that meets what would in other cities be even minimum standards of acceptability.

On the upper West Side, many thousands of renters and owners still pay less for their apartments than do their counterparts on the East

Manhattan's last public stables are in West 89th Street (1986 photo)

Side. Increasingly, however, the area's older buildings are coming down or being remodeled into luxury homes; lower-income residents are being displaced by new or remodeled buildings whose occupants appreciate the West Side's attractions and will pay East Side prices to enjoy living in what they consider the most exciting part of town.

XX. Whither the West Side?

Nowhere is the legendary provincialism of New Yorkers more evident than in the attitudes that people of one borough hold toward those of another—even of one part of the same borough toward another part. In Manhattan, despite a recent growth in mutual acceptance, East Siders and West Siders still glower at each other across Central Park.

This intolerance has the effect, in part, of keeping rents and property values lower on the West Side than on the East. It has helped make it possible for families to obtain large West Side apartments on a rental basis, whereas on the East Side they would have had to buy such apartments. It has contributed to the pluralism of an area where students and young married people flock to see film classics at the Thalia while the elderly—a considerable and valuable part of the West Side's population mix—continue to live in the neighborhoods where they have always lived, meeting each other on number 5, 7, 10, 11, and 104 buses.

The upper West Side has come a long way in the century-plus since Edward Clark pioneered luxury housing with his Dakota on Central Park West. When the San Remo, two blocks north of the Dakota, celebrated its fiftieth anniversary in 1980, tenants included songwriter Harold Arlen, screenwriter Marshall Brickman, singer Barry Manilow, and actors Dustin Hoffman, Diane Keaton, and Tony Randall (who moved to the Beresford in July 1985 after decades at the San Remo). Living at the Gainsborough on Central Park South were film director Louis Malle and his wife, actress Candice Bergen. The century-old Osborne, at 57th Street and Seventh Avenue, included among its tenants the East Side café society entertainer Bobby Short and the concert pianist Gary Graffman. Herbert Schmertz, the Mobil Oil bigwig responsible for funding television's Masterpiece Theatre, had a flat on the top floor of the Normandy at 86th Street and Riverside Drive. Faye Dunaway and Tuesday Weld lived at the Eldorado, as did New York City comptroller Harrison Goldin. So many celebrities live on the upper West Side that people tend to forget the fact that most West Siders have trouble making ends meet.

It is hard to say exactly what Edward S. Clark had in mind when he envisioned his "city of the future," in which apartment buildings combined with single-family dwelling would house rich and poor, "Some splendidly, many elegantly, and all comfortably." "The principle of economic combination," Clark said, "should be employed to the greatest possible extent." Does "economic combination" translate into mixed-income housing?

Columbus Avenue window-shoppers are only part of today's upper West Side story
(1985 photo)

In the West Side Urban Renewal Area, where developers once balked at putting up luxury housing, the 1980s have seen a surge in luxury apartment construction. Many such buildings are required to have one-fifth of their units available to the elderly at reduced rates; but market forces, uncontrolled by government restraints, make the dream of mixed-income housing less and less realizable. Apartment prices have been climbing dramatically for decades, pushed up by rising labor and material costs and by a demand that far exceeds supply. Propelling real estate prices into the stratosphere in recent years has been frantic speculation—"contract flipping" in the trade. Fortunes have been made not by building but by merely buying and reselling. As land prices rose, it became impossible for builders to contemplate construction of anything but office towers or luxury housing. Nothing else would justify the cost of the property, much less the cost of construction.

Broadway benches at Verdi Square accommodate a population mix . . . (1985 photo)

And as apartment building prices have risen, buyers have acquired properties not necessarily with the idea of razing existing houses or renovating them but merely of reselling at a higher price. A vacant building fetches a higher price than an occupied building. As a consequence, some buyers have bent their efforts on emptying their newly acquired buildings. Workers hired by the owners have on occasion been sent into unoccupied apartments with sledgehammers and ordered to make the rooms uninhabitable.

. . . matched only by the one on Riverside Drive benches (1986 photo)

It is relatively easy for a landlord to accumulate vacancies in a single room occupancy hotel (SRO) and thereby either facilitate its conversion to a co-op or rent units at market rates rather than as rent-stabilized apartments. Many speculators have "warehoused" rooms in SROs in anticipation of reaping large profits. More and more SRO occupants have been forced into the street—sometimes by landlords who hired prostitutes, pimps, and other undesirables in illegal efforts to frighten tenants out of their homes.

Two philosophies collide in any discussion of the West Side's future. They are not very different from the opposing philosophies that dominate national politics.

The manager of a solid upper West Side SRO may serve as spokesman for the school of thought that holds that the rights of property owners are paramount:

"I'm a firm believer in the private sector. With appropriate government controls. I repeat: appropriate. Not restrictive to the point where the private sector doesn't want to become involved. With good government policing and the ability for the proprietary sector to make a legitimate return on its investment.

"I'm not an expert in rent controls. I'm for some limits when and if there is a housing crisis and prices are skyrocketing, but only if this is true in every part of the city. If there is adequate housing available in Brooklyn or Queens, and people insist on living in Manhattan, and in Manhattan the prices are four, five, six, seven times as much as in Brooklyn or Queens, I say that's just too bad. I believe in market supply-and-demand philosophy. You don't have to live in Manhattan. You can live a forty-five-minute ride away on the subway. I didn't grow up in Manhattan. I grew up in another borough, probably because it was cheaper living in another borough. It still is.

"When the housing supply is adequate I do not believe that controls or limits are necessary. When there is a very definite shortage of housing and the prices across the board are so high that the general working class and middle class cannot afford it, then I believe there should be some sensible limits, but limits that do not make it impossible for the landlord to make an honest return on his investment. It all depends on your philosophy."

Although opinions vary on what constitutes an "honest" or "legitimate" return on investment, the philosophy that market forces should determine the future of the West Side is widely shared. Property owners and developers, whatever their political sympathies, generally favor whatever will increase the value of their property. And who can blame them?

As the man said, it depends on your philosophy. In some people's view, a major reason for the city's financial crisis of the mid–1970s was that it had too much subsidized housing. To remain economically viable, they said, New York must receive full taxes on more residential buildings and must have more tenants in higher tax brackets. Robert Moses subscribed to this philosophy when he and his slum clearance committee drew up their plan in the 1950s calling for only four hundred low-income public-housing units in the West Side Urban Renewal Area. As finally amended, the plan called for 2,500 low-income units, 5,421 middle-income units, and a mere 151 luxury units—too few, said some, for a healthy tax base.

A quarter-century later, while thousands of apartments in upper West Side buildings were kept vacant, three thousand displaced families were being housed at city expense in such West Side hotels as the Martinique in West 32nd Street and the Carter (originally the Dixie) in West 43rd. Purchased in October 1977 for an estimated $1.5 million, the Carter was being used in 1985 to house 120 families at a cost to the city of $7,450 per day—$2.7 million per year—for accommodations that made the old SROs look almost luxurious. Six people, mostly women and children, shared two single beds and cots in a ten-by-ten-foot room, and the city paid $2,842 per month in rent. To house a family of ten in two small rooms at the Carter cost the city $4,878 per month.

Something was clearly wrong with the city's approach to the problem of the homeless, many of whom preferred to sleep in the street rather than risk the crime encountered in city shelters.

As the ranks of New York's homeless swelled, political pressures forced Mayor Edward I. Koch in January 1985 to put into effect what was to be an eighteen-month moratorium on SRO conversions. This was to give the city time to study ways to protect whatever SROs remained. When the City Council finally put a modification of the mayor's proposal into law nearly seven months later, landlords protested. Simon Felder, who managed the Benjamin Franklin for a developer who wanted to convert the building into condominium units, told an interviewer, "The moratorium is not an appropriate way to deal with the problems of the homeless. Homelessness is a social problem. Solving it is the responsibility of the community and the local government. Dumping it in the laps of the landlords may have a short-term political impact, but it's not going to solve anything.

"There are so many empty buildings in this city, including some on the West Side, that the city took over years ago for nonpayment of taxes and that could be used to house the homeless. Why doesn't the city just rehabilitate those buildings and staff them minimally with a superintendent and a social worker or somebody to guide these people instead of putting them up at hotels and paying exorbitant amounts of money? It's a matter of management. I believe that the city does not know how to manage the problem. By imposing a moratorium on SRO conversions the city is laying the problem at someone else's door, and it doesn't solve a thing. There are landlords who own SROs with not a single occupied room; because of the moratorium they can't make any sort of conversion. That's not helping the homeless or anyone else. The buildings are licensed as SROs and are not being used as SROs. The moratorium penalizes landlords who conduct legitimate businesses; it puts a restriction on people who own property and want to do with their property as they please. The

There is lingering anger as social tensions persist on the upper West Side (1985 photo)

moratorium has very little going for it other than the short-term impact it may have for those who seek political gain by it."

The developer later gave up and sold the building with 210 vacancies to someone who rented out rooms on a weekly basis. Meanwhile, apartments were being warehoused not only in SROs but also in some of the fanciest apartment houses. The Century at 25 Central Park West was preparing for conversion to condominium status after more than fifty-five years as a rental building. The Lincoln Towers buildings were being renovated for co-op conversion. Other buildings were going the same way. In June 1985, the State Court of Appeals ruled that Harry Helmsley, a hotel owner and real estate developer who had acquired Park West Village from the Zeckendorf interests, could sell the development's eight hundred rental units as condominiums—even though Title I federal money had been used to acquire the land for the buildings. The ruling also applied to the 575 units in the Coliseum Park Apartments whose four partner-owners put them on the market as co-operatives.

*   *   *

Standing in opposition to the philosophy stated earlier in this chapter is another philosophy. It is underlined by the fact that New York City recognizes an obligation to find housing for those residents who cannot house themselves. Whether as a matter of compassion or of political self-interest, city administrations past and present have committed themselves to helping our less fortunate residents.

The city has also at times taken a firm stand against developers and landlords, recognizing a responsibility to protect its neighborhoods from excess density, its streets from sunless gloom, its citizenry from exploitation. Developers and landlords bring political pressure on city officials to let them have their way, waving the banner of freedom from government interference. City officials, mindful of the need to increase revenues from property taxes, are inclined to listen, especially when co-operating with the developers can mean big election campaign contributions. This is how it has always been in big cities. Only a Pollyanna believes anything will change with respect to developers' having undue influence on city planners. Politicians grant variances and temporary tax abatements to people who hardly need financial relief, people who are permitted large tax write-offs for "depreciation" on land that is manifestly appreciating in value month by month. (New York property has occasionally depreciated; land in the south Bronx is now worth far less than it was a quarter-century ago. And although even upper West Side property has depreciated at times, this is hardly the case today.)

"Don't let the West Side become the East Side," wail those who cherish its traditional ambience of relaxed livability at affordable prices in rental apartments. Yet change is inevitable, and the West Side, which has seen so much change, will see more of it.

The Hispanic minority will, despite itself, be assimilated as other minorities have been assimilated. Norman Podhoretz has spoken of assim-

Veteran West Siders live side by side with affluent young newcomers (1986 photo)

ilated Jews as "facsimile WASPS." The same will be said of another generation of Hispanics: Yuppies of the next century will in many cases have Spanish surnames. And, far more than at present, many will be black. Despite the handicaps of going to school in an environment that encourages everything except education, a growing number of blacks will shrug off peer pressure not to succeed and will enjoy the fruits of their innate skill and intelligence.

Today's youth will outgrow spray-can graffiti vandalism and ghetto blasters; future generations will disdain such antisocial behavior as kid stuff. Society will find constructive ways to employ the creative energies of minority youth, which will respond by taking its rightful role in the productive life of the city.

The West Side, while retaining some of its old character, will surely become more like the East Side. Higher rents and rising apartment prices will change the character of the population as subsidized housing reverts in time to market value housing. Yet even as more West Side buildings become co-ops or condominiums, mounting demand will encourage more building, which will lead to inevitable overbuilding, which will reverse (or at least slow) the upward course of prices. And tax law changes will eventually make it as advantageous to rent as to own. At the same time public pressure—including pressure from merchants and from corporations now obliged to pay outrageous starting salaries in order to compete with cities whose housing is less costly—will force an enlightened new breed of city administrators to stop giving in to developers and landlords whose only concern is obtaining the greatest possible return—however unconscionable—from their investments.

And, in the sardonic words of a longtime West Sider, "You should live so long."

Appendix I

Representative West Side Apartment Houses and Hotels: A Chronology
Turn-of-the-century buildings are listed under 1900, although that
date is in many cases approximate.

1884	Dakota	1 West 72nd Street NW corner Ctrl Park W	10 stories
1885	Osborne	205 West 57th Street NW corner Seventh Ave	10 stories
1885	Dundonald Flats	71 West 83rd Street	5 stories
1886	Evelyn	101 West 78th Street NW corner Ninth Ave	7 stories
1889	Endicott Hotel	101 West 81st Street SW corner Ninth Avenue	7 stories
1890	Greylock	61 West 74th Street NW corner Columbus	7 stories
1890	Brockholst	101 West 85th Street NW corner Columbus	6 stories
1891	Colorado	76 West 82nd Street	5 stories
1891	Lyndhurst	78 West 82nd Street	5 stories
1891	Nebraska	80 West 82nd Street	5 stories
1891	Kenmar	101 West 77th Street	5 stories
1891	Renfrew	103 West 77th Street	5 stories
1891	Juanita	105 West 77th Street	5 stories
1893	Sevillia Hotel (later Ctrl Pk Mews)	117 West 58th Street	12 stories
1895	Hohenzollern	495 West End Avenue SW corner 84th Street	9 stories
1896	La Rochelle	57 West 75th Street NE corner Columbus Ave	9 stories
1898	Hotel Orleans	100 West 80th Street SW corner Columbus Ave	10 stories
1900	Norfolk (later Remington) Hotel	129-131 West 46th Street	9 stories
1900	Collinson	225 West End Avenue NW corner 70th Street	6 stories
1900	West View (later Riverside Studios)	342 West 71st Street	7 stories

1900	Venice	350 West 71st Street	7 stories
1900	St. Charles	101 West 72nd Street	6 stories
1900	Westport (later Vendome)	48 West 73rd Street Columbus - Amsterdam	7 stories
1900	Plymouth	101 West 74th Street NE corner Columbus	6 stories
1900	Sylvia	59 West 76th Street NE corner Columbus	6 stories
1900	Aylsmere	60 West 76th Street SE corner Columbus	7 stories
1900	Indiana	117 West 79th Street	7 stories
1900	New Century	401 West End Avenue NW corner 79th Street	9 stories
1900	Hawkins	204 West 81st Street	5 stories
1900	Forrest	251 West 81st Street	7 stories
1900	Beverly	265 West 81st Street	8 stories
1900	Saxony	250 West 82nd Street SW corner Broadway	7 stories
1900	Rexton	320 West 83rd Street	7 stories
1900	Cayuga	324 West 83rd Street	7 stories
1900	Turrets	125 Riverside Drive NE corner 84th Street	9 stories
1900	Martha	200 West 84th Street SW corner Amsterdam	6 stories
1900	Hyperion	320 West 84th Street	6 stories
1900	Clinton	74 West 85th Street	5 stories
1900	Sudeley	76-78 West 85th Street	5 stories
1900	St. Elmo	170 West 85th Street SE corner Amsterdam	5 stories
1900	Stratton	342 West 85th Street	6 stories
1900	Lancashire	353-355 W 85th Street	8 stories
1900	Euclid Hall	2349 Broadway west side, 85th St to 86th	7 stories
1900	Elliott	61 West 86th Street NE corner Columbus Ave	5 stories
1900	Ormonde	101 West 86th Street NW corner Columbus Ave	5 stories
1900	Prague	77 West 87th Street SE corner Columbus	5 stories
1900	Fife Arms	251 West 87th Street NW corner Broadway	7 stories
1900	Chatillion	214 Riverside Drive SE corner 94th St	7 stories
1900	Iroquois	201 West 94th Street NW corner Amsterdam	5 stories
1900	Bonta-Narragansett	210 West 94th Street SE corner Broadway	7 stories

1900	Fremont	310 West 94th Street	7 stories
1900	Orlando	311 West 94th Street	6 stories
1900	Georgean Court	315 West 94th Street	7 stories
1900	Beau Rivage	316 West 94th Street	6 stories
1900	St. Louis	319 West 94th Street	6 stories
1900	Avalon Hall	227 Riverside Drive SE corner 95th Street	7 stories
1900	Sans Souci	200 West 95th Street SW corner Amsterdam	5 stories
1900	Valencia Court	317 West 95th Street	7 stories
1900	West Point	336 West 95th Street	7 stories
1900	Wollaston	231 West 96th Street NE corner Broadway	7 stories
1900	317 West 95th St	off Riverside Drive	7 stories
1900	Victoria	250 Riverside Drive NE corner 97th Street	9 stories
1900	Hartcourt	258 West 97th Street	7 stories
1900	Von Colon	311 West 97th Street	7 stories
1900	Holland Court	315-317 West 98th Street NW corner Amsterdam Ave	8 stories
1900	Marion	2612 Broadway 98th Street to 99th	9 stories
1900	La Riviera	230 West 99th Street SE corner Broadway	7 stories
1900	Strand View	309 West 99th Street	8 stories
1900	Paramount	315 West 99th Street	8 stories
1900	Emahrel	317 West 99th Street	8 stories
1900	West End Hall	840 West End Avenue NE corner 101st St	6 stories
1900	Kent	216 West 102nd Street SE corner Broadway	7 stories
1900	Westbourne	930 West End Avenue SE corner 106th Street	7 stories
1900	Lancaster Apts	936 West End Avenue NE corner 106th Street	7 stories
1900	River Mansion	337 Riverside Drive SE corner 106th Street	5 stories
1900	Waumbek	300 West 107th Street SW corner Broadway	7 stories
1900	Loyola	477 Central Park West SW corner 108th Street	5 stories
1900	Metropolitan	235-239 West 108th St	6 stories
1900	Hartley Hall	482-484 Central Park West, SW corner 109th	7 stories
1900	Irving Hall	500 Cathedral Parkway SW corner Amsterdam	6 stories

1900	Miramar	452 Riverside Drive SW corner 119thSt	9 stories
1901	Patterson (later Wentworth) Hotel	59 West 46th Street	13 stories
1901	Coronet	57 West 58th Street NE corner Sixth Avenue	10 stories
1901	Harperly Hall	41 Central Park West NW corner 64th Street	12 stories
1901	Brentmore	88 Central Park West SW corner 69th Street	12 stories
1901	Van Horne	300 West End Avenue NE corner 74th Street	13 stories
1901	Astor Apts	2141-2157 Broadway 245 West 75th Street	12 stories
1901	Bretton Hall	2350 Broadway east side, 85th St to 86th	12 stories
1901	De Soto	215 West 91st Street NE corner Broadway	13 stories
1901	Stratford-Avon	210 Riverside Drive NE corner 93rd Street	12 stories
1901	Central Park View	414 Central Park West NW corner 101st Street	16 stories
1901	Graham Court	SW corner 116th St and Seventh Ave (later Adam Clayton Powell, Jr, Blvd)	8 stories
1902	Ansonia Hotel	2107 Broadway, west side, 73rd St to 74th	17 stories
1902	Dorilton	171 West 71st Street NE corner Broadway	12 stories
1902	Central Park Studios	15 West 67th Street	14 3-bed- room du- plexes, 20 simplexes
1903	Woodward Hotel	SE corner 55th St and Bwy	12 stories
1903	Sixty-Seventh Street Studios	27 West 67th Street	14 stories
1903	Belleclaire	250 West 77th Street	10 stories
1903	Schuyler Arms	305 West 98th Street	7 stories
1904	Walton	104 West 70th Street SW corner Columbus Ave	11 stories
1904	Chatsworth	346 West 72nd Street SE corner Riverside Dr	13 stories
1904	Orienta	302-304 West 79th St at Riverside Drive	8 stories
1904	Lucerne Hotel	201 West 79th Street NW corner Amsterdam	12 stories

1904	51 West 81st St (later Galaxy 51)	NE corner Columbus Ave	12 stories
1904	Red House	350 West 85th Street	6 stories
1904	Marseilles Hotel	SW corner 103rd Street and Broadway	9 stories
1904	Manhasset	301 West 108th Street 300 West 109th Street	11 stories
1904	St. Urban	285 Central Park West SW corner 89th Street	12 stories
1904	Terrace Court	202-208 Riverside Dr SE corner 93rd Street	9 stories
1905	Knickerbocker Hotel (later an office bldg)	SE corner Broadway and 42nd Street	12 stories, 550 rooms
1905	Santa Monica	345 West 70th Street	6 stories (2 bldgs)
1905	Van Dyck	175 West 72nd Street NW corner Amsterdam	13 stories
1905	Severn Arms	170 West 73rd Street SW corner Amsterdam	12 stories
1905	Langham	135 Central Park West 73rd to 74th Streets	12 stories
1905	Central Pk View (later Orwell House)	SW corner 86th Street 257 Central Pk West	12 stories
1905	Riverdale	67 Riverside Drive SE corner 79th Street	9 stories
1905	St. Denis	200 Riverside Drive NE corner 92nd Street	9 stories
1905	Vancouver	314 West 94th Street	6 stories
1906	Spencer Arms (later Lincoln Tower) Hotel	140 West 69th Street SE corner Broadway	12 stories
1906	Lasanno (later Imperial) Court	307 West 79th Street	10 stories
1906	Rossleigh Court	1 West 85th Street NW corner Ctrl Park West	12 stories
1906	Camden	206 West 95th Street	6 stories
1906	Piedmont	316 West 97th Street	6 stories
1906	Concord Hall	468 Riverside Drive SE corner 119th Street	9 stories
1906	Wyoming	166 West 55th Street NE corner Seventh Ave.	12 stories
1907- 1911	Henry Phipps Houses	63rd and 64th Streets west of Amsterdam	6 stories
1907	Prasada	50 Central Park West SW corner 65th Street	12 stories
1907	Hartford	60 West 75th Street SE corner Columbus	6 stories

1907	Evanston	272 West 90th Street SE corner West End Ave	12 stories
1907	Rhineland	244 Riverside Drive SE corner 97th Street	6 stories
1907	Peter Stuyvesant	252 Riverside Drive SE corner 98th Street	12 stories
1907	Stanley Court	945 West End Avenue NW corner 106th Street	12 stories
1907	Chester Hall	201 West 107th Street NW corner Amsterdam	6 stories
1907	Pontchartrain	312-316 West 109th St	8 stories
1907	Hendrik Hudson	380 Riverside Drive NE corner 110th Street	8 stories
1907	Strathmore	404 Riverside Drive SE corner 113th Street	12 stories
1908	Gainsborough Studios	222 Central Park South	16 stories (8 duplex floors)
1908	Ormonde (later Embassy) Hotel	Broadway, 69th Street to 70th, east side	10 stories
1908	Hargrave Hotel	112 West 72nd Street	12 stories
1908	Kenilworth	151 Central Park West NW corner 75th Street	12 stories
1908	Churchill	252 West 76th Street	10 stories
1908	Apthorp	2207 Broadway 78th to 79th Streets	12 stories
1908	Bownett (later Hayden)	11 West 81st Street	12 stories
1908	Clarendon	137 Riverside Drive SE corner 86th Street	12 stories
1908	Irving Arms (Westsider)	222 Riverside Drive NE corner 94th Street	7 stories
1908	Lucetine	35 West 96th Street	8 stories
1908	Peter Stuyvesant	252 Riverside Drive SE corner 98th Street	10 stories
1908	Allenhurst Apts (later Midway)	216 West 100th Street SE corner Broadway	12 stories
1909	Netherlands	340 West 86th Street	12 stories
1909	Alwyn Court	180 West 58th Street SE corner Seventh Ave	12 stories
1909	44 West 74th St	just east of Columbus	5 stories
1909	44 West 77th St	just east of Columbus	14 stories
1909	Belnord	225 West 86th Street Broadway to Amsterdam	13 stories
1909	Cornwall	255 West 90th Street NW corner Broadway	12 stories

1909	Turin	333 Central Park West, NW corner 93rd Street	12 stories, four sections with two open courts
1909	509-515 Cathedral Parkway	(110th Street)	12 stories, two inverted U-shaped buildings
1909	Fowler Court	400 Riverside Drive 621 West 112th Street	6 stories
1910	200 West 58th St	SW corner 7th Avenue	12 stories
1910	Lucania	235 West 71st Street	9 stories
1910	Lathrop	101 West 77th Street	8 stories
1910	Kelmscott	316 West 79th Street	12 stories
1910	Dorset	150 West 79th Street	12 stories
1910	Wayne	309 West 86th Street	12 stories
1910	155 Riverside Dr	SE corner 88th Street	12 stories
1910	Gramont	215 West 98th Street	9 stories
1910	Chesterfield	260 Riverside Drive NE corner 98th Street	10 stories
1910	Glen Cairn	270 Riverside Drive NE corner 99th Street	12 stories
1910	North and South Pennington	801 West End Avenue NW corner 99th Street	12 stories
1910	276 Riverside Dr	SE corner 100th Street	13 stories
1910	305 Riverside Dr	SE corner 103rd Street	13 stories
1910	Colosseum	435 Riverside Drive SE corner 116th Street	12 stories
1911	Wellsmore (later Benjamin Franklin)	222 West 77th Street SE corner Broadway	12 stories
1911	Barrington	209 West 81st Street	9 stories
1911	Umbria	465 West End Avenue NW corner 82nd Street	12 stories
1911	Chautauqua	574 West End Avenue SE corner 88th Street	12 stories
1911	600 West End Ave	NE corner 89th Street	12 stories
1911	Evanston	610 West End Avenue (272 West 90th Street)	12 stories
1911	640 West End Ave	NE corner 91st Street	12 stories
1911	645 West End Ave	SW corner 92nd Street	12 stories
1911	780 West End Ave	SE corner 98th Street	12 stories
1911	782 West End Ave	NE corner 98th Street	12 stories
1911	Marc Antony	514 Cathedral Parkway	12 stories
1911	Prince Humbert	520 Cathedral Parkway	12 stories
1911	Sethlow (later Bancroft) Apts	509 West 121st Street	8 stories
1912	530 West End Ave	SE corner 86th Street	13 stories

1912	Chepstow	215-217 W 101st Street	13 stories
1913	135 West 58th St	west of Sixth Avenue	9 stories
1913	Hotel Cardinal	240 West End Avenue	16 stories
		NW corner 71st Street	
1913	271 Ctrl Park W	SW corner 87th Street	13 stories
1913	562 West End Ave	87th Street to 88th	12 stories
1913	838 West End Ave	SE corner 101st Street	12 stories
1913	839 West End Ave	SW corner 101st Street	12 stories
1913	895 West End Ave	SW corner 104th Street	12 stories
1913	Clebourne	924 West End Ave	13 stories
		NE corner 105th Street	
1914	838 West End Ave	SE corner 101st Street	12 stories
1914	Della Robbia	740 West End Avenue	13 stories
		NE corner 96th Street	
1914	Cliff Dwellers'	243 Riverside Drive	15 stories
	Apartments	NW corner 96th Street	
1915	126 West 73rd St	west of Columbus	13 stories
1915	Bellguard	216 West 89th Street	12 stories
		SE corner Broadway	
1915	Astor Court	east side of Broadway	12 stories
		89th Street to 90th	
1915	Rutherford	360 Riverside Drive	13 stories
		NE corner 108th Street	
1916	100 Ctrl Park S	SW corner Sixth Ave	15 stories
1916	Hotel Margrave	Broadway, midblock	10 stories
		between 71st and 72nd	
1916	590 West End Ave	SE corner 89th Street	13 stories
1916	789 West End Ave	SW corner 99th Street	13 stories
1917	885 West End Ave	NW corner 103rd Street	12 stories
1917	895 West End Ave	SW corner 104th Street	12 stories
1917	905 West End Ave	NW corner 104th Street	12 stories
1918	Robin Studios	100 West 57th Street	14 stories
	(later office bldg)	SW corner Seventh Ave	
1918	Hotel des Artistes	1 West 67th Street	20 stories
			(10 duplex
			floors)
1919	Cambridge	60 West 68th Street	11 stories
1920	19-21 W 69th St	near Central Park West	14 stories
1920	Hotel Esplanade	NW corner 74th Street	14 stories
		and West End Avenue	
1920	Manhill	222 West 83rd Street	14 stories
		SE corner Broadway	
1920	The Towers	250 West 85th Street	14 stories
		SW corner Broadway	
1921	Kimberly	201 West 74th Street	15 stories
	(later Fitzgerald)		
1921	180 Riverside Drive	NE corner 90th Street	14 stories

1922	Hotel Pennsylvania (later Statler, later Penta)	east side of Seventh Ave between 32nd and 33rd	20 stories, 2200 rooms
1922	Empire Hotel	Broadway - Columbus at 63rd Street	15 stories
1922	Jerome Palace	221 West 82nd Street 222 West 83rd Street	two Bwy buildings, each 15 stories
1922	Dexter House	345 West 86th Street	15 stories
1922	Oxford	205 West 88th Street	15 stories
1923	Marboro	171 West 79th Street	15 stories
1923	Excelsior Hotel	45 West 81st Street	15 stories
1923	Bedford	168 West 86th Street	14 stories
1923	Greystone Hotel	SE corner Broadway and 91st Street	14 stories, 500 rooms
1923	Armsted (later Regent) Hotel	NE corner Broadway and 104th Street	17 stories
1924	128 Ctrl Park S	west of Sixth Ave	15 stories
1924	Bradford Hotel	210 West 70th Street	15 stories
1924	522 West End Ave	SW corner 85th Street	15 stories
1924	Edna Court	SW corner 90th Street and Amsterdam	14 stories
1924	Herbert Arms	124 West 93rd Street	9 stories
1924	Ralph Arms	134 West 93rd Street	9 stories
1924	875 West End Ave	SW corner 103rd Street	15 stories
1924	Charlton Apts	SW corner Bwy and 108th St	15 stories
1924	390 Riverside Dr	NE corner 111th Street	15 stories
1924	395 Riverside Dr	SE corner 112th Street	15 stories
1925	101 West 55th St (later called Claridge's)	NW corner Sixth	16 stories
1925	Buckingham Hotel	NW corner 57th and Sixth	16 stories
1925	Alamac Hotel	160 West 71st Street SE corner Broadway	21 stories, more than 600 rooms
1925	Olcott	27 West 72nd Street	17 stories
1925	260 West End Ave	SE corner 72nd Street	15 stories
1925	316 West 72nd St	off West End Avenue	15 stories
1925	Wellston	161 West 75th Street 174 West 76th Street	15 stories
1925	Surrey	215 West 83rd Street	15 stories
1925	Cambridge House	337 West 86th Street	17 stories
1925	173-175 Riv Dr	89th to 90th Street	16 stories
1925	Mirabeau	165 West 91st Street	15 stories
1925	250 West 94th St	SW corner Broadway	15 stories
1925	755 West End Ave	SW corner 97th Street	15 stories
1925	415 Ctrl Park W	NW corner 101st Street	16 stories

1925	Walter Arms	216 West 101st Street SE corner Broadway	15 stories
1925	898 West End Ave	SE corner 104th Street	15 stories
1925	910 West End Ave	SE corner 105th Street	15 stories
1925	209-212 W 106th St	between Bwy and Amstrdm	15 stories
1926	Taft Hotel (Executive Plaza)	50th Street to 51st east side of Seventh Ave	20 stories
1926	Park Central (later Omni) Hotel	NW corner 56th Street and Seventh Avenue	31 stories
1926	Windsor Hotel	SW corner 58th St and Sixth	15 stories
1926	Mayflower Hotel	Central Park West 61st Street to 62nd	15 stories and tower
1926	277 West End Ave	SW corner 72nd Street	15 stories
1926	Bancroft Hotel	40 West 72nd Street	16 stories
1926	Ruxton	50 West 72nd Street	16 stories
1926	Park Royal Hotel	23 West 73rd Street	16 stories
1926	Level Club	253 West 73rd Street	16 stories
1926	Hotel Milburn	242 West 76th Street	15 stories
1926	6 and 16 W 77th St	facing the museum	15 stories
1926	Alden Hotel	225 Central Park West north of 82nd Street	17 stories, more than 600 rooms
1926	Hotel Brewster	21 West 86th Street	15 stories
1926	John Muir	27 West 86th Street	14 stories
1926	150 Riverside Dr	NE corner 87th Street	16 stories
1926	698 West End Ave	NE corner 94th Street	15 stories
1927	Warwick Hotel	NE corner Sixth Ave and 54th Street	30 stories
1927	Navarro (later Ritz-Carlton) Hotel	112 Central Park West	25 stories
1927	Chalfonte Hotel	200 West 70th Street	15 stories
1927	Oliver Cromwell	12 West 72nd Street	29 stories
1927	Beacon Hotel	2128 Broadway NE corner 75th Street	24 stories, 500 rooms
1927	Manchester House	145 West 79th Street	18 stories
1927	Hotel Bolivar	230 Central Park West SW corner 83rd Street	27 stories
1927	Windermere Hotel	666 West End Avenue NE corner 92nd Street	19 stories plus tower
1927	Kipling Arms	145 West 96th Street	16 stories
1927	Envoy	781 West End Avenue NW corner 98th Street	16 stories
1927	Trafalgar	233 West 99th Street NE corner Broadway	16 stories
1927	Hotel Broadmoor	225 West 102nd Street NW corner Broadway	16 stories
1927	White House	262 Central Park West NW corner 86th Street	14 stories

1928	261 Ctrl Park W	SW corner 86th Street	14 stories
1928	Westover	253 West 72nd Street	25 stories
1928	160 West 73rd St	west of Columbus	14 stories
1928	Richmond	147 West 79th Street	16 stories
1928	175 West 93rd St	NE corner Amsterdam	16 stories
1929	Hotel Edison	228-248 West 47th St	25 stories, 1,000 rooms
1929	Hotel Dorset	30 West 54th Street	19 stories
1929	Wellington Hotel	NE corner Seventh Avenue and 55th Street	27 stories, 410 rooms plus 307 in older bldg
1929	Henry Hudson Hotel	353 West 57th Street Women's Assn Clubhouse	27 stories
1929	55 Central Park W	SW corner 66th Street	19 stories
1929	91 Central Park W	NW corner 69th Street	16 stories
1929	101 Ctrl Park W	70th Street to 71st	19 stories
1929	Parkway	49 West 72nd Street	16 stories
1929	Beresford	211 Central Park West 81st to 82nd Streets	22 stories
1929	110 Riverside Dr	NE corner 83rd Street	17 stories
1929	118 Riverside Dr	SE corner 84th Street	16 stories
1929	336 Ctrl Park W	SW corner 94th Street	16 stories
1929	Master Apartments	310 Riverside Drive NE corner 103rd St	29 stories
1929	444 Ctrl Park W	NW corner 104th St	19 stories
1930	London Terrace	23rd Street to 24th Ninth Avenue to Tenth	fourteen buildings, more than 1,600 units
1930	Salisbury Hotel	123-41 West 57th St	16 stories
1930	San Remo	145 Central Park West 74th Street to 75th	27 stories
1930	Manhattan Towers Hotel (The Opera)	2162-2168 Broadway NE corner 76th Street	26 stories
1931	Parc Vendome	340 West 57th Street east of Ninth Avenue	20 stories
1931	Essex House	160 Central Park South	45 stories, 1,286 rooms
1931	St. Moritz Hotel	50 Central Park South	36 stories, 950 rooms
1931	Barbizon Plaza (later Trump Parc)	106 Central Park South NW corner 58th Street	40 stories, 1,400 rooms
1931	Century Apts	25 Central Park West 62nd to 63rd Streets	31 stories
1931	Hotel Majestic	115 Central Park West 71st Street to 72nd	29 stories

1931	Eldorado	300 Central Park West 90th Street to 91st	30 stories
1931	Ardsley	320 Central Park West SW corner 92nd Street	21 stories
1931	Paris Hotel	SE corner West End Avenue and 97th St	23 stories, 790 rooms
1936	Rockefeller Apts	17 West 54th Street	12 stories
1936	411 West End Ave	SW corner 80th Street	18 stories
1937	Hampshire House	150 Central Park South	37 stories
1937	565 West End Ave	NW corner 87th Street	18 stories
1939	Normandy	140 Riverside Drive NE corner 86th Street	19 stories
1940	40 Central Park S	between Fifth Avenue and Sixth	20 stories
1941	240 Central Park S	SE corner Broadway at Columbus Circle	20 stories
1945	Hudson Towers	301 West 72nd Street NW corner West End Ave	23 stories
1948	Amsterdam Houses	61st Street to 64th west side of Amsterdam	twelve buildings, 6 to 13 stories each
1948	Schwab House	11 Riverside Drive 73rd Street to 74th	17 stories
1957	Coliseum Park	345 West 58th Street and 30 West 60th St	two 14-story Columbus Ave bldgs with a garden
1957	The Westmore	340 West 58th Street	8 stories
1957-1970	Frederick Douglass Houses	100th Street to 104th Manhattan Avenue to Amsterdam	twenty-nine buildings, 4 to 20 stories each, 2,462 units
1957-1962	Park West Village	97th Street to 100th Central Park West to Amsterdam	seven buildings, 17 to 20 stories each, 2,700 units
1962	116 Central Park South	fronts mostly on 58th St west of Sixth Ave	15 stories
1962-1970	Lincoln Towers	66th to 70th Streets Amsterdam Avenue to Freedom Place	eight buildings, 29 stories each, 3,897 units

1963	Mayfair Towers	15 West 72nd Street	27 stories
1963	Wesley Towers	210 West 89th Street	12 stories
1964	200 Central Park South	NW corner Seventh Ave	35 stories
1965	Park Towers South	315 West 57th Street & 330 West 58th Street	19 stories
1965	Dorchester Towers	155 West 68th Street Broadway to Amsterdam	33 stories
1965	50 Riverside Drive	NE corner 78th Street	21 stories
1965	Stephen Wise Towers	124 West 91st Street	two 19-story towers, 398 units
1965	Goddard Riverside Towers	74 West 92nd Street	22 stories, 168 units
1967	220 Central Park South	half a block east of Columbus circle	18 stories
1967	80 Central Park W	NW corner 68th Street	25 stories
1967	Strykers Bay Houses	689 Columbus Avenue and 66 West 94th St	two build-ings, one of 17 stories, one of 21, 220 units
1967	Columbus Park Towers	100 West 94th Street on Columbus Avenue	27 stories, 163 units
1967	Goddard Tower	711 Amsterdam Avenue NE corner 94th Street	27 stories, 194 units
1967	RNA Houses	150, 160 West 96th St Columbus to Amsterdam	14 stories, 208 units
1968	Hemisphere House	60 West 57th Street SE corner Sixth Ave	20 stories
1968	210 Ctrl Park S	west of Seventh Ave	23 stories
1968	Jefferson Towers	700 Columbus Avenue 94th Street to 95th	21 stories, 190 units
1968	West Side Manor	70 West 95th Street	27 stories, 246 units
1968	Westgate Houses	120, 140, and 160 West 97th Street	three 14-story buildings, 417 units
1969	Trinity House	100 West 92nd Street 91st Street to 92nd	29 stories, 200 units
1969	Eugenio Maria De Hostos Apts	201 West 93rd Street	22 stories, 223 units
1970	Columbus House	386 Columbus Avenue 95th to 96th Streets	33 stories, 248 units
1971	Carnegie Mews	211 West 56th Street NE corner Broadway	32 stories

1971	Park Lane Hotel	36 Central Park South	46 stories, 640 rooms
1971	1 Lincoln Plaza	east side of Broadway 63rd Street to 64th	40 stories
1971	1 Sherman Square	201 West 70th Street NW corner Broadway	41 stories
1971	St. Martin's Tower	65 West 90th Street, east side of Columbus Avenue, 90th to 91st	27 stories, 179 units
1971	Columbus Manor	70 West 93rd Street along Columbus Avenue	30 stories, 210 units
1971	New Amsterdam Houses	733 Amsterdam Avenue 95th to 96th Streets	27 stories, 228 units
1972	Turin House	609 Columbus Avenue 89th Street to 90th	18 stories, 95 units
1972	5 West 91st Street	off Central Park West	6 stories
1972	Leader House	100 West 93rd Street Columbus, 92nd to 93rd	30 stories, 280 units
1973	130 West 67th Street		25 stories
1973	Lincoln Plaza Towers	44 West 62nd Street SE corner Columbus	30 stories
1974	Millicent V. Hearst House	Eleventh Avenue 64th Street to 65th	33 stories
1974	Heywood Broun Plaza (later Heywood Tower)	175 West 90th Street Amsterdam Avenue 90th Street to 91st	20 stories, 192 units
1975	Clinton Towers	790 Eleventh Avenue 54th Street to 55th	39 stories
1975	2 Lincoln Square	60 West 66th Street SE corner Columbus	37 stories
1975	30 Lincoln Plaza	east side of Broadway 62nd Street to 63rd	34 stories
1975	Glenn Gardens	175 West 87th Street NE corner Amsterdam 65 West 96th Street	32 stories, 266 units
1975	Tower West	65 West 96th Street NE corner Columbus	29 stories, 217 units
1975	Cathedral Parkway Towers	125 West 109th Street and 124 West 110th between Columbus and Amsterdam	two buildings, 12 and 22 stories, respectively, 309 units total
1976	Lincoln-Amsterdam House	110 West End Avenue	25 stories, 188 units

1976	Gloucester	200 West 79th Street SW corner Amsterdam	19 stories
1977	Harbor View Terrace	54th Street to 56th Tenth Avenue to Eleventh	14 stories
1977	Nevada Towers	70th Street between Bwy and Amsterdam	29 stories
1980	Harkness	61 West 62nd Street	27 stories
1981	Regent	45 West 60th Street	34 stories
1982	Beaumont	30 West 61st Street	32 stories
1982	Le Premier	112 West 56th Street	32 stories
1982	Colonnade 57	347 West 57th Street	45 stories
1982	West River House	424 West End Avenue SE corner 81st Street	23 stories
1982	Columbia	2275 Broadway, NW corner 96th Street	31 stories
1983	45 West 67th St	NE corner Columbus Avenue	32 stories ABC uses first 6 floors
1983	Columbus House	386 Columbus Avenue SW corner 79th Street	16 stories
1983	Phelps House	595 Columbus Avenue 88th Street to 89th	11 stories, 168 units
1984	Museum Tower	15 West 53rd Street	52 stories MOMA uses first 6 floors
1984	Montana	247 West 87th Street east side of Bwy	27-storied twin towers
1985	Lincoln Park	211 West 71st Street	17 stories
1985	Park Belvedere	101 West 79th Street NW corner Columbus	34 stories
1985	Centra	100 West 89th Street SW corner Columbus	9 stories
1986	Symphony House	1755 Broadway NW corner 56th Street	44 stories incl offices
1986	Metropolitan Tower	146 West 57th Street	66 stories incl offices
1986	Park South Tower	124 West 60th Street	52 stories, 498 units
1986	Alfred	161 West 61st Street between Columbus and Amsterdam	38 stories incl offices, 224 units
1986	Tower 67	145 West 67th Street	48 stories, 450 units
1986	Bel Canto	1991 Broadway 67th-68th Street	27 stories

1986	Copley	2000 Broadway	28 stories
		SE corner 68th Street	
1986	Bromley	225 West 83rd Street	23 stories,
		83rd Street to 84th,	306 units
		east side of Broadway	
1986	Packard	SE corner 86th and	11 stories,
		Amsterdam	48 units
1986	Columbus Green	NW corner 87th Street	9 stories,
		and Columbus Avenue	95 units
1986	Savannah	250 West 89th Street, SW cor-	18 stories
		ner Broadway	
1986	600 Columbus Ave	NW corner 89th Street	13 stories,
			166 units
1986	James Tower	SW corner 90th Street	22 stories,
		and Columbus Avenue	201 units
			plus 11 in
			3 town-
			houses
1986	New West	2209 Broadway	22 stories
		SW corner 90th Street	
1986	Princeton House	NE corner Broadway and	17 stories,
		95th Street	212 units
1986	Westmont	730 Columbus Avenue	16 stories,
		95th Street and 96th	175 units
1986	Parkgate	750 Columbus Avenue	11 stories
		96th Street to 97th	207 units

(Note: some 1986 buildings not occupied until 1987)

Appendix II

Broadway Theaters, Past and Present: A Chronology

Republic, September 27, 1900, at 207 West 42nd Street

Majestic, January 21, 1903, at 5 Columbus Circle

Lyric, October 12, 1903, at 213 West 42nd Street

Hudson, October 19, 1903, at 139 West 44th Street

New Amsterdam, November 2, 1903, at 214 West 42nd Street

Lyceum, November 6, 1903, at 149 West 45th Street

Liberty, October 10, 1904, at 234 West 42nd Street

Hippodrome, April 12, 1905, on Sixth Avenue between 43rd and 44th streets

*Astor, September 21, 1906, at 1537 Broadway (corner of 45th Street)

Stuyvesant (later the Belasco), October 16, 1907, at 111 West 44th Street

*Gaiety, September 4, 1909, at 1547 Broadway (between 45th and 46th streets)

New (later Century), November 8, 1909, Central Park West between 62nd and 63rd streets

Globe (later Lunt-Fontanne), January 10, 1910, at 205 West 46th Street

George M. Cohan's, February 12, 1911, at 1482 Broadway (main entrance in 43rd Street)

Winter Garden, March 20, 1911, at 1634 Broadway (between 50th and 51st streets)

Playhouse, April 15, 1911, at 137 West 48th Street.

*Folies Bergere (later Fulton, later Helen Hayes), May 1, 1911, at 210 West 46th Street (opened as a a theater-restaurant, became a legitimate theater in October 1911)

Little (later second Helen Hayes), March 12, 1912, at 238 West 44th Street

48th Street, August 12, 1912, at 157 West 48th Street

Eltinge (later Empire), September 11, 1912, at 236 West 42nd Street

Cort, December 20, 1912, at 148 West 48th Street

Weber and Fields Music Hall (later the 44th Street), January 23, 1913, at 216 West 46th Street

Palace, March 24, 1913, at 1564 Broadway (between 46th and 47th streets)

Longacre, May 1, 1913, at 234 West 48th Street

Shubert, September 29, 1913, at 225 West 44th Street

Booth, October 16, 1913, at 222 West 45th Street

* Razed in 1982 to make room for the Marriott Marquis Hotel.

Candler (later Harris) May 7, 1914, at 226 West 42nd Street (opened as a movie house but was converted to a legitimate theater for the August 19 opening of *On Trial* by the twenty-one-year-old playwright Elmer Rice)

*Morosco, February 5, 1917, at 217 West 45th Street

*Bijou, April 12, 1917, at 209 West 45th Street

Plymouth, October 10, 1917, at 236 West 45th Street

Broadhurst (named for a turn-of-the-century playwright), September 27, 1917, at 235 West 44th Street

Vanderbilt, March 7, 1918, at 148 West 48th Street

Henry Miller's, April 1, 1918, at 124 West 43rd Street

Selwyn, October 2, 1918, at 229 West 42nd Street

Times Square, September 30, 1920, at 219 West 42nd Street

Ambassador, February 11, 1921, at 215 West 49th Street

Klaw (later Avon), March 2, 1921, at 251 West 45th Street (with a play starring Katharine Cornell, Tallulah Bankhead, and Francine Larrimore)

National (later Billy Rose, later Nederlander), September 1, 1921, at 208 West 41st Street

Music Box, September 22, 1921, at 239 West 45th Street

Jolson (later Century), October 6, 1921, at 932 Seventh Avenue (between 58th and 59th streets)

Imperial, December 25, 1923, at 249 West 45th Street

Martin Beck, November 11, 1924, at 302 West 45th Street

46th Street, December 24, 1924, at 226 West 46th Street

Colony (later Broadway), December 25, 1924, at 1681 Broadway (53rd Street) as a movie house; opened as a legitimate theater December 8, 1930

Guild (later ANTA, later still Virginia), April 13, 1925, at 245 West 52nd Street

Mansfield (later Brooks Atkinson), February 15, 1926, at 256 West 47th Street

Royale, January 11, 1927, at 242 West 45th Street

Ziegfeld, February 2, 1927, on Sixth Avenue at 54th Street

Theatre Masque (later John Golden's), February 24, 1927, at 252 West 45th Street (built as the Eighth Avenue subway was under construction)

Erlanger (later St. James), September 26, 1927, at 246 West 44th Street

Gallo (later San Carlos Opera House, later still New Yorker), November 7, 1927, at 245 West 54th Street (it became a legitimate theater in May 1930)

Alvin (later Neil Simon), November 22, 1927, at 250 West 52nd Street

Ethel Barrymore, December 20, 1928, at 243 West 47th Street

Mark Hellinger, April 22, 1930, at 237 West 51st Street (movie house; reopened December 13, 1934, as a legitimate theater)

Vivian Beaumont, October 21, 1965, at Lincoln Center

* Razed in 1982 to make room for the Marriott Marquis Hotel.

Mitzi E. Newhouse, October 21, 1965, at Lincoln Center

American Place (off-Broadway), December 6, 1971, in the new J. P. Stevens Building, 111 West 46th Street

Circle-in-the-Square, November 15, 1972, below ground level in the Uris Building, 1633 Broadway (50th Street)

Uris Theater, November 19, 1972, at 1633 Broadway

Minskoff, March 13, 1973, in the new Astor Plaza at 1515 Broadway between 44th and 45th streets

Bibliography

Alpern, Andrew, *Apartments for the Affluent*. New York: McGraw-Hill, 1975.

Bard, Adrienne G., "Straus Park and The Sinking of the Titanic," *West Side Spirit*, April 6, 1985.

Barnard, Eunice Fuller, "Ten-Cent Fare Once Was Paid by New York," *New York Times*, May 1, 1927.

Bettmann, Otto L., *The Good Old Days—They Were Terrible!* New York: Random House, 1974.

Birmingham, Stephen, *Life at the Dakota, New York's Most Unusual Address*. New York: Random House, 1979.

Bonavoglia, Angela, "Birthplace of a Writers' Movement," *West Side Spirit*, April 15, 1985.

Bosworth, Patricia, *Diane Arbus: A Biography*. New York: Alfred A. Knopf, 1984.

Boyer, M. Christine, *Manhattan Manners: Architecture and Style, 1850–1900*. New York: Rizzoli, 1985.

Chavez, Lydia, "On West Side, Barrio Life Vanishing," *New York Times*, May 24, 1986.

Collins, Glenn, "Behind Zabar's Counters, Three Feuding Partners," *New York Times*, March 16, 1985.

Duggan, Dennis, "Big Apartments of '20s Recalled," *New York Times*, September 2, 1962.

Edmiston, Susan, and Linda D. Cirino, *Literary New York: A History and Guide*. Boston: Houghton Mifflin, 1976.

Ellis, Edward Robb, *The Epic of New York City*. New York: Coward-McCann, 1966.

Fortune magazine, July 1939. (Entire issue dedicated to New York City for opening of World's Fair.)

Garney, Cynthia, "The Bilingual Education Battle," *Washington Post*, July 29, 1985, national weekly edition.

Gilbertson, Elsa, The Apthorp and Belnord: Grandes Dames of the Upper East Side, Working Paper No. 2, New York Neighborhoods, 1981? (unpublished)

Goldberger, Paul, *The City Observed: New York. A Guide to the Architecture of Manhattan*. New York: Vintage Books, 1979.

———— "Trump Announces Plan to Construct World's Tallest Building," *New York Times*, November 19, 1985.

Goldfarb, Carl, "Empty Rooms Wait for a Few Dollars More," *Chelsea-Clinton News*, May 2, 1985.

Goldstone, Harmon H., and Martha Dalrymple, *History Preserved: A Guide to New York City Landmarks and Historic Districts*. New York: Simon & Schuster, 1974.

Goodman, George W., "West Side Housing Boom Splits City and Community," *New York Times*, February 17, 1985.

——— "Condominium Plan Upheld by Court," *New York Times*, June 9, 1985.

Gottlieb, Martin, "Trump Planning 66th St. Tower, Tallest in World," *New York Times*, November 19, 1985.

——— "Trump Plan: Wide Impact on West Side," *New York Times*, April 30, 1986.

Grafton, John, *New York in the Nineteenth Century*. New York: Dover, 1980.

Greskes, Michael, "On 20th Anniversary, Landmarks Panel Is Strong But Controversial Force in City," *New York Times*, April 24, 1985.

Guitar, Mary Ann, "Good Gracious! Living at the Decibel Arms," *New York Times Magazine*, December 1, 1963.

Hamilton, Ian, *Robert Lowell: A Biography*. New York: Random House, 1982.

Henderson, Mary C., *The City and the Theatre: New York Playhouses from Bowling Green to Times Square*. Clifton, N.J.: James T. White, 1973.

Hinds, Michael deCourcy, "Adapting to the High Cost of Housing," *New York Times*, February 3, 1985, VIII.

——— "Along Upper Broadway, A Revival," *New York Times*, May 26, 1985, VIII.

——— "West Side School Opposed On Plan to Build Tower," *New York Times*, November 12, 1985.

Johnson, Kirk, "J–51 Rule Change Brings Confusion," *New York Times*, August 18, 1985.

Joyce, Fay S., "Income Limits for Mitchell-Lama Tenants Increased," *New York Times*, August 18, 1985.

Lockwood, Charles, *Bricks & Brownstone, The New York Row House, 1783–1929*. New York: McGraw-Hill, 1972.

——— *Manhattan Moves Uptown, An Illustrated History*. Boston: Houghton Mifflin, 1976.

Longstreet, Stephen, *City on Two Rivers; Profiles of New York—Yesterday and Today*. New York: Hawthorn, 1975.

Lyman, Susan Elizabeth, *The Story of New York*. New York: Crown, 1964.

Lyons, Richard D., "The Long Battle for Approval of City Center Tower," *New York Times*, September 1, 1985.

Mandell, Jonathan, "Lox, Stock and Bagel," *New York Daily News Magazine*, June 23, 1985.

Mannes, David, *Music is My Faith; An Autobiography*. New York: W. W. Norton, 1938.

Mannes, Marya, *The New York I Know*. Philadelphia: J.B. Lippincott, 1961.

—— *Out of My Time*. Garden City, N.Y.: Doubleday, 1971.

Manso, Peter, *Mailer: His Life and Times*. New York: Simon and Schuster, 1985.

Mayer, Grace M., *Once Upon a City*. New York: Macmillan, 1958.

McQuillan, Alice, "Residents-Developer Compromise Set," *West Side Spirit*, June 10, 1985.

Miller, J., *Miller's New York As It Is*, 1866; New York: Schocken, 1975.

Morris, Lloyd R., *Incredible New York: High Life and Low Life of the Last Hundred Years*. New York: Random House, 1951.

Morrisroe, Patricia, "The New Class," *New York Magazine*, June 13, 1985.

Moscow, Henry, *The Street Book: An Encyclopedia of Manhattan's Street Names and Their Origins*. New York: Hagstrom, 1978

Mumford, Lewis, *Sketches from Life*. New York: Dial Press, 1982.

Norton, Thomas E., and Jerry E. Patterson, *Living It Up, A Guide to the Named Apartment Houses of New York*. New York: Atheneum, 1984.

Oliver, Dick, "Horrors of Welfare Hotels," *West Side Spirit*, August 5, 1985.

—— "Did the Pentagon Bankroll One American Dream?," *West Side Spirit*, August 12, 1985.

Patterson, Jerry E., *The City of New York*. New York: Harry N. Abrams, 1978.

Perlman, Geanne, "A Primer for Public School Excellence," *West Side Spirit*, November 11, 1985.

Podhoretz, Norman, *Making It*. New York: Random House, 1967.

Real Estate Record and Builders' Guide, 1884–1929.

Rimer, Sara, "A Towering Oasis on the West Side Ponders Its Conversion to Co-ops," *New York Times*, February 9, 1985.

Ross, Don, *New York Herald-Tribune*, four-part series, June 25–29, 1961.

Sanders, Bob, "Prostitution on the West Side," *West Side Spirit*, June 17, 1985.

—— "Broadway Boom Is Hitting Full Stride," *West Side Spirit*, August 19, 1985.

Schanberg, Sydney H., "Home-Truth Report," *New York Times*, March 16, 1985.

—— "Let 'Em Move Wherever," *New York Times*, May 4, 1985.

Schickel, Richard, *The World of Carnegie Hall*. New York: Julian Messner, 1960.

Schoen, Douglas, *Pat: A Biography of Daniel Patrick Moynihan*. New York: Harper and Row, 1979.

Starr, Roger, *The Rise and Fall of New York City*. New York: Basic Books, 1985.

Stein, Susan R., ed., *The Architecture of Richard Morris Hunt*. Chicago: University of Chicago Press, 1986.

Stern, Ellen, "When Hell Was a 'Mild Climate' Here," *Chelsea-Clinton News*, May 16, 1985.

Stern, Robert A.M., Gregory Gilmartin and John Massengale, *New York 1900: Metropolitan Architecture and Urbanism 1890–1915*. New York: Rizzoli, 1983.

Stokes, I.N. Phelps, *The Iconography of Manhattan Island, 1498–1909*. New York: Robert H. Dodd, 1915–1928 (6 volumes)

Swanberg, William A., *Citizen Hearst*. New York: Charles Scribner's Sons, 1961.

Tauranac, John, and Christopher Little, *Elegant New York: The Builders and the Buildings, 1885–1910*. New York: Abbeville Press, 1985.

Trager, James, "Fainter Toots From Atlantic Liners," *New York Times*, April 20, 1985.

Waterbury, Jean Parker, *A History of Collegiate School, 1638–1963*. New York: Clarkson Potter, 1965.

White, Norval, and Elliot Willensky, *AIA Guide to New York City*, revised edition. New York: Macmillan, 1978.

Wiseman, Carter, "Sky High," *New York Magazine*, May 13, 1985.

Young, Sarah Gilman, *European Modes of Living, or The Question of Apartment Houses (French Flats)*. New York: G. P. Putnam's Sons, 1881.

Index

Untermeyer, Louis, 156, 166
Upjohn, Richard, 8, 32
Urban, Joseph, 71
Uris, Harris H. and Percy, 79

Valentino, Rudolph, 66, 76
Vancouver, The, 200; photo, 201
Vanderbilt, Cornelius II, 52
Van Doren, Mark, 154
Vaux, Calvert, 19
Veblen, Thorstein, 27
Verdi Park, 73
Verdon, Gwen, 115
Viele, Egbert L., 13, 14
Virginia Theater, 45
Vivian Beaumont Theater, 115

Wagner, Robert F., Jr., 100, 121
Walden School, 55, 166, 169
Walker and Gillette, 73
Wall Street Journal, 223
Walton, The, 123
Ware, James E., 19
Warren and Wetmore, 32
Warwick Hotel, 71
Washington Heights, 67
Weber and Fields, 44
Weekes, E. Hobart, 56
Weld, Tuesday, 227
Wentworth Hotel, 39
West End Avenue, 4, 18, 26, 28, 29, 61, 62, 73, 109, 121, 192
Westgate, The, 111
Westmore, The, 97
West, Nathanael, 157
West Park Apartments, 103
West-Park Presbyterian Church, 27
West Side Community Gardens, 125, 127; photo, 126
West Side Highway, 86, 129

West Side Industrial Synagogue, 27
West Side Tennis Club, 70
West Side Urban Renewal Area, 101, 104–106, 111, 113, 125, 128, 199, 229
White Hall Hotel, 70
White, Stanford, 23, 27, 45
White, Theodore, 95, 96
Williams Residence, 199
Williams, Tennessee, 154
Windsor Hotel, 72
Winter Garden Theater, 43, 96
Wolfe, Thomas, 154
Woodward Hotel, 39, 72
Wouk, Herman, 5, 158
Wright, Richard, 154
Wylie, Elinor, 154

Yacht Club, New York, 32
Yeshiva Chofetz Chaim, 49, 173
Yevtushenko, Yevgeni, 154
YMCA, 75, 160
York and Sawyer, 55, 73
Youmans, Vincent, 183
Young, Sarah Gilman, 11

Zabar's, 143, 150–153; shopping bag photo, 151
Zeckendorf, Arthur, 183
Zeckendorf, William, 102, 109, 192
Zeisloft, E. Idell, 5
Ziegfeld, Florenz, 36
Ziegfeld Theater, 45, 71, 76
zoning laws, 22, 66, 110, 116, 122, 128, 187n., 191
Zucker, Alfred, 23
Zuckerman, Eugenia, 175
Zuckerman, Mortimer, 192
Zuckerman, Pinchas, 175

JAMES TRAGER studied city planning under Richard Hudnut at Harvard, became a writer rather than an architect or urban engineer, and moved to the West Side in 1966 after fifteen years on the other side. He is the author of books on a variety of subjects including agriculture and world trade, food and nutrition, Japanese society, and world history. He is married to the photographer Chie Nishio, whose work accounts for most of the illustrations in this book.